Quizlet 사용법

스마트폰, 태블릿, 컴퓨터에서 재미있고 효과적인 어휘 공부
Flash Card와 Spell Check, 게임 등의 서비스를 제공하며,
자리잡은 학습 시스템

01 Quizlet 사용방법

Step 1. 네이버 QR 인식기 또는 별도의 QR 인식기를 실행시켜
페이지 상단의 QR코드를 인식합니다.

ⓐ 네이버 앱에서 마이크 아이콘 클릭합니다.

ⓑ QR 코드 인식기를 클릭합니다.

Step 2. 원하는 학습 일차를 선택합니다.

Step 3. 원하는 어휘의 MP3 음원을 선택하여 듣습니다.

02 Quizlet의 다양한 학습기능

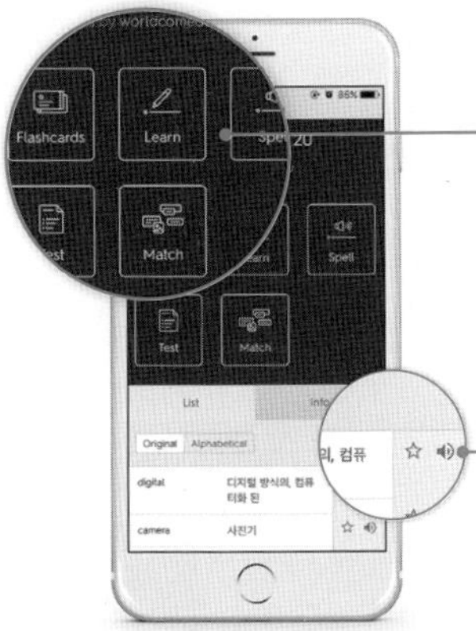

STUDY와 PLAY를 통해 다양한 방식으로
재밌게 학습할 수 있습니다.

- STUDY : Flashcard, Learn, Spell, Test
- PLAY : Match

단어 혹은 스피커 버튼을 누르면
음성을 들을 수 있습니다.

* Google Play에서 Quizlet 어플리케이션 다운로드 및 이용이 가능합니다.

QR 코드 사용법

보다 쉽고 간편하게 접근할 수 있는 학습 방법!
QR코드 인식을 통한 Word Max 6단계 시리즈 음원 바로 듣고 학습하기

01 첫 번째, 네이버 앱을 통해 QR코드 사용하기

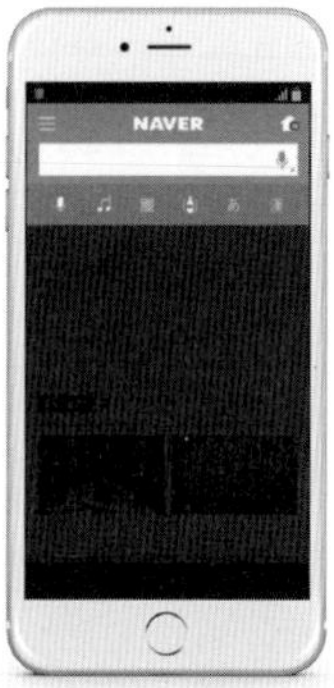

Step 1. 네이버 QR 인식기 또는 별도의 QR 인식기를 실행시킵니다.

ⓐ 네이버 앱에서 마이크 아이콘 클릭합니다.
ⓑ QR 코드 인식기를 클릭합니다.

Step 2. 내지의 QR 코드를 인식합니다.

Step 3. MP3 음원이 유튜브를 통해 다운로드 없이 이용 가능합니다.

02 두 번째, 콜롬북스 앱을 통해 MP3파일 다운받기

Step 1. 구글 플레이에서 콜롬북스를 검색하여 앱을 설치합니다.

Step 2. 콜롬북스 앱을 실행하여 워드맥스를 검색합니다.
(검색어 : WORD MAX, Word Max, 워드맥스)

Step 3. MP3를 다운로드 받아 이용합니다.

* 아이폰 사용시 표지의 QR 코드 인식을 통해 별도의 어플 설치 없이 웹에서 바로 사용이 가능합니다.

WORD MAX 4 5300

WorldCom Edu

WORD MAX 5300 4

초판	2016년 10월 31일
지은이	김 지 훈, 김 채 원
영문검수	Kenneth Drenen
책임편집	신 은 진
편집팀	월드컴 에듀 편집팀
펴낸이	임 병 업
디자인	임 예 슬, 김 지 현, 차 지 원
펴낸곳	(주)월드컴 에듀
등록	2016년 10월 31일
주소	서울시 강남구 남부순환로 2706, 5층 (도곡동, 차우빌딩)
전화	02)3273-4300(대표)
팩스	02)3273-4303
홈페이지	www.wcbooks.co.kr
이메일	wc4300@wcbooks.co.kr

WORD MAX 5300 여는 글

언어를 배울 때 어휘 학습은 모든 언어 학습자가 가장 먼저 시작하는 분야이면서 동시에 가장 숙달하기 어려운 분야입니다. 이는 문법이나 읽기, 듣기와는 다른 어휘 학습의 독특한 측면이며 다른 학습 방식이 필요한 이유이기도 합니다. 수능을 비롯한 최근의 영어 시험 경향은 결국 어휘사용능력이 전반적인 문제 해결의 핵심 요소가 되고 있습니다.
WORD MAX 5300은 최신 경향에 맞추어 가장 효율적인 어휘 학습 방식을 제공하고자 합니다.

WORD MAX 5300시리즈는 과학적인 방법으로 최대의 효과를 얻을 수 있도록 어휘를 엄선했습니다.

WORD MAX 5300시리즈는 총 6권의 수준별 구성으로 최신 출제 경향과 엄선된 예문 및 다양하고 풍부한 리뷰 테스트를 통해 어휘 활용 능력을 최대화 할 수 있도록 구성했습니다.
최근 12년의 수능 및 각종 시험 기출 문제와 교과서 자료를 중심으로 자체 데이터베이스를 통해 학습 대상 어휘를 엄선했습니다. 특히 기출 빈도와 출제 예상도를 고려하여 선정한 어휘들은 효율적인 어휘 학습을 도와 줄 것입니다.

단계별로 세분화되고 실용성 있는 어휘 학습 환경을 제공합니다.

Level 1~3은 핵심적인 어휘를 풍부한 예문과 리뷰 테스트를 통해 예비중학 과정부터 중등 내신 대비까지 학생들의 기본적 영어 능력 향상에 도움이 되도록 구성했습니다.
Level 4~6은 최근 12년간의 수학능력시험, 모의고사, 학력평가의 기출문제를 토대로 어휘를 선정하였습니다. 더불어 각 어휘의 출제 맥락을 연구하고 수준별 분류 및 보정과정을 통해 단순 어휘 학습을 넘어 전반적인 영어 활용 능력을 향상 시킬 수 있게 구성했습니다.

다양한 어휘 활용 연습 기회를 제공하여 전반적인 영어 실력의 향상을 목표로 합니다.

WORD MAX 5300시리즈는 일일 테스트를 비롯한 Review Test의 총 8개 섹션의 다양한 테스트를 통해 학습한 어휘를 완전히 이해하고 활용할 수 있도록 했습니다. 쓰임에 따라 다양한 뜻을 가진 어휘들과 이에 대한 실용성 높은 예문들은 영어 사용 능력 향상에 확실한 도움이 될 것입니다.

어휘 학습 방법에 대한 이견은 많지만 어휘 학습 대상 선정의 중요성에 대해서는 연구자와 일선 교육자 모두 공감하고 있습니다. WORD MAX 5300시리즈를 충실히 학습한다면 어휘를 학습하는 재미 뿐만 아니라 영어 전반에서 실력 향상을 성취 할 수 있을 것이라 자부합니다.

WORD MAX 5300시리즈와 함께 어휘 학습에 최고의 결과를 얻을 수 있기를 기원합니다.

- 월드컴 에듀 편집팀 일동

구성 및 활용

1 단계별 30일 구성의 계획적 어휘 학습!

'단어 → 어구 → 예문' 순으로 자연스럽게 확장되는 학습을 통해 어휘력을 향상합니다.

하루 30개
단계별 30일 구성

유의어, 반의어, 연관 단어 등의
제시를 통해 어휘력을 확장합니다.

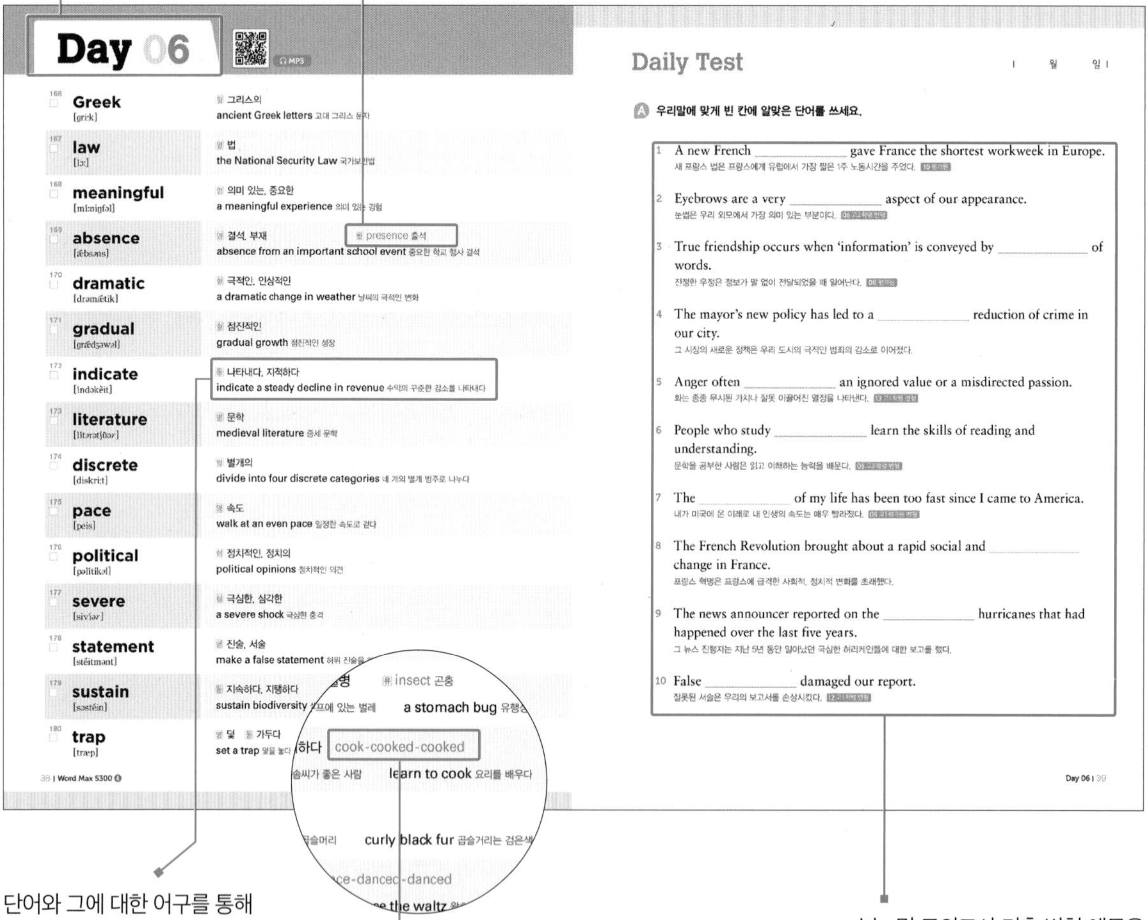

단어와 그에 대한 어구를 통해
다양한 어휘 학습을 가능하게 합니다.

수능 및 모의고사 기출 변형 예문을
통해 표제어를 응용 학습합니다.

동사의 3단 변화형과 비교형 제시를 통해
시제별 동사 형태를 연습합니다.

2 Review Test 7가지 유형으로 학습 점검하기!

2일마다 학습한 어휘를 다양한 유형의 문제를 통해 반복 학습합니다.

한영 빈칸 채우기
우리말 해석에 따라 어구를 완성합니다.

영한 빈칸 채우기
영어 문장에 알맞은 단어를 찾아 빈 칸에 씁니다.

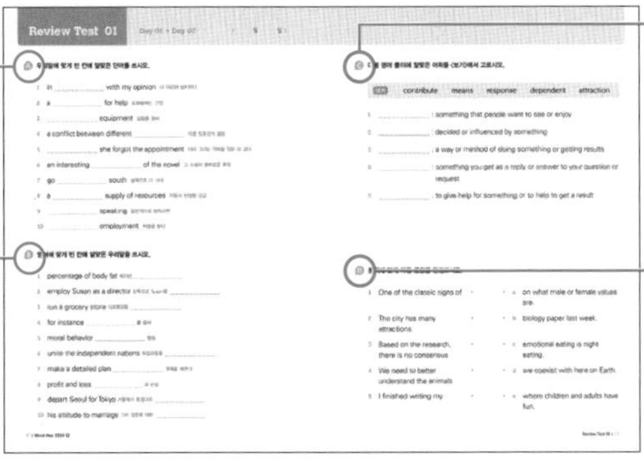

영영 풀이
보기에서 영영 풀이에 해당하는 단어를 찾아봅니다.

문장 완성
문맥상 알맞은 문장끼리 연결하여 완성된 문장을 학습합니다.

영영 어휘활용
문장에서 문맥상 알맞은 단어를 선택합니다.

문장 완성
우리말에 따라 보기에서 알맞은 단어를 골라 문장을 완성합니다.

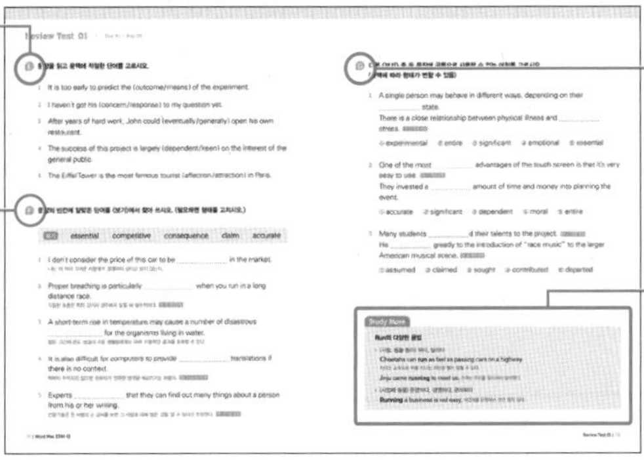

공통 어휘 찾기
두 문장에 공통으로 들어가는 다양한 형태의 어휘를 찾아봅니다.

Study More
표제어에 대한 확장된 개념을 제시함으로써 다양한 관점에서 어휘력을 향상 시킬 수 있습니다.

3 Work Book

워크북을 활용하여 단어의 철자와 뜻을 한번 더 반복 학습합니다.

쓰기 노트

일일 테스트

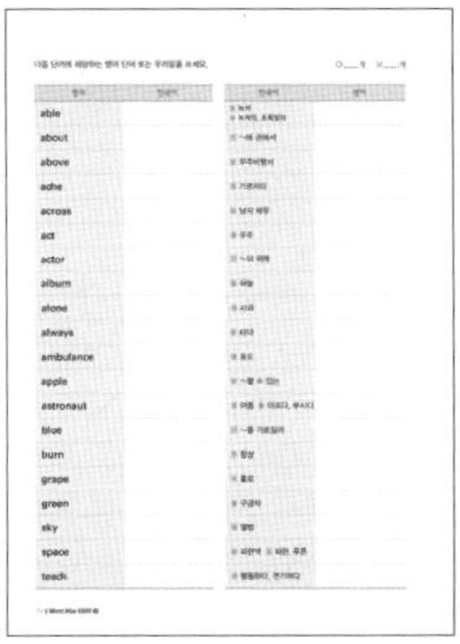

목차

★ 책 속의 책 Workbook 제공

WORD MAX 4 5300

Day 01

MP3

001 **accord** [əkɔ́ːrd]
명 일치 동 일치하다
in accord with my opinion 내 의견과 일치하다

002 **percentage** [pərséntidʒ]
명 백분율
percentage of body fat 체지방 율

003 **emotional** [imóuʃənəl]
형 감동적인, 정서의
emotional stress 정서적 스트레스

004 **plea** [pliː]
명 애원, 간청
plea for help 도와달라는 간청

005 **continuous** [kəntínjuəs]
형 계속되는, 끊임없는
continuous pain 계속되는 고통

006 **response** [rispɑ́ns]
명 반응, 응답
immune response 면역 반응   make a response 응답하다

007 **employ** [implɔ́i]
동 고용하다
employ Susan as a director 감독으로 Susan을 고용하다

008 **means** [miːnz]
명 수단, 방법
means of communication 의사소통의 수단

009 **term** [təːrm]
명 용어, 기간
scientific terms 과학 용어

010 **run** [rʌn]
동 경영하다, 운영하다
run a grocery store 식료품점을 운영하다

011 **experimental** [ikspèrəméntəl]
형 실험의
experimental equipment 실험용 장비

012 **benefit** [bénəfit]
명 이점, 혜택 동 유익하다
the benefits of exercising 운동의 이점

013 **attraction** [ətrǽkʃən]
명 명소, 매력
various tourist attractions in Korea 한국에 다양한 관광 명소

014 **competitive** [kəmpétitiv]
형 경쟁의, 경쟁력 있는
competitive rate 경쟁률

015 **affection** [əfékʃən]
명 애정
a deep affection for her daughter 그녀의 딸에 대한 깊은 애정

Daily Test

| 월 일 |

A 우리말에 맞게 빈 칸에 알맞은 단어를 쓰세요.

1 His opinion was not in ______________ with the doctors' own views.
그의 견해는 의사들 자신의 견해와 일치하지 않았다. 10 고3학평 변형

2 The ______________ of boys who liked playing sports was more than three times that of girls.
운동하는 것을 좋아하는 소년들의 비율은 소녀들에 비해 세 배가 넘었다. 14 고1학평 변형

3 One of the classic signs of ______________ eating is night eating.
감정적 식사의 전형적인 신호 중 하나는 밤에 먹는 것이다. 2012 수능

4 The ______________ noise of construction work in front of my house made me annoyed.
우리 집 앞 공사 현장의 끊임없는 소음은 나를 짜증나게 했다.

5 People have found many ways to reduce stress or control their ______________ to it.
사람들은 스트레스를 줄이거나 그에 대한 반응을 조절할 수 있는 여러 가지 방법을 발견하였다. 13 평가원

6 We should press the fashion industry not to ______________ very skinny models.
우리는 패션 업계가 더 이상 너무 마른 모델을 고용하지 못하도록 해야 한다. 08 고2학평 변형

7 The president's ______________ in office is five years in Korea.
한국에서 대통령의 임기 기간은 5년이다.

8 For his experiments, Tim took 6-week-old mice and moved them to an ______________ enclosure.
그의 실험을 위해, Tim은 6주일 된 생쥐들을 가져 와서 그의 실험용 울타리로 옮겨두었다. 2015 수능 변형

9 Reading classical texts ______________ the mind by triggering moments of self-reflection.
고전을 읽는 것은 자기 반성을 이끌어 내어 정신적으로 이롭게 한다. 15 평가원

10 The city has many ______________ where children and adults have fun.
그 도시는 아이들과 어른들이 즐겁게 시간을 보낼 수 있는 많은 명소들이 있다. 09 고1학평 변형

Day 01

MP3

016 □ **condition** [kəndíʃən]
명 상태, 조건, 상황
financial condition 재정 상태

017 □ **personal** [pə́ːrsənəl]
형 개인의, 개인적인
gain personal confidence 개인적 신뢰를 얻다

018 □ **dependent** [dipéndənt]
형 의존하는, 의지하는
mostly dependent on your fortune 운에 전적으로 의존하는

019 □ **motivate** [móutəvèit]
동 동기를 부여하다
motivate us to study physics 우리가 물리학을 공부하도록 동기를 부여하다

020 □ **pressure** [préʃər]
명 압박, 압력
high blood pressure 고혈압 under pressure 압박을 받는

021 □ **race** [reis]
명 인종
a conflict between different races 다른 인종간의 갈등

022 □ **consequence** [kánsəkwèns]
명 결과, 중요성
as a consequence of the accident 그 사고의 결과로서

023 □ **efficiently** [ifíʃəntli]
부 효율적으로, 능률적으로
do one's work efficiently ~의 일을 효율적으로 하다

024 □ **female** [fíːmèil]
형 여성의
a female candidate for the presidency 여자 대통령 후보

025 □ **instance** [ínstəns]
명 예, 사례
for instance 예를 들어

026 □ **react** [riǽkt]
동 반응하다
react angrily to the news 그 소식에 격하게 반응하다

027 □ **concept** [kánsept]
명 개념
a basic concept 기초 개념

028 □ **entire** [intáiər]
형 전체의, 내내
the entire staff of the school 학교의 전 직원

029 □ **moral** [mɔ́(ː)rəl]
형 도덕의, 도덕적인
moral behavior 도덕적인 행동

030 □ **perhaps** [pərhǽps]
부 아마, 어쩌면
Perhaps she forgot the appointment. 아마 그녀는 약속을 잊은 것 같다.

Daily Test

| 월 일 |

A 우리말에 맞게 빈 칸에 알맞은 단어를 쓰세요.

1 Hundreds of thousands of refugees are ______________ on food aid.
수 십만 명의 난민들이 식량 원조에 의지하고 있다.

2 The match finished over an hour ago and there is no need for me to feel under ______________.
경기는 한 시간 전에 끝났고 더 이상 난 압박감을 느낄 필요가 없다. 14 고1평가원 변형

3 The belief that different ______________ of people have different characters and abilities is wrong.
다른 인종의 사람들은 다른 특징과 능력을 가질 거라는 믿음은 잘못되었다. 05 고3학평 변형

4 If you want to change your lifestyle, you must accept the ______________ of that decision.
만약 당신의 생활 방식을 바꾸고 싶다면, 너는 그 결정의 결과를 받아들여야만 한다. 14 평가원

5 The title of the book is "How to Develop Brain Function ______________."
그 책의 제목은 "뇌의 기능을 효율적으로 개발하는 법" 이다. 15 고2학평 변형

6 Based on the research, there is no actual consensus on what male or ______________ values are.
그 조사에 의하면 무엇이 남성적 가치 혹은 여성적 가치인지에 대해 실질적인 의견일치는 없다.

7 I want to travel to some European countries, for ______________, to Spain and to France.
나는 유럽 국가를 예를 들면, 스페인과 프랑스로 여행을 가고 싶다.

8 There are few people who do not ______________ to music to some degree.
음악에 어느 정도 반응하지 않는 사람은 거의 없다. 2008 수능

9 These days, the ______________ of seasonal fruit is starting to fade away.
요즈음은 계절과일이라는 개념이 약해지고 있다. 09 고3학평 변형

10 ______________ his next travel destination will be France.
아마도 그의 다음 여행 목적지는 프랑스일 것이다.

Day 02

MP3

031 **feature** [fíːtʃər]
명 특징
an interesting feature of the novel 그 소설의 흥미로운 특징

032 **significant** [signífikənt]
형 중요한, 상당한
a significant discovery 중요한 발견

033 **throughout** [θru(ː)áut]
전 내내, ~동안
throughout the month 1달 내내

034 **unite** [juːnáit]
동 통합하다, 단결하다
unite the independent nations 독립국들을 통합하다

035 **assume** [əsjúːm]
동 추정하다, 추측하다
assume he is guilty 그가 유죄라고 추측하다

036 **detailed** [ditéild]
형 상세한
make a detailed plan 상세한 계획을 세우다

037 **following** [fálouiŋ]
형 그 다음의
answer the following question 다음 질문에 답하시오

038 **predict** [pridíkt]
동 예측하다, 예견하다
predict the result of the game 경기의 결과를 예측하다

039 **concern** [kənsə́ːrn]
명 관심, 우려 동 걱정시키다
concern about violence in movies 영화의 폭력성에 대한 우려

040 **eventually** [ivéntʃuəli]
부 마침내, 결국
eventually arrived two hours late 결국 두 시간 늦게 도착했다

041 **further** [fə́ːrðər]
부 더, 멀리, 추가의
go further south 남쪽으로 더 가다

042 **outcome** [áutkʌ̀m]
명 결과, 성과
guess the outcome of a game 경기의 결과를 추측하다

043 **profit** [práfit]
명 이익, 수익
profit and loss 이익과 손실

044 **reward** [riwɔ́ːrd]
명 보상 동 보상하다
reward for a good grade 좋은 성적에 대한 보상

045 **coexist** [kòuigzíst]
동 공존하다
coexist peacefully 평화로이 공존하다

Daily Test

| 월 일 |

Ⓐ 우리말에 맞게 빈 칸에 알맞은 단어를 쓰세요.

1 Gravity has a ______________ effect on the number of objects juggled.
중력은 던져 올리는 물건의 숫자에 상당한 영향을 미친다. 05 고2 평가원 변형

2 ______________ the 20th century, global temperatures have gone up by just under one degree Celsius.
20세기 내내, 세계 온도는 약 섭씨 1도 이하 정도만 올랐다. 14 평가원

3 Our ancestors needed to be ______________ to protect their food from enemies.
우리 선조는 적들로부터 그들의 음식을 지키기 위해 단결해야 했다. 11 고2 학평 변형

4 Let's ______________ for a while that the plan will fail.
잠깐 동안 그 계획이 실패할 것이라고 추측해 보자.

5 For more ______________ information, email us at master@ecotoy.
더 자세한 정보를 원하신다면, master@ecotoy로 메일을 보내주세요. 15 고1 학평 변형

6 It is hard to ______________ what the judge's sentence will be.
그 판사의 선고가 어떨 지는 예측하기 어렵다.

7 He was deeply ______________ about the safety of his family.
그는 가족의 안전이 몹시 염려되었다. 11 고1 학평

8 Minji and Jinju compared the final ______________ to their initial expectations.
민지와 진주는 그들의 처음 기대치와 그들의 최종 결과를 비교했다. 14 고1 평가원 변형

9 To increase our chances of earning a ______________, we need sensible planning.
이익을 올릴 수 있는 가능성을 향상시키기 위해 우리는 합리적인 계획이 필요하다.

10 We need to better understand the animals we ______________ with here on Earth.
우리는 지구에 우리와 공존하는 동물들을 더 잘 이해할 필요가 있다.

Day 02

MP3

046 essential [əsénʃəl]
형 필수적인, 본질적인
prepare essential goods 필수품을 준비하다

047 contribute [kəntríbjuːt]
동 기증하다, 기여하다
contribute books to a school library 학교 도서관에 책을 기증하다

048 invest [invést]
동 투자하다
invest in stocks 주식에 투자하다

049 limited [límitid]
형 제한된
a limited supply of resources 자원의 한정된 공급

050 claim [kleim]
명 주장 동 주장하다, 요구하다
an exaggerated claim 과장된 주장

051 occasion [əkéiʒən]
명 때, 행사
on occasion 때때로 a special occasion 특별한 행사

052 generally [dʒénərəli]
부 일반적으로, 대개, 보통
generally speaking 일반적으로 말하자면

053 accurate [ǽkjərit]
형 정확한
an accurate description 정확한 묘사

054 biology [baiálədʒi]
명 생물학
study marine biology 해양 생물학을 공부하다

055 principle [prínsəpl]
명 원리, 원칙
a man of high moral principles 높은 도덕적 원칙을 가진 사람

056 seek [siːk]
동 찾다, 추구하다
seek employment 직장을 찾다

057 depart [dipáːrt]
동 출발하다, 떠나다
depart Seoul for Tokyo 서울에서 동경으로 출발하다

058 myth [miθ]
명 신화
a creation myth 창조 신화

059 range [reindʒ]
명 (변화, 차이, 거리의) 범위, 다양성
in a range of experiences 경험의 범위 내에서

060 attitude [ǽtitjùːd]
명 태도
his attitude to marriage 그의 결혼에 대한 태도

Daily Test

| 월 일 |

A 우리말에 맞게 빈 칸에 알맞은 단어를 쓰세요.

1 Families don't grow strong unless parents _____________ precious time in them.
부모님이 가족들에게 소중한 시간을 투자하지 않는다면, 그들은 강하게 자랄 수 없다. 16 고1학평 변형

2 Almost every man _____________ he was innocent.
거의 모든 사람들이 그가 무죄라고 주장했다. 13 평가원

3 On _____________, Susan would ask James directly, "What's intelligence?"
때때로, Susan은 James에게 직접적으로 무엇이 지능인지 물어보았다. 14 고1 평가원 변형

4 People _____________ believe the conscious mind constantly directs their actions.
사람들은 대개 의식적인 마음이 끊임없이 그들의 행동을 지시한다고 믿는다. 14 고1학평 변형

5 I finished writing my _____________ paper last week.
난 지난 주말에 생물학 보고서를 다 작성했다. 2014 수능

6 One of the main _____________ I follow when I draw outside is not to select a subject that is too odd.
내가 야외에서 그릴 때 따르는 주요 원칙 중 하나는 너무 이상한 대상을 선택하지 않는 것이다. 2009 수능

7 If you are _____________ a different kind of information, ask for it by calling us.
만약 당신이 다른 종류의 정보를 원한다면, 우리에게 전화로 요청하십시오. 2010 수능

8 Our tour plan is to _____________ from Inchon Airport on April 1 and return on April 20.
우리의 여행 계획은 4월 1일 인천 공항에서 출발해서 4월 20일에 돌아오는 것이다.

9 We're sure we can find the right paint color within the _____________ of colors in the store.
우리는 그 상점에 있는 색들의 범위 내에서 알맞은 물감 색을 찾을 수 있다고 확신한다.

10 I decided to focus more on building positive _____________ within the classroom.
나는 교실 안에서 긍정적인 태도를 구축하는데 더 집중하기로 결심했다. 2015 수능

Review Test 01

Day 01 + Day 02 | 월 일 |

A 우리말에 맞게 빈 칸에 알맞은 단어를 쓰시오.

1 in ______________ with my opinion 내 의견과 일치하다

2 a ______________ for help 도와달라는 간청

3 ______________ equipment 실험용 장비

4 a conflict between different ______________ 다른 인종간의 갈등

5 ______________ she forgot the appointment. 아마 그녀는 약속을 잊은 것 같다.

6 an interesting ______________ of the novel 그 소설의 흥미로운 특징

7 go ______________ south 남쪽으로 더 가다

8 a ______________ supply of resources 자원의 한정된 공급

9 ______________ speaking 일반적으로 말하자면

10 ______________ employment 직장을 찾다

B 영어에 맞게 빈 칸에 알맞은 우리말을 쓰시오.

1 percentage of body fat 체지방 ______________

2 employ Susan as a director 감독으로 Susan을 ______________

3 run a grocery store 식료품점을 ______________

4 for instance ______________를 들어

5 moral behavior ______________ 행동

6 unite the independent nations 독립국들을 ______________

7 make a detailed plan ______________ 계획을 세우다

8 profit and loss ______________과 손실

9 depart Seoul for Tokyo 서울에서 동경으로 ______________

10 his attitude to marriage 그의 결혼에 대한 ______________

C 다음 영어 풀이에 알맞은 어휘를 〈보기〉에서 고르시오.

보기	contribute	means	response	dependent	attraction

1 ______________ : something that people want to see or enjoy

2 ______________ : decided or influenced by something

3 ______________ : a way or method of doing something or getting results

4 ______________ : something you get as a reply or answer to your question or request

5 ______________ : to give help for something or to help to get a result

D 문맥에 맞게 다음 문장을 완성하시오.

1	One of the classic signs of •	• a	on what male or female values are.
2	The city has many attractions •	• b	biology paper last week.
3	Based on the research, there is no consensus •	• c	emotional eating is night eating.
4	We need to better understand the animals •	• d	we coexist with here on Earth.
5	I finished writing my •	• e	where children and adults have fun.

E 문장을 읽고 문맥에 적절한 단어를 고르시오.

1 It is too early to predict the (outcome/means) of the experiment.

2 I haven't got his (concern/response) to my question yet.

3 After years of hard work, John could (eventually/generally) open his own restaurant.

4 The success of this project is largely (dependent/keen) on the interest of the general public.

5 The Eiffel Tower is the most famous tourist (affection/attraction) in Paris.

F 문장의 빈칸에 알맞은 단어를 〈보기〉에서 찾아 쓰시오. (필요하면 형태를 고치시오.)

보기 essential competitive consequence claim accurate

1 I don't consider the price of this car to be ______________ in the market.
나는 이 차의 가격은 시장에서 경쟁력이 있다고 보지 않는다.

2 Proper breathing is particularly ______________ when you run in a long distance race.
적절한 호흡은 특히 장거리 경주에서 달릴 때 필수적이다. 11 고1학평 변형

3 A short-term rise in temperature may cause a number of disastrous ______________ for the organisms living in water.
짧은 기간의 온도 상승이 수중 생물들에게는 여러 치명적인 결과를 초래할 수 있다.

4 It is also difficult for computers to provide ______________ translations if there is no context.
맥락이 주어지지 않으면 컴퓨터가 정확한 번역을 제공하기는 어렵다. 09 고2평가원 변형

5 Experts ______________ that they can find out many things about a person from his or her writing.
전문가들은 한 사람의 손 글씨를 보면 그 사람에 대해 많은 것을 알 수 있다고 주장한다. 07 고1학평 변형

G 다음 〈보기〉 중 두 문장에 공통으로 사용할 수 있는 어휘를 고르시오.

1 A single person may behave in different ways, depending on their ___________ state.
There is a close relationship between physical illness and ___________ stress. 13 고1학평 변형

① experimental ② entire ③ significant ④ emotional ⑤ essential

2 One of the most ___________ advantages of the touch screen is that it's very easy to use. 06 고1학평 변형
They invested a ___________ amount of time and money into planning the event.

① accurate ② significant ③ dependent ④ moral ⑤ entire

3 Many students ___________ their talents to the project. 08 고1학평 변형
He ___________ greatly to the introduction of "race music" to the larger American musical scene. 15 고1학평 변형

① assumed ② claimed ③ sought ④ contributed ⑤ departed

Study More

run의 다양한 용법

- (사람, 동물 등이) 뛰다, 달리다
  Cheetahs can **run** as fast as passing cars on a highway.
  치타는 고속도로 위를 지나는 차만큼 빨리 달릴 수 있다.
  Jinju came **running** to meet us. 진주는 우리를 맞이하러 달려왔다.
- (사업체 등을) 운영하다, 경영하다, 관리하다
  Running a business is not easy. 사업체를 운영하는 것은 쉽지 않다.

Day 03

MP3

061 □ **contrast** [kántræst]
명 대조, 차이 동 대조하다, 대비되다
a contrast between A and B A와 B 사이의 차이

062 □ **aspect** [ǽspekt]
명 측면, 양상
various aspects of a child's imagination 아이들 상상력의 다양한 양상

063 □ **entertain** [èntərtéin]
동 즐겁게 하다, 접대하다
entertain his son with fairy tales 동화로 그의 아들을 즐겁게 해주다

064 □ **frequent** [fríːkwənt]
형 잦은, 빈번한 부 frequently 자주, 빈번히
frequent occurrence 자주 일어나는 일

065 □ **promote** [prəmóut]
동 승진 시키다, 홍보하다
be promoted to manager 매니저로 승진하다

066 □ **refer** [rifə́ːr]
동 언급하다, 참조하다, 나타내다
refer to the matter again 그 문제를 다시 언급하다

067 □ **capacity** [kəpǽsəti]
명 능력, 수용력
intellectual capacity 지적 능력

068 □ **crop** [krap]
명 농작물, 작물
major crops in Korea 한국의 주요 작물

069 □ **detect** [ditékt]
동 발견하다, 탐지하다
detect the odor of a gas 가스 냄새를 탐지하다

070 □ **explanation** [èksplənéiʃən]
명 설명, 해설
a detailed explanation 상세한 설명

071 □ **lack** [læk]
명 부족 동 부족하다, 결핍되다
a lack of nutrition 영양 부족

072 □ **addition** [ədíʃən]
명 추가, 덧셈
make an addition 첨가하다 in addition 게다가

073 □ **advanced** [ədvǽnst]
형 선진의, 상급의
advanced technology 선진 기술

074 □ **factor** [fǽktər]
명 요인, 요소
an important factor 중요한 요인

075 □ **goods** [gudz]
명 상품, 물건
goods and services 상품과 서비스

Daily Test

| 월 일 |

Ⓐ 우리말에 맞게 빈 칸에 알맞은 단어를 쓰세요.

1 There is a sharp _______________ between knowing and doing.
아는 것과 행하는 것에는 명확한 차이가 있다.

2 My writing assignment is to write about one interesting _______________ of social media.
나의 글쓰기 숙제는 소셜 미디어에 대해 하나의 흥미로운 측면을 쓰는 것이다.

3 Your dogs have plenty of items to keep them _______________ while you are gone.
당신의 강아지들은 당신이 없는 동안에 그들을 재미있게 해 줄 많은 아이템을 가지고 있다. 08 고2 평가원 변형

4 _______________ repetition of positive experiences change your self-concept in a positive manner.
긍정적인 경험의 빈번한 반복은 당신의 자아개념을 긍정적인 방식으로 변화시킨다. 05 고3 평가원 변형

5 Habitat diversity _______________ to the variety of places where life exists.
서식지 다양성은 생물들이 살 수 있는 다양한 장소들을 나타낸다. 2011 수능

6 The main _______________ of the country is wheat.
그 나라의 주된 작물은 밀이다.

7 I _______________ the odor of something bad and saw the pot was burning.
나는 무언가 이상한 냄새를 탐지했고, 냄비가 타고 있는 것을 보았다.

8 Before you start your _______________, it is important to think about your audience.
당신의 설명을 시작하기 전에, 당신의 관객을 생각하는 것은 중요하다. 04 고2 평가원 변형

9 Failure may be due to _______________ of ability or to lack of motivation.
실패는 능력의 부족 혹은 동기의 부족 때문일 수 있다. 13 고1 평가원 변형

10 Ann argued in favor of the _______________ of more computers to the computer lab.
Ann은 컴퓨터실에 더 많은 컴퓨터의 추가를 주장했다. 06 고2 학평

Day 03

MP3

076 □ **manufacture** [mæ̀njəfǽktʃər]
동 제조하다 명 제조
manufacture Smartphone parts 스마트폰 부품을 제조하다

077 □ **satisfaction** [sæ̀tisfǽkʃən]
명 만족
customer satisfaction 고객 만족

078 □ **responsibility** [rispɑ̀nsəbíləti]
명 책임, 책무
take responsibility for animals 동물에 대한 책임

079 □ **analysis** [ənǽləsəs]
명 분석
make an analysis of human behavior 사람 행동에 관한 행동

080 □ **demonstrate** [démənstrèit]
동 입증하다, 시위하다
demonstrate a chemical phenomenon 화학적 현상에 대해 입증하다

081 □ **completely** [kəmplí:tli]
부 완전히, 전적으로
completely different colors 완전히 다른 색깔

082 □ **environmental** [invàiərənméntəl]
형 환경의
environmental adaptation 환경 적응

083 □ **appeal** [əpí:l]
명 간청, 호소 동 간청하다, 호소하다
make an emotional appeal 감정적인 호소를 하다

084 □ **generation** [dʒènəréiʃən]
명 세대, 시대
overcome the generation gap 세대차이를 극복하다

085 □ **operate** [ápərèit]
동 가동하다, 조작하다, 작동하다
operate machinery 기계를 작동하다

086 □ **yield** [ji:ld]
명 수확(량), 생산 동 산출하다, 생산하다
a poor crop yield 빈약한 농작물 수확량

087 □ **accomplish** [əkámpliʃ]
동 성취하다, 완수하다
accomplish a mission 업무를 완수하다

088 □ **classic** [klǽsik]
형 일류의, 전형적인, 고전적인
classic novels 최고의 소설들 a classic error 전형적인 실수

089 □ **conscious** [kánʃəs]
형 의식하는, 자각하는
be conscious of your own problem 자기 자신의 문제를 의식하고 있다

090 □ **firm** [fə:rm]
명 기업, 회사 형 단단한, 확고한
work at a law firm 법률 회사에서 일하다

Daily Test

| 월 일 |

A 우리말에 맞게 빈 칸에 알맞은 단어를 쓰세요.

1 Most plastic is ______________ using oil by-products and natural gas.
대부분의 플라스틱은 오일의 부산물과 천연 가스를 사용하여 제조된다. 11 평가원

2 The greatest communication ______________ comes from close relationships.
가장 큰 의사소통의 만족은 친밀한 관계로부터 온다. 14 평가원

3 I scrubbed the surface of the timber until it was ______________ smooth.
나는 그 목재의 표면이 완전히 매끄러울 때까지 문질러 닦았다.

4 Each cell must obtain its energy from some outside ______________ source.
각각의 세포는 그들의 에너지를 외부 환경적 자원으로부터 얻어야 한다. 08 평가원

5 The presidential candidate ______________ to the people for support.
대통령 후보는 사람들에게 지지를 호소했다.

6 In order to ______________ the printer, you need either electricity or a battery.
그 인쇄기를 작동시키기 위해서, 전기 또는 건전지가 필요해요. 09 평가원

7 For a better ______________ of mustard seeds, pollination is necessary.
더 나은 겨자씨의 수확을 위해서 수분은 필수적이다. 15 평가원

8 Focus on one task at a time, and you'll ______________ each task better, and probably faster.
한 번에 한 가지 일에 집중해라, 그러면 당신은 각각의 일을 훌륭하고 더 빠르게 완수할 것이다. 15 고1학평 변형

9 "You made a ______________ mistake, as I did," he told me.
"너는 나와 마찬가지로 전형적인 실수를 했구나," 라고 그가 나에게 말했다. 14 고2학평

10 I am much more ______________ of the need to exercise regularly.
나는 규칙적으로 운동하는 것에 대한 필요성을 더 잘 인지하고 있다.

Day 04

MP3

091 **intelligence** [intélidʒəns]
명 지능
an intelligence test 지능 검사

092 **necessity** [nəsésəti]
명 필요성, 필수품
necessity of saving 저축의 필요성

093 **recall** [rikɔ́:l]
동 상기하다, 기억해내다
recall happy memories 행복한 기억을 상기하다

094 **replace** [ripléis]
동 교체하다, 대체하다
replace an old chair with a new one 낡은 의자를 새 것으로 교체하다

095 **adjust** [ədʒʌ́st]
동 조절하다, 적응하다
adjust the volume on a radio 라디오 음량을 조절하다

096 **contain** [kəntéin]
동 포함하다, 함유하다
contain high levels of caffeine 많은 카페인을 함유하다

097 **exception** [iksépʃən]
명 예외, 제외
make an exception 예외를 두다

098 **frustrated** [frʌ́strèitid]
형 낙담한, 좌절한
be frustrated with the exam result 시험 결과에 낙담하다

099 **per** [pər]
전 ~마다
grow 2 centimetres per year 1년에 2센티미터씩 자라다

100 **practical** [prǽktikəl]
형 현실적인, 실용적인
need a practical solution 현실적인 해결책이 필요하다

101 **pursue** [pərsjú:]
동 추구하다, 뒤쫓다
pursue an objective 목표를 추구하다

102 **relatively** [rélətivli]
부 비교적으로, 상대적인
relatively low cost 비교적 낮은 가격

103 **setting** [sétiŋ]
명 환경, 배경
an ideal setting 이상적인 환경

104 **academic** [æ̀kədémik]
형 학업의, 학문적인
high academic standards 높은 학업 수준

105 **citizen** [sítizən]
명 시민
a citizen movement 시민 운동

Daily Test

| 월 일 |

A 우리말에 맞게 빈 칸에 알맞은 단어를 쓰세요.

1 Emotional ______________ travels through an organization like electricity over telephone wires.
감정적 지능은 전화 선에 흐르는 전기와 같이 조직 전체로 퍼져 나간다. 13 고1학평 변형

2 When people are depressed, ______________ their problems makes things worse.
사람들이 우울해 할 때, 그들의 문제를 상기시키는 것은 상황을 더 나쁘게 만든다. 12 고1학평 변형

3 Many jobs might be ______________ by robots in the future.
미래에는 많은 직업들이 로보트에 의해 대체될 지 모른다.

4 Alex said Joe helped him ______________ to the new school.
Alex는 Joe가 자신이 새로운 학교에 적응할 수 있도록 도와줬다고 말했다. 16 고3학평 변형

5 Lemonade ______________ a lot of vitamin C.
레모네이드는 많은 양의 비타민 C를 포함하고 있다. 14 고3평가원 변형

6 They don't accept late applications, but since John was so sick, they made an ______________.
그들은 늦은 신청서를 받지 않지만, John은 너무 아팠기 때문에 예외를 두었다.

7 Think of specific times when you were mad or ______________.
당신이 매우 화가 났거나 좌절했던 특정한 때를 생각해 보아라. 13 고1학평 변형

8 Solar energy can be a ______________ alternative energy source for us in the future.
우리에게 태양 에너지는 미래에 합리적인 대체 에너지 자원이 될 수 있다. 2015 수능

9 Great successes come when you ______________ and obtain what you want.
위대한 성공은 당신이 원하는 것을 추구하고 얻을 때 따라온다. 16 고2학평 변형

10 The ______________ standards of the students at Harvard are very high.
하버드의 학생들의 학문적 수준은 매우 높다.

Day 04

MP3

106 **exposure** [ikspóuʒər]
명 노출
exposure to the natural environment 자연 환경에 노출됨

107 **inner** [ínər]
형 내면의, 내부의
inner peace 내적 평화

108 **perceive** [pərsíːv]
동 인식하다, 인지하다
perceive change 변화를 인식하다

109 **lawyer** [lɔ́ːjər]
명 변호사
consult a lawyer 변호사에게 상담하다

110 **agriculture** [ǽgrəkʌ̀ltʃər]
명 농사, 농업
the Department of Agriculture 농업부

111 **conventional** [kənvénʃənəl]
형 전통적인, 관습적인
conventional wisdom 전통적인 지혜

112 **directly** [diréktli]
부 곧장, 직접적으로
answer directly 직설적으로 대답하다

113 **innovation** [ìnəvéiʃən]
명 혁신
stimulate constant innovation 지속적인 혁신을 자극하다

114 **mark** [mɑːrk]
명 자국, 흔적 동 표시하다
a scratch mark 긁힌 자국

115 **objective** [əbdʒéktiv]
명 목적 형 객관적인
the principal objective 주된 목적

116 **overall** [òuvərɔ́ːl]
형 종합적인
overall results 종합적인 성과

117 **rural** [rú(ː)ərəl]
형 시골의, 지방의
a rural economy 지방 경제

118 **deplete** [dipliːt]
동 고갈시키다, 다 써버리다
deplete natural resources 천연 자원을 고갈시키다

119 **sort** [sɔːrt]
명 종류 동 분류하다
favorite sort of music 좋아하는 음악의 종류

120 **acquire** [əkwáiər]
동 습득하다, 얻다
acquire good social knowledge 좋은 사회지식을 습득하다

Daily Test

| 월 일 |

A 우리말에 맞게 빈 칸에 알맞은 단어를 쓰세요.

1 Direct ______________ to ultraviolet light can cause negative effects on the skin.
자외선에 직접적인 노출은 피부에 부정적인 영향을 미칠 수 있다. 15 고1학평 변형

2 The ______________ had a unique place within American society.
변호사는 미국 사회 내에서 독특한 위치에 있었다. 09 평가원

3 ______________ is the most important part of many countries' economies.
농업은 많은 나라들의 경제에 있어 아주 중요한 항목이다.

4 Long hairs could reveal freedom from ______________ expectations.
긴 머리는 관습적 기대로부터의 자유를 드러낸다. 08 고1학평 변형

5 ______________ and cultural exchange can expand Earth's capacity.
혁신과 문화적 교류는 세계의 수용력을 확장 시킬 수 있다. 16 평가원 변형

6 If you do not put a question ______________ at the end of this sentence, your answer will be wrong.
만약 네가 이 문장 끝에 물음표를 넣지 않는다면, 너의 답은 틀린 것이 될 수 있다.

7 Most people who live in ______________ areas usually work in agriculture.
시골 지방에 살고 있는 대부분의 사람들은 보통 농업에 종사한다.

8 Light recreational exercise does little to adversely ______________ bodily nutrients.
가벼운 운동은 신체 영양소를 고갈시키는 데 악영향을 거의 끼치지 않는다.

9 Children who grow up experiencing all ______________ of cultures tend to be less biased.
모든 종류의 문화를 경험하면서 자라는 아이들은 덜 편향적인 경향이 있다. 09 고3평가원 변형

10 What helps the child ______________ a mother tongue?
무엇이 아이들이 모국어를 배울 수 있도록 돕나요? 15 고1학평 변형

A 우리말에 맞게 빈 칸에 알맞은 단어를 쓰시오.

1 a ______________ between A and B A와 B 사이의 차이
2 major ______________ in Korea 한국의 주요 작물
3 a ______________ of nutrition 영양 부족
4 make an ______________ of human behavior 사람 행동에 관한 행동
5 a poor crop ______________ 빈약한 농작물 수확량
6 an ______________ test 지능 검사
7 ______________ the volume on a radio 라디오 음량을 조절하다
8 ______________ to the natural environment 자연 환경에 노출됨
9 the Department of ______________ 농업부
10 a scratch ______________ 긁힌 자국

B 영어에 맞게 빈 칸에 알맞은 우리말을 쓰시오.

1 entertain his son with fairy tales 동화로 그의 아들을 ______________
2 be promoted to manager 매니저로 ______________
3 take responsibility for animals 동물에 대한 ______________
4 make an emotional appeal 감정적인 ______________를 하다
5 work at a law firm 법률 ______________에서 일하다
6 necessity of saving 저축의 ______________
7 need a practical solution ______________ 해결책이 필요하다
8 high academic standards 높은 ______________ 수준
9 stimulate constant innovation 지속적인 ______________을 자극하다
10 a rural economy ______________ 경제

C 다음 영어 풀이에 알맞은 어휘를 〈보기〉에서 고르시오.

보기	promote	crop	practical	refer	factor

1 ______________ : to lead attention to something; to speak of something

2 ______________ : to encourage people to be aware of something

3 ______________ : a plant grown by farmers such as rice or wheat

4 ______________ : something that causes or contributes to a result

5 ______________ : useful and applicable to a real situation

D 문맥에 맞게 다음 문장을 완성하시오.

1 Habitat diversity refers to •

2 Most plastic is manufactured using •

3 In order to operate the printer, •

4 Lemonade contains •

5 Think of specific times •

• a the variety of places where life exists.

• b a lot of vitamin C.

• c you need either electricity or a battery.

• d when you were mad or frustrated.

• e oil by-products and natural gas.

E 문장을 읽고 문맥에 적절한 단어를 고르시오.

1 What (aspect/exception) of the new school do you like most?

2 Tom's family makes (overall/frequent) visits to the restaurant.

3 She has (completely/efficiently) forgotten our appointment today.

4 My shoes are wearing down. They need to be (replaced/innovated) soon.

5 The main (exposure/objective) of this class is to learn the basic terms of physics.

F 문장의 빈칸에 알맞은 단어를 〈보기〉에서 찾아 쓰시오. (필요하면 형태를 고치시오.)

보기	inner	recall	demonstrate	contain	relatively

1 Human beings are very good at ______________ faces they have seen before.
인간은 자신이 이전에 본 얼굴을 상기하는 것에 아주 능하다. 09 고1 평가원 변형

2 The early part of their marriage were ______________ peaceful.
그들 결혼생활 초기는 비교적 평온했다. 14 고1 학평 변형

3 She cut a page out of the magazine, which ______________ a picture of red roses.
그녀는 붉은 장미 꽃을 포함하고 있는 페이지 하나를 잡지에서 오려 냈다. 12 고1 학평 변형

4 The child was curious to see the ______________ side of the hut.
아이는 오두막의 안쪽은 어떤지 보고 싶어했다.

5 Joe successfully ______________ his ability to serve as a science teacher.
Joe는 과학 선생님으로 근무할 능력을 갖추고 있다는 것을 성공적으로 입증했다.

G 다음 〈보기〉 중 두 문장에 공통으로 사용할 수 있는 어휘를 고르시오.

1 It is becoming clear that ____________ problems should be seen a global issue. 10 고2학평 변형
Many people have become aware of the connection between ____________ pollution and climate change. 13 고1학평 변형

① practical ② advanced ③ dependent ④ environmental ⑤ continuous

2 I was extremely ____________ with the poor quality of his history essay.
He was ____________ with the negative comments of his friends.

① detailed ② lack ③ rural ④ responsible ⑤ frustrated

3 ____________ being a scientist, he was also a famous signer.
He speaks three foreign languages ____________ English.

① in terms of ② in spite of ③ in contrast with
④ regardless of ⑤ in addition to

Study More

혼동하기 쉬운 단어 mess vs. mass

- [mess] 명 지저분하고 엉망인 상태
  make a **mess** in the kitchen 부엌을 엉망인 상태로 만들다
- [mass] 명 덩어리
  be full of dark **masses** of clouds 먹구름 덩어리가 가득하다

Day 05

MP3

121 **decade** [dékeid]
명 10년간
for the last three decades 지난 30년 동안

122 **disaster** [dizǽstər]
명 재앙, 재해
a natural disaster like an earthquake 지진과 같은 자연재해

123 **equipment** [ikwípmənt]
명 장비, 기기
equipment for soccer 축구 장비

124 **extent** [ikstént]
명 정도, 범위
the extent of the damage 손상의 정도

125 **gender** [dʒéndər]
명 성, 성별
gender equality 성 평등

126 **central** [séntrəl]
형 중앙의, 중심의
in the central part of the city 도시의 중심부

127 **content** [kəntént]
명 내용물, 목차
a table of contents 책의 목차

128 **excessive** [iksésiv]
형 과도한, 지나친
excessive spending 과도한 소비

129 **expand** [ikspǽnd]
동 확장하다, 확대하다
expand a business 사업을 확장하다

130 **instruction** [instrʌ́kʃən]
명 지시, 교육, 교수
follow the instructions 지시를 따르다

131 **mass** [mæs]
명 덩어리, 대량
a mass of snow 눈 덩어리

132 **narration** [næréiʃən]
명 서술, 화법
the manner of narration 서술법, 화법

133 **reproduce** [rìːprədjúːs]
동 번식하다, 복제하다
help flowers reproduce 꽃이 번식하는 것을 돕다

134 **additional** [ədíʃənəl]
형 추가의
pay additional expenses 추가 비용을 지불하다

135 **regarding** [rigɑ́ːrdiŋ]
전 ~에 관하여
information regarding the education system 교육 시스템에 관한 정보

Daily Test

| 월 일 |

A 우리말에 맞게 빈 칸에 알맞은 단어를 쓰세요.

1 During the ______________ of the 1840s, a lot of people from all over the world moved to California to find gold.
1840년대의 10년 동안 전 세계로부터 많은 사람들이 금을 찾기 위해 캘리포니아로 이동했다.

2 Some people have lost their homes due to natural ______________.
몇몇 사람들은 자연 재해 때문에 그들의 집을 잃었다. 15 고1학평 변형

3 We accept donations of used medical ______________ such as wheelchairs and shower chairs.
우리는 휠체어나 샤워 의자 같은 중고 의료 장비들의 기부를 받고 있다. 2016 수능

4 The ______________ of Edison's scientific knowledge was amazing.
Edison의 과학에 대한 지식의 범위는 놀라울 정도였다.

5 ______________ America has been hit hard by a series of hurricanes.
중앙 아메리카는 일련의 허리케인들에 의해 심하게 타격을 받았다. 16 고1학평 변형

6 Bottles can reveal their ______________ without being opened.
병들은 열지 않아도 그들의 내용물을 그대로 드러낼 수 있다. 2008 수능

7 ______________ greed can give rise to unexpected disasters.
과도한 탐욕은 기대치 않은 재난을 일으킬 수 있다. 15 고1학평 변형

8 Following Jenny's ______________, Richard made a flower with the cream.
Jenny의 지시에 따라서, Richard는 크림으로 꽃을 만들었다.

9 Before taking on a ______________ of tasks, always remember "one task at a time."
많은 일을 하기 전에, 항상 "한 번에 한 가지 일"을 기억하라. 08 고1학평 변형

10 ______________ charges apply if you wish to use the express delivery service.
빠른 배달 서비스를 이용하면 추가 요금이 적용됩니다.

Day 05

MP3

136 □ **architecture** [ɑ́:rkitèktʃər]
명 건축학, 건축양식
study architecture 건축학을 공부하다

137 □ **convey** [kənvéi]
동 전달하다
convey personal opinions 개인적인 의견을 전달하다

138 □ **convince** [kənvíns]
동 납득시키다, 설득하다
convince Frank to sign the contract 계약서에 서명하도록 Frank를 설득하다

139 □ **crucial** [krú:ʃəl]
형 중대한, 결정적인
a crucial factor 결정적인 요인

140 □ **generate** [dʒénərèit]
동 발생시키다, 일으키다
generate heat 열을 발생시키다

141 □ **identify** [aidéntəfài]
동 확인하다, 알아보다
identify the exact reason 정확한 이유를 파악하다

142 □ **internal** [intə́:rnəl]
형 내부의
the internal structure of the room 방의 내부 구조

143 □ **relation** [riléiʃən]
명 관계
diplomatic relations between two countries 두 나라의 외교적 관계

144 □ **struggle** [strʌ́gl]
동 투쟁하다, 분투하다
struggle for independence 독립을 위해 투쟁하다

145 □ **phenomenon** [finɑ́mənɑ̀n]
명 현상
a natural phenomenon 자연 현상

146 □ **colleague** [kɑ́li:g]
명 동료
Cindy's long-time colleague Cindy의 오랜 동료

147 □ **be engaged in** [bi ingéidʒd in]
~에 종사하고 있다
be engaged in newspaper work 신문 업무에 종사하다

148 □ **delight** [diláit]
명 기쁨 동 즐겁게 하다
cry with delight 기뻐서 울다

149 □ **destruction** [distrʌ́kʃən]
명 파괴, 파멸
the destruction of the environment 환경 파괴

150 □ **fundamental** [fʌ̀ndəméntəl]
형 근본적인, 기본적인
a fundamental change 근본적인 변화

Daily Test

| 월 일 |

A 우리말에 맞게 빈 칸에 알맞은 단어를 쓰세요.

1 Steven enrolled at Cornell University to study ______________.
Steven은 건축학을 공부하기 위해 Cornell 대학교에 등록했다. 15 고2학평 변형

2 Some species use alarm calls to ______________ information about potential predators.
몇몇 종들은 잠재적 천적에 대한 정보를 전달하기 위해 위험 신호를 사용한다. 15 고1학평 변형

3 One way to ______________ your values is to look at what frustrates you.
당신의 가치를 확인하기 위한 방법 중 하나는 무엇이 당신을 좌절시키는지 보는 것이다. 13 고1학평 변형

4 ______________ peace is what enables a startup to survive.
내부적인 평화는 신생 기업이 살아남는 것을 가능케 한다. 15 고2학평 변형

5 Faith and encouragement can lead to the positive ______________ between a husband and wife.
믿음과 격려는 부부 사이의 긍정적인 관계로 이끌 수 있다.

6 History is littered with examples of people who have ______________ for the freedom and independence.
역사는 자유와 독립을 위해 투쟁해 온 사람들의 예로 점철되어 있다.

7 Many people do not understand that hypnosis is a natural ______________.
많은 사람들은 최면이 자연적인 현상임을 이해하지 못한다. 10 고1학평 변형

8 Mark gave a presentation about the new project without consulting his ______________.
Mark는 그의 동료들과 상의도 없이 새 프로젝트에 관한 발표를 했다.

9 I'm ______________ you're fully recovered from your illness.
나는 너의 병세가 완전히 회복 되어서 기쁘구나. 2012 수능

10 I believe mystery plays a ______________ role in experiencing the great things in life.
나는 미스터리가 인생에서 위대한 것들을 경험하는데 근본적인 역할을 한다고 믿는다. 08 평가원

Day 06

MP3

151 **insight** [ínsàit]
명 통찰력
a leader of great insight 대단한 통찰력을 지닌 지도자

152 **persuade** [pərswéid]
동 설득하다
persuade her to come back 그녀에게 돌아오라고 설득하다

153 **security** [sikjú(:)ərəti]
명 보안, 안전
a potential threat to security 보안에 잠재적인 위협

154 **truly** [trú:li]
부 정말로
truly memorable experience 정말로 기억에 남는 경험

155 **unexpected** [ʌ̀nikspéktid]
형 예기치 않은, 예상 밖의
an unexpected result 예기치 않은 결과

156 **attach** [ətǽtʃ]
동 붙이다, 첨부하다
attach a name tag 이름표를 붙이다 attach a file 파일을 첨부하다

157 **barrier** [bǽriər]
명 장벽, 장애물
stand behind the barrier 장벽 뒤에 서다

158 **ceremony** [sérəmòuni]
명 의식, 식
the opening ceremony of the Olympics 올림픽의 개막식

159 **dozen** [dʌ́zən]
명 12개짜리, 십여 개(명)
study a dozen species of ants 개미 12종을 연구하다

160 **import** [ímpɔ̀:rt]
동 수입하다 명 수입(품)
import agricultural products 농산품을 수입하다

161 **nutritious** [nju:tríʃəs]
형 영양가 있는, 영양분이 높은
serve a nutritious meal 영양가 있는 식사를 하다

162 **insomnia** [insámniə]
명 불면증
induce insomnia 불면증을 유도하다

163 **pound** [paund]
동 두드리다
pound on the roof 지붕 위를 두드리다

164 **restrict** [ristríkt]
동 제한하다
restrict freedom of expression 표현의 자유를 제한하다

165 **unpleasant** [ʌnplézənt]
형 불쾌한
an unpleasant smell 불쾌한 냄새

Daily Test

| 월 일 |

A 우리말에 맞게 빈 칸에 알맞은 단어를 쓰세요.

1 His new novel was full of ______________ about human nature.
그의 새로운 소설은 인간 본성에 대한 통찰력으로 가득 차 있다.

2 Miranda ______________ her mother to allow her to go to the senior prom.
Miranda는 졸업반 무도회에 가게 해달라고 그녀의 어머니를 설득했다.

3 Do you fear that war will disrupt the economy and your ______________?
당신은 전쟁이 경제나 당신의 안전을 파괴할까 두려움을 느낍니까? 2012 수능

4 These are examples of ______________ great discoveries.
이들은 예상치 못한 위대한 발견들의 예시이다. 12 고1학평 변형

5 The graduation ______________ will be held next Friday in Hutt High School's Assembly Hall.
졸업식은 다음주 금요일 Hutt 고등학교 강당에서 열릴 것이다. 2008 수능

6 ______________ of people were waiting in long lines at checkout counters to purchase products.
수십 명의 사람들이 상품을 구입하기 위해 계산 카운터에서 길게 줄을 지어 기다리고 있다. 15 고2학평 변형

7 Experts say that a ______________ breakfast is the brain's fuel.
전문가는 영양가 있는 아침식사가 뇌의 연료라고 말했다. 15 고1학평 변형

8 The man ______________ on the front door urgently.
그 남자는 다급하게 현관문을 두드렸다.

9 The narrow neck of a bottle ______________ the flow of liquid.
병의 좁은 목은 액체의 흐름을 방해한다. 14 고3평가원 변형

10 A very ______________ smell came into my nostrils.
매우 불쾌한 냄새가 내 콧구멍으로 들어왔다. 16 고1학평 변형

Day 06

MP3

166 □ **Greek** [gri:k]
형 그리스의
ancient Greek letters 고대 그리스 문자

167 □ **law** [lɔː]
명 법, 법률, 법칙
the National Security Law 국가보안법

168 □ **meaningful** [míːniŋfəl]
형 의미 있는, 중요한
a meaningful experience 의미 있는 경험

169 □ **absence** [ǽbsəns]
명 결석, 부재　반 presence 출석
absence from an important school event 중요한 학교 행사 결석

170 □ **dramatic** [drəmǽtik]
형 극적인, 인상적인
a dramatic change in weather 날씨의 극적인 변화

171 □ **gradual** [grǽdʒəwəl]
형 점진적인
gradual growth 점진적인 성장

172 □ **indicate** [índəkèit]
동 나타내다, 지적하다
indicate a steady decline in revenue 수익의 꾸준한 감소를 나타내다

173 □ **literature** [lítərətʃùər]
명 문학
medieval literature 중세 문학

174 □ **discrete** [diskriːt]
형 별개의
divide into four discrete categories 네 개의 별개 범주로 나누다

175 □ **pace** [peis]
명 속도, 발걸음
walk at an even pace 일정한 속도로 걷다

176 □ **political** [pəlítikəl]
형 정치적인, 정치의
political opinions 정치적인 의견

177 □ **severe** [sivíər]
형 극심한, 심각한
a severe shock 극심한 충격

178 □ **statement** [stéitmənt]
명 진술, 서술
make a false statement 허위 진술을 하다

179 □ **sustain** [səstéin]
동 지속하다, 지탱하다
sustain biodiversity 생물학적 다양성을 지속하다

180 □ **trap** [træp]
명 덫　동 가두다
set a trap 덫을 놓다

Daily Test

| 월 일 |

A **우리말에 맞게 빈 칸에 알맞은 단어를 쓰세요.**

1 A new French ______________ gave France the shortest work week in Europe.
새 프랑스 법은 프랑스에게 유럽에서 가장 짧은 1주 노동시간을 주었다. 10 평가원

2 Eyebrows are a very ______________ aspect of our appearance.
눈썹은 우리 외모에서 가장 의미 있는 부분이다. 06 고2학평 변형

3 True friendship occurs when 'information' is conveyed by ______________ of words.
진정한 우정은 정보가 말 없이 전달되었을 때 일어난다. 08 평가원

4 The mayor's new policy has led to a ______________ reduction of crime in our city.
그 시장의 새로운 정책은 우리 도시의 극적인 범죄의 감소로 이어졌다.

5 Anger often ______________ an ignored value or a misdirected passion.
화는 종종 무시된 가치나 잘못 이끌어진 열정을 나타낸다. 13 고1학평 변형

6 People who study ______________ learn the skills of reading and understanding.
문학을 공부하는 사람은 읽고 이해하는 능력을 배운다. 05 고3학평 변형

7 The ______________ of my life has been too fast since I came to America.
내가 미국에 온 이래로 내 인생의 속도는 매우 빨라졌다. 05 고1평가원 변형

8 The French Revolution brought about rapid social and ______________ change in France.
프랑스 혁명은 프랑스에 급격한 사회적, 정치적 변화를 초래했다.

9 The news announcer reported on the ______________ hurricanes that had happened over the last five years.
그 뉴스 진행자는 지난 5년 동안 일어났던 극심한 허리케인들에 대한 보고를 했다.

10 False ______________ damaged our report.
잘못된 서술이 우리의 보고서에 피해를 입혔다. 12 고1학평 변형

Review Test 03

Day 05 + Day 06 | 월 일 |

A 우리말에 맞게 빈 칸에 알맞은 단어를 쓰시오.

1 a natural ______________ like an earthquake 지진과 같은 자연재해

2 the ______________ of the damage 손상의 정도

3 follow the ______________ 지시를 따르다

4 ______________ heat 열을 발생시키다

5 a natural ______________ 자연 현상

6 a leader of great ______________ 대단한 통찰력을 지닌 지도자

7 ______________ a name tag 이름표를 붙이다

8 serve a ______________ meal 영양가 있는 식사를 하다

9 ______________ growth 점진적인 성장

10 ______________ opinions 정치적인 의견

B 영어에 맞게 빈 칸에 알맞은 우리말을 쓰시오.

1 gender equality ______________ 평등

2 expand a business 사업을 ______________

3 the manner of narration ______________

4 diplomatic relations between two countries 두 나라의 외교적 ______________

5 cry with delight ______________ 울다

6 persuade her to come back 그녀에게 돌아오라고 ______________

7 the opening ceremony of the Olympics 올림픽의 ______________

8 induce insomnia ______________ 을 유도하다

9 medieval literature 중세 ______________

10 make a false statement 허위 ______________ 을 하다

C 다음 영어 풀이에 알맞은 어휘를 〈보기〉에서 고르시오.

보기 decade law colleague crucial dozen

1 ______________ : a period of ten years

2 ______________ : very important or absolutely necessary

3 ______________ : a group of twelve people or things

4 ______________ : official rules that people in a country must follow

5 ______________ : a person who you work with

D 문맥에 맞게 다음 문장을 완성하시오.

1 Excessive greed can give	•	• a	a startup to survive.
2 Bottles can reveal their contents	•	• b	unexpected great discoveries.
3 Internal peace is what enables	•	• c	rise to unexpected disasters.
4 These are examples of	•	• d	came into my nostrils.
5 A very unpleasant smell	•	• e	without being opened.

E 문장을 읽고 문맥에 적절한 단어를 고르시오.

1 A (mass/absence) of snow blocked the entrance of the school.

2 Suzie could (identify/restrict) her son's handwriting at a glance.

3 Korea (expands/imports) oil mostly from Middle Eastern countries.

4 This teddy bear is very (dramatic/meaningful) to my daughter.

5 What was the (crucial/gradual) factor in the success of his new album?

F 문장의 빈칸에 알맞은 단어를 〈보기〉에서 찾아 쓰시오. (필요하면 형태를 고치시오.)

보기	additional	unexpected	indicate	internal	central

1 The ______________ sound startled him, so he began to run away.
예기치 못했던 소리에 그는 깜짝 놀라서 도망가기 시작했다. 14 고1학평 변형

2 The results of the study ______________ that lack of sleep increases food intake and promotes fatness.
이 연구의 결과는 수면 부족이 음식물 섭취를 증가시키고 비만을 조장하는 요인이 될 수 있음을 보여준다. 09 고1학평 변형

3 The ______________ temperature of this house is controlled by a computer system.
이 집의 내부 온도는 컴퓨터 시스템에 의해서 조정된다.

4 Could you could give me an ______________ week to consider your offer.
당신 제안을 검토하는데 추가적인 일주일을 더 주실 수 있습니까? 15 고1학평 변형

5 The ______________ issue of this book is how animals communicate.
이 책의 주된 주제는 어떻게 동물들이 의사소통을 하는 가이다.

G 다음 〈보기〉 중 두 문장에 공통으로 사용할 수 있는 어휘를 고르시오.

1 In addition to airplanes, ships are also used to ________ goods around the world.
Like language, facial expression and body movement can also ________ information. 06 고1학평 변형

① expand ② adjust ③ generate ④ convey ⑤ restrict

2 When a virus is inside a living cell, it can ________ more of itself. 2002 수능 변형
Many animals, such as birds or reptiles, ________ by laying eggs.

① struggle ② sustain ③ reproduce ④ trap ⑤ persuade

3 Jeremy is trying to ________ me that he is the best candidate for the task.
Nobody could ________ him that other people do not care about his nose. 2004 수능 변형

① recall ② convince ③ perceive ④ pursue ⑤ attach

Study More

혼동하기 쉬운 단어 identify vs. identity

- [identify] 동 (신원 등을) 확인하다, 알아보다
  The police **identified** fingerprints and handwriting simultaneously.
  경찰은 지문과 필체를 동시에 확인했다.
- [identity] 명 정체성, 신분
  Some teenagers undergo an **identity** crisis. 몇몇 10대들은 정체성 위기를 겪는다.

Day 07

MP3

181 □ **wander** [wɑ́ndər]
동 거닐다, 돌아다니다
wander along the street 거리를 거닐다

182 □ **commercial** [kəmə́ːrʃəl]
형 상업적인
commercial purposes 상업적 목적

183 □ **merely** [míərli]
부 단지, 그저
merely as a joke 단지 농담으로서

184 □ **badly** [bǽdli]
부 심하게, 나쁘게
be damaged badly 심하게 손상을 입다

185 □ **biological** [bàiəlɑ́dʒikəl]
형 생물학의
biological factor 생물학적 요소

186 □ **authority** [əθɔ́ːrəti]
명 권한, 권위
abuse your authority 권한을 남용하다

187 □ **category** [kǽtəgɔ̀ːri]
명 범주, 부문, 종류
belong to the same category 같은 범주에 속하다

188 □ **celebration** [sèləbréiʃən]
명 축하, 기념
throw a celebration party 축하 파티를 열다

189 □ **cell** [sel]
명 세포
red blood cells 적혈구

190 □ **childhood** [tʃáildhùd]
명 어린 시절, 유년기
in his early childhood 그의 어린 시절에

191 □ **consult** [kɑ́nsʌlt]
동 상담하다
consult a professor 교수와 상담하다

192 □ **cultivate** [kʌ́ltəvèit]
동 경작하다, 재배하다
cultivate a field 밭을 경작하다

193 □ **defense** [diféns]
명 방어, 방위, 수비
play defence for the Italian soccer team 이탈리아 축구팀의 수비를 맡다

194 □ **emission** [imíʃən]
명 (가스 등의)배출물 (주로 복수형), 방출
reduce emissions of harmful gases 유독 가스 배출량을 줄이다

195 □ **mess** [mes]
명 엉망 동 엉망으로 만들다
mess up a room 방을 어지르다 make a mess 엉망으로 만들다

Daily Test

| 월 일 |

Ⓐ 우리말에 맞게 빈 칸에 알맞은 단어를 쓰세요.

1 I ______________ into my neighbor's backyard.
나는 옆집의 뒷마당을 돌아다녔다. 12 고1학평 변형

2 Each year, ______________ fishing kills more than 100 million sharks globally.
매년 상업적인 어업은 세계적으로 1억 마리 이상의 상어들을 죽인다. 11 고2학평 변형

3 Advertising does more than ______________ sell products and form consumption patterns.
광고는 단순히 상품을 팔고 소비 형태를 형성하는 것 이상을 한다. 12 고3학평 변형

4 The boss was angry because his employees managed the important project ______________.
직원들이 중요한 프로젝트를 잘못 관리했기에 그 사장은 화가 났다.

5 The antique store divided its artifacts into two main ______________: wood and stone.
그 골동품 가게는 공예품을 목재와 석재, 두 주요 부문으로 나누었다.

6 The programs run Monday to Friday with ______________ performances every Friday.
그 프로그램은 매주 금요일에 축하 행사를 포함하여 월요일부터 금요일까지 운영된다. 15 고2학평 변형

7 Memories of his ______________ in the countryside still make him happy.
시골에서 보낸 그의 어린 시절의 추억은 여전히 그를 행복하게 한다.

8 Mrs. Lee has her own gardens nearby, in which she ______________ sweet potatoes.
Mrs. Lee는 근처에 그녀가 고구마를 재배하는 정원을 갖고 있다. 14 고1학평 변형

9 The easiest way to reduce carbon dioxide ______________ is simply change our mind-set.
탄소 배출을 줄이는 가장 쉬운 방법은 간단히 우리의 태도를 바꾸는 것이다. 10 고3평가원 변형

10 Don't worry about spills and ______________. They can always be cleaned up.
엎지르고 어지르는 것을 걱정하지 마렴. 그들은 항상 치울 수 있단다. 15 고2학평 변형

Day 07

MP3

196 □ **physician** [fizíʃən]
명 (내과) 의사
consult a physician 의사에게 진찰받다

197 □ **random** [rǽndəm]
형 무작위의, 임의의
a random selection 무작위 선발

198 □ **resistance** [rizístəns]
명 저항(력)
resistance to violence 폭력에 대한 저항

199 □ **sufficient** [səfíʃənt]
형 충분한
a sufficient quantity 충분한 양

200 □ **verbal** [vəːrbəl]
형 말의, 구두의
a verbal agreement 구두 합의

201 □ **ancestor** [ǽnsestər]
명 조상
ancestor worship 조상 숭배

202 □ **burst into** [bəːrst íntə]
갑자기 ~을 터뜨리다, 내뿜다
burst into tears 갑자기 울음을 터뜨리다

203 □ **counselor** [káunsələr]
명 상담원
become a career counselor 직업 상담원이 되다

204 □ **devote** [divóut]
동 헌신하다, 바치다
devote your life to photography 사진 찍는데 일생을 바치다

205 □ **fade** [feid]
동 바래다, 천천히 사라지다
begin to fade 희미해지기 시작하다

206 □ **hence** [hens]
부 따라서, 그러므로
Hence he won the marathon. 따라서 그가 마라톤에서 우승했다.

207 □ **frighten** [fráitən]
동 놀라게하다, 무섭게하다
be frightened easily 쉽게 놀라다

208 □ **grab** [græb]
동 붙잡다, 움켜잡다
grab the chance 기회를 붙잡다

209 □ **grocery** [gróusəri]
명 식료품, 잡화점
a grocery bill 식료품 계산서

210 □ **load** [loud]
명 짐, 화물 동 짐을 싣다
load up your luggage 짐을 싣다

Daily Test

| 월 일 |

A 우리말에 맞게 빈 칸에 알맞은 단어를 쓰세요.

1 Global ______________ to GM foods is growing.
세계적으로 유전자 변형 음식에 대한 저항은 늘어가고 있다. 04 평가원

2 ______________ interaction between parents and babies is important.
부모와 아기간의 구두적 상호작용은 중요하다. 14 고2 학평 변형

3 When Louis finished the race, everybody ______________ tears.
Louis가 경주를 끝냈을 때, 모두가 울음을 터트렸다. 16 고1 학평 변형

4 A ______________ helped Emma cope with her personal problems.
상담자가 Emma가 그녀의 개인적인 문제를 대처하는데 도움을 주었다.

5 Emily has ______________ her last 22 years to teaching students.
Emily는 지난 22년 동안 학생들을 가르치는 데 헌신해왔다. 16 고3 학평 변형

6 She looked out the window and saw the rain slowly beginning to ______________.
그녀는 창밖을 보았고 비가 천천히 그치는 것을 보았다. 15 고1 학평 변형

7 ______________, studying history trains us not to accept everything we read or hear as the truth.
따라서, 역사를 공부하는 것은 우리가 읽고 듣는 모든 것을 진실로 받아들이지 않게 훈련시킨다. 13 평가원

8 The sound of howling wolves ______________ us, but we carefully came out from the jungle.
늑대들의 울음 소리가 우리를 무섭게 했지만, 우리는 조심스럽게 정글에서 빠져 나왔다.

9 His father ______________ a broomstick and chased him.
그의 아버지는 빗자루를 들고 그의 아들을 뒤쫓았다. 16 고2 학평 변형

10 Consumers usually buy seafoods in ______________ stores.
고객들은 대개 식료품점에서 해산물을 산다. 15 고2 학평 변형

Day 08

MP3

211 **release** [rilíːs]
동 방출하다, 석방하다
release heat 열을 방출하다

212 **remarkable** [rimɑ́ːrkəbl]
형 놀라운, 주목할만한
a remarkable change 주목할만한 변화

213 **reverse** [rivə́ːrs]
형 (정)반대의 동 뒤바꾸다
walk in the reverse direction 반대 방향으로 걷다

214 **ritual** [rítʃuəl]
명 의식, 절차
perform religious rituals 종교적 의식을 거행하다

215 **seal** [siːl]
동 봉(인)하다 명 도장, 봉인
seal the envelope 봉투를 봉하다

216 **settle** [sétl]
동 해결하다, 정착하다
settle an economic dispute 경제적 분쟁을 해결하다

217 **stimulate** [stímjəlèit]
동 자극하다, 촉진하다
stimulate the sensory nerves 감각 신경을 자극하다

218 **transform** [trænsfɔ́ːrm]
동 바꾸다, 변형시키다
transform salt into energy 소금을 에너지로 바꾸다

219 **translate** [trænsléit]
동 번역하다
translate the letter into Korean 한국말로 편지를 번역하다

220 **wheat** [hwiːt]
명 밀
grow wheat 밀을 재배하다

221 **suffering** [sʌ́fəriŋ]
명 고통 형 고통을 겪는
endure suffering 고통을 견디다

222 **enthusiasm** [inθjúːziæ̀zəm]
명 열광, 열정
arouse enthusiasm 열정을 깨우다

223 **acknowledge** [əknɑ́lidʒ]
동 인정하다
acknowledge the need for renovations 혁신의 필요성을 인정하다

224 **approximately** [əprɑ́ksəmətli]
부 대략
approximately four decades later 대략 40년 뒤에

225 **brilliant** [bríljənt]
형 훌륭한, 빛나는
a brilliant exhibition 훌륭한 전시회

Daily Test

| 월 일 |

A 우리말에 맞게 빈 칸에 알맞은 단어를 쓰세요.

1 Heat ______________ an aroma that attracts certain insects.
그 열은 특정 곤충들을 끌어당기는 향을 방출한다. 2009 수능

2 In Australia a few years ago, I met a ______________ man named John Walton.
몇 년 전 호주에서, 나는 John Walton이라는 놀라운 남자를 만났다. 14 평가원

3 His poor attempt to win friends had the ______________ effect.
친구를 얻으려는 그의 어설픈 시도는 정반대의 효과를 가져왔다.

4 Jane and I ______________ the storeroom into a shop selling vintage goods.
Jane과 나는 그 창고를 빈티지 상품들을 판매하는 가게로 바꾸었다.

5 The book was ______________ from Arabic into Latin, three hundred years after the author's death.
그 책은 저자가 죽은 뒤 300년 후에, 아랍어에서 라틴어로 번역되었다. 11 고1학평 변형

6 About 265 gallons of water is needed to produce two pounds of ______________.
약 265 갤런의 물이 2파운드의 밀을 생산하는데 필요하다. 16 고1학평 변형

7 Why are people in a certain area ______________ from malaria more often than others?
왜 특정 지역 사람들이 다른 사람들보다 더 말라리아로 인해 고통을 받나요? 10 고1학평 변형

8 John went back to work with ______________ and confidence.
John은 열정과 자신감을 가지고 다시 일하러 돌아갔다. 10 고1학평 변형

9 The newly discovered fossil is ______________ 500 years old.
그 새롭게 발견된 화석은 대략 500년 전의 것이다.

10 Eric Clapton is one of the most ______________ guitarists in the world.
Eric Clapton은 세계에서 가장 훌륭한 기타리스트 중의 한 명이다.

Day 08

MP3

226 □ **chase** [tʃeis]
동 뒤쫓다, 추구하다 명 추적, 추구
chase the criminal 범인을 쫓다

227 □ **contract** [kántrækt]
명 계약(서) 동 계약하다
a contract to build a new library 새 도서관 건설 계약

228 □ **desperate** [déspərit]
형 절망적인, 필사적인
a desperate decision 절망적인 결정

229 □ **disturb** [distə́:rb]
동 방해하다
disturb his study 그의 공부를 방해하다

230 □ **edit** [édit]
동 편집하다, 교정하다
the edited version of the script 원고 편집본

231 □ **enormous** [inɔ́:rməs]
형 거대한, 막대한
enormous wealth 막대한 재산

232 □ **exhaust** [igzɔ́:st]
동 기진맥진하게 하다, 지치다
exhaust himself running 달리기로 기진맥진하다

233 □ **external** [ikstə́:rnəl]
형 외부의, 외관의
external pressure 외적 압력

234 □ **likewise** [láikwàiz]
부 똑같이, 마찬가지로
do likewise 똑같이 하다

235 □ **metaphor** [métəfɔ̀:r]
명 은유, 비유
talk by metaphor 비유를 사용해서 얘기하다

236 □ **pause** [pɔ:z]
동 잠시 멈추다 명 멈춤
pause for a moment 잠시 멈추다

237 □ **phrase** [freiz]
명 구
a memorable phrase 기억에 남는 구절

238 □ **sequence** [sí:kwəns]
명 연속, 순서
the sequence of events 사건의 연속

239 □ **pasture** [pǽstʃər]
명 목초지
high mountain pasture 고산지대의 목초지

240 □ **output** [áutpùt]
명 생산량
the total output 총 생산량

Daily Test

| 월 일 |

A 우리말에 맞게 빈 칸에 알맞은 단어를 쓰세요.

1 Refugees from war zones were ______________ to find safe refuge.
전쟁지역에서 오는 난민들은 안전한 도피처를 찾기 위해 필사적이었다. 15 고1학평 변형

2 What ______________ me is the idea that good behavior must be reinforced with incentives.
나를 혼란스럽게 하는 것은 좋은 행동은 보상에 의해 강화되어야 한다는 생각이었다. 2011 수능

3 James started to ______________ four Greek plays written by Euripides.
James는 Euripides가 쓴 네 가지 그리스 희극을 편집하기 시작했다. 16 평가원

4 Peter was ______________ when he finally opened the front door of his apartment.
마침내 Peter가 그의 아파트 현관문을 열었을 때 그는 지쳐 있었다. 16 평가원

5 There is a problem with the computer's ______________ speakers.
그 컴퓨터는 외부 스피커에 문제가 있는 것 같다.

6 "I beat him in the game." is a ______________ in which the word "beat" means "defeated".
"나는 그를 게임에서 이겼다."는 "beat"가 "이겼다"는 뜻으로 사용된 은유이다.

7 He ______________ and scanned the field, but he could not see anything familiar.
그는 멈추고 언덕을 훑어보았지만, 어떠한 익숙한 것도 볼 수 없었다. 14 고1학평 변형

8 The last chapter describes the ______________ of events that led to solving the problem.
마지막 장은 문제해결로 이끈 사건의 순서에 대해 설명한다.

9 Tom spends time cutting hay and carring piles of it to the ______________.
Tom은 목초지에서 건초를 베고, 그 더미들을 나르는 것으로 시간을 보낸다.

10 Fortunately, my company's monthly ______________ has increased due to the new medicine.
다행히도, 내 회사의 월간 생산량은 신약 때문에 증가하게 되었다.

Review Test 04

Day 07 + Day 08 | 월 일 |

A 우리말에 맞게 빈 칸에 알맞은 단어를 쓰시오.

1 ________________ along the street 거리를 거닐다

2 abuse your ________________ 권한을 남용하다

3 in his early ________________ 그의 어린 시절에

4 begin to ________________ 희미해지기 시작하다

5 ________________ up your luggage 짐을 싣다

6 walk in the ________________ direction 반대 방향으로 걷다

7 ________________ the sensory nerves 감각 신경을 자극하다

8 arouse ________________ 열정을 깨우다

9 ________________ himself running 달리기로 기진맥진하다

10 talk by ________________ 비유를 사용해서 얘기하다

B 영어에 맞게 빈 칸에 알맞은 우리말을 쓰시오.

1 merely as a joke ________________ 농담으로서

2 cultivate a field 밭을 ________________

3 resistance to violence 폭력에 대한 ________________

4 ancestor worship ________________ 숭배

5 be frightened easily 쉽게 ________________

6 seal the envelope 봉투를 ________________

7 translate the letter into Korean 한국말로 편지를 ________________

8 approximately four decades later ________________ 40년 뒤에

9 do likewise ________________ 하다

10 high mountain pasture 고산지대의 ________________

C 다음 영어 풀이에 알맞은 어휘를 〈보기〉에서 고르시오.

보기	translate	chase	verbal	ancestor	category

1 ______________ : of or relating to speech; spoken rather than written

2 ______________ : a group of things with similar features

3 ______________ : to run after a person or animal with the purpose of catching it.

4 ______________ : a person who lived many generations ago

5 ______________ : to change words or text from one language into another language

D 문맥에 맞게 다음 문장을 완성하시오.

1 When Louis finished the race, •	• a cope with her personal problems.
2 A counselor helped Emma •	• b that attracts certain insects.
3 Heat releases an aroma •	• c were desperate to find safe refuge.
4 Refugees from war zones •	• d everybody burst into tears.
5 James started to edit four •	• e Greek plays written by Euripides.

Review Test 04 | Day 07 + Day 08

E 문장을 읽고 문맥에 적절한 단어를 고르시오.

1 The company made (desperate/approximate) efforts to develop a new type of car.

2 We don't have (verbal/sufficient) time to do the work this week.

3 She (devoted/stimulated) all her time and energy to writing a new novel.

4 The country made (remarkable/external) progress environmentally.

5 We (consulted/wandered) a professor to get advice for our new business.

F 문장의 빈칸에 알맞은 단어를 〈보기〉에서 찾아 쓰시오. (필요하면 형태를 고치시오.)

보기	biological	emission	commercial	suffering	random

1 Researchers want to know whether ______________ factors can affect human relationships.
연구자들은 생물학적 요소들이 인간 관계에 영향을 미칠 수 있는지 알고 싶어 한다.

2 We will discuss ways to reduce gas ______________ from cars.
우리는 자동차로부터 나오는 가스 배출물들을 줄일 방법을 토론할 것이다.

3 The results of this study should not be used for ______________ purposes.
이 연구 결과는 상업적인 목적을 위해서 사용되어서는 안 된다.

4 Raised in a poor family, Confucius truly understood the ______________ of the people.
가난한 가정에서 자랐기 때문에 공자는 백성들의 고통을 진심으로 이해했다. 10 고1학평 변형

5 It turns out that coin tosses are never truly ______________.
동전 던지기 결과는 결코 임의적이지 않다는 것이 드러났다. 10 고1학평 변형

G 다음 〈보기〉 중 두 문장에 공통으로 사용할 수 있는 어휘를 고르시오.

1 Sara ______________ that it took time to learn all the aspects of word processing. 08 고1학평 변형
It is widely ______________ that thinking well is a time-consuming process. 13 고3평가원 변형

① cultivated ② acknowledged ③ chased ④ frightened ⑤ emission

2 When a person experiences stress, stress hormones are ____________ from the brain. 09 고1학평 변형
A year later, she ____________ her first pop album. 05 고1평가원

① faded ② disturbed ③ grabbed ④ released ⑤ translated

3 The newly married couple is planning to ____________ in a nearby village.
A special committee was set up to ____________ student disputes.

① indicate ② exhaust ③ settle ④ reverse ⑤ contract

Study More

'trans-' : [형용사에서] '횡단', '초월'의 뜻을 나타낸다.
[동사에서] '다른 장소 · 상태로 변화, 이전'을 나타낸다.

- [transcontinental] 형 대륙 횡단의
  a **transcontinental** flight 대륙 횡단 비행
- [transform] 동 변형시키다 [translate] 동 번역하다
  The machine **transforms** solar energy into electricity. 그 기계는 태양력을 전기로 바꾼다.
  She started to **translate** the letter into French. 그녀는 그 편지를 불어로 번역하기 시작했다.

Day 09

MP3

241 **commitment** [kəmítmənt]
명 약속, 신념
meet a commitment 약속을 지키다

242 **multiple** [mʌ́ltəpl]
형 많은, 다수의 명 배수
multiple personalities 다중 인격

243 **vulnerable** [vʌ́lnərəbl]
형 취약한, 연약한
vulnerable to attack 공격에 취약한

244 **correspond** [kɔ̀(:)rispɑ́nd]
동 일치하다, 부합하다
correspond closely 밀접하게 일치하다

245 **enroll** [inróul]
동 등록하다, 입학하다
enroll in a basic class 초급 반에 등록하다

246 **export** [ékspɔːrt]
동 수출하다 명 수출
export oranges and apples 오렌지와 사과를 수출하다

247 **imaginative** [imǽdʒənətiv]
형 창의적인, 상상력이 풍부한
an imaginative solution to the problem 창의적인 문제해결

248 **launch** [lɔːntʃ]
동 시작하다, 출시하다
launch a new Smartphone 새 스마트폰을 출시하다

249 **mine** [main]
동 채굴하다 명 광산
mine for coal 석탄을 채굴하다

250 **motion** [móuʃən]
명 움직임, 행동
Newton's laws of motion 뉴턴의 운동 법칙

251 **passage** [pǽsidʒ]
명 한 절, 통로, (시간의)흐름
a secret passage 비밀 통로

252 **register** [rédʒistər]
동 등록하다, 신고하다
register for the intensive course 심화 과정에 등록하다

253 **scarce** [skɛərs]
형 부족한, 드문
scarce in vitamins 비타민이 부족한

254 **sensitive** [sénsətiv]
형 민감한, 섬세한
sensitive skin 민감한 피부

255 **strategy** [strǽtidʒi]
명 전략, 계획
marketing strategy 마케팅 전략

Daily Test

| 월 일 |

A 우리말에 맞게 빈 칸에 알맞은 단어를 쓰세요.

1 As time passed, his _______________ and passion seemed to fade gradually.
시간이 지나면서, 그의 신념과 열정은 점점 옅어지는 듯 했다. 16 평가원

2 Remember that life is a game where there are _______________ winners.
인생은 많은 승자가 있는 게임이라는 걸 기억하라. 2011 수능

3 These plants are highly _______________ to frost, so you must take them inside at night.
이 식물들은 서리에 매우 약하기 때문에, 너는 그것들을 밤에는 안으로 들여놔야 한다.

4 Once upon a time, there was only one way to _______________ a hit album: radio.
옛날에는 크게 성공하는 앨범을 발매하는 유일한 방법은 라디오였다. 2013 수능

5 Most sharks must stay in continuous _______________ in order to survive.
대부분의 상어들은 살기 위해 계속해서 계속 움직여야 한다. 07 고3학평 변형

6 Unlike the _______________ of time, biological aging resists easy measurement.
시간의 흐름과 다르게, 생물학적인 노화는 쉬운 측정을 방해한다. 2016 수능

7 You'll pay from $920 to $1,140 depending on how many classes you _______________ for.
얼마나 많은 수업을 등록하는가에 따라 당신은 920 달러에서 1140 달러까지 수업료를 내게 될 것이다. 15 고1학평 변형

8 Jobs for the young will be _______________ in the future.
젊은이들의 일자리가 미래에는 부족해 질 것이다.

9 If a person is already _______________ and upset about something, delaying feedback can be wise.
어떤사람이 무언가에 대해 이미 예민하고 화가 났다면, 피드백을 늦게 주는 것이 현명할 수 있다. 16 평가원

10 Implementing a sound urban development _______________ is very important.
건실한 도시 개발 전략을 시행하는 것은 매우 중요하다.

Day 09

MP3

256 **absolutely** [ǽbsəlùːtli]
부 절대적으로
absolutely impossible 절대적으로 불가능한

257 **cognitive** [kágnitiv]
형 인지의
cognitive reaction 인지 반응

258 **independent** [ìndipéndənt]
형 독립적인
be financially independent 경제적으로 자립하다

259 **leadership** [líːdərʃip]
명 지도력, 지도권
have strong leadership 강한 지도력을 갖다

260 **instantly** [ínstəntli]
부 즉각, 즉시
respond instantly 즉각 반응하다

261 **be concerned about** [bi kənsə́ːrnd əbáut]
~에 대해 걱정하다
be concerned about the environment 환경에 대해 걱정하다

262 **superior** [sjuː(ː)pí(ː)əriər]
형 우수한, 상급의
the superior classes 상위 계층

263 **surrounding** [səráundiŋ]
형 인근의, 주변의
consider the surrounding environment 주변 환경을 고려하다

264 **accompany** [əkʌ́mpəni]
동 동반하다, 동행하다
accompany my mother 어머니를 동반하다

265 **admit** [ədmít]
동 인정하다, 입장을 허락하다
admit your mistake 실수를 인정하다

266 **appoint** [əpɔ́int]
동 임명하다, 지명하다
appoint a new chairman 새 의장을 임명하다

267 **attribute** [ǽtrəbjùːt]
동 ~의 탓으로 돌리다 명 자질, 속성
attribute his failure to bad luck 그의 실패를 불운의 탓으로 돌리다

268 **complicated** [kámpləkèitid]
형 복잡한
solve a complicated puzzle 복잡한 수수께끼를 풀다

269 **deny** [dinái]
동 부인하다, 부정하다
deny his accusation 그의 혐의를 부인하다

270 **document** [dákjəmənt]
명 문서, 서류
forge a formal document 공식 문서를 위조하다

Daily Test

| 월 일 |

A 우리말에 맞게 빈 칸에 알맞은 단어를 쓰세요.

1 You have ______________ no evidence - only a suspicion based on coincidence.
당신은 오직 우연의 일치에서 오는 의심 말고는 절대적인 증거가 없다. 11 평가원

2 Helen thought that '______________ load' might influence self-control.
Helen은 인지의 부하가 자제력에 영향을 미칠 수 있다고 생각했다. 15 고2학평 변형

3 Mary got a new job with a high salary, so she can be financially ______________.
Mary는 높은 연봉의 직업을 구했기 때문에 그녀는 경제적으로 자립할 수 있다.

4 Jenny's ______________ has been contributing to the success of the company.
Jenny의 리더십은 회사의 성공에 기여해왔다. 12 고1학평 변형

5 We can contact people ______________, wherever they are via the Internet.
우리는 사람들이 어디에 있던지 인터넷을 통해 그들과 즉시 접촉할 수 있다.

6 I ______________ my team members to the workshop.
나는 나의 팀원들과 연수회에 동행했다.

7 It is easy to find fault in others, but difficult to ______________ our own.
다른 사람의 결점을 찾는 것은 쉽지만 우리 자신의 결점을 인정하는 것은 어렵다. 04 고3학평 변형

8 Early in her career, Cindy was ______________ the store manager.
경력 초기에 Cindy는 가게 매니저로 임명됐었다. 14 평가원

9 The man strongly ______________ all charges against him, but the jury still found him guilty.
그 남자는 자신에 대한 모든 혐의를 강하게 부인했지만 배심원단은 그에게 유죄 판결을 내렸다.

10 Would you fax me the ______________ right away?
지금 바로 서류를 팩스로 보내줄 수 있나요? 2014 수능

Day 10

MP3

271 **steady** [stédi]
형 꾸준한, 지속적인
make steady progress 꾸준한 발전을 이루다

272 **fascinate** [fǽsənèit]
동 매료시키다, 황홀하게 하다
fascinate the audience 관중을 매료시키다

273 **sum** [sʌm]
명 액수, 합계
a large sum of money 많은 양의 돈

274 **depression** [dipréʃn]
명 우울증, 우울함
suffer from severe depression 심한 우울증에 시달리다

275 **skilled** [skild]
형 숙련된, 능숙한
a skilled craftsman 숙련된 공예가

276 **overlook** [óuvərlùk]
동 간과하다, 눈감아주다
overlook an important fact 중요한 사실을 간과하다

277 **eager** [íːgər]
형 열망하는, 열심인
be eager to meet again 다시 만나기를 열망하다

278 **ingredient** [ingríːdiənt]
명 재료, 성분
the main ingredients of this medicine 이 약의 주요 성분

279 **fate** [feit]
명 운명
his tragic fate 그의 비극적인 운명

280 **remote** [rimóut]
형 먼, 외딴
restrict remote access 원격 접근을 제한하다

281 **moderate** [mádərit]
형 적당한, 중도의
moderate temperature 적당한 온도

282 **carriage** [kǽridʒ]
명 마차, 객차
a first-class carriage 일등 객차

283 **endless** [éndlis]
형 끝없는, 무한한
endless possibility 끝없는 가능성

284 **resolve** [rizálv]
동 해결하다, 결심하다
resolve a dispute 논쟁을 해결하다

285 **scent** [sent]
명 향기, 향내
a sweet scent 달콤한 향기

Daily Test

| 월 일 |

A 우리말에 맞게 빈 칸에 알맞은 단어를 쓰세요.

1 I am ______________ by the beauty of roses.
나는 장미의 아름다움에 매료된다. 2004 수능

2 A few years ago, I established a healing group to treat anxiety and ______________.
몇 년 전에 나는 불안과 우울증을 치료하기 위한 치료 그룹을 만들었다. 11 고2학평 변형

3 She was both highly ______________ and a great team player.
그녀는 상당히 숙련되었고 협동을 잘 하는 사람이다.

4 What we have ______________ is the ant's environment.
우리가 간과했던 것은 개미의 환경이었다. 15 평가원

5 He was ______________ to talk about his life as a film director.
그는 영화 감독으로서의 자신의 삶에 대해 이야기 하기를 열망했다.

6 Your challenge is to use a seasonal ______________ to create a delicious dish.
당신의 도전은 계절 재료를 이용하여 맛있는 음식을 만드는 것이다. 16 고1학평 변형

7 King Lear cursed his tragic ______________ and killed himself in the last chapter.
리어왕은 마지막 장에서 그의 비극적 운명을 저주했고 자결했다.

8 They welcomed me with ______________ promises.
그들은 끝없는 약속들로 나를 환영해주었다. 2013 수능

9 The United States ______________ to enter World War II after the attack on Pearl Harbor.
진주만 공격 후에 미국은 세계2차 대전에 참전하기로 결정했다.

10 The bottles are just too small to hold the flowers' ______________.
그 병들은 꽃 향기를 한 곳에 모으기엔 너무 작다. 09 고3평가원 변형

Day 10

MP3

286 □ **instinct** [instíŋkt]
명 본능
maternal instinct 모성본능

287 □ **revenue** [révənjùː]
명 매출, 수입
annual revenue 연 매출

288 □ **mutual** [mjúːtʃuəl]
형 상호간의, 서로의
a mutual agreement 상호간의 동의　　a mutual enemy 공공의 적

289 □ **obstacle** [ábstəkl]
명 장애, 장애물
a major obstacle to success 성공의 주된 장애물

290 □ **requirement** [rikwáiərmənt]
명 필요 조건, 요구
requirement for graduation 졸업 필요 조건

291 □ **gravity** [grǽvəti]
명 중력
the law of gravity 중력의 법칙

292 □ **productive** [prədʌ́ktiv]
형 생산하는, 생산적인, 이익을 내는
productive capacity 생산력

293 □ **aid** [eid]
명 원조, 지원　동 돕다
emergency aid 긴급 지원

294 □ **surgery** [sə́ːrdʒəri]
명 수술
undergo surgery 수술을 받다

295 □ **reputation** [rèpjə(ː)téiʃən]
명 평판, 명성
have a good reputation 평판이 좋다

296 □ **conserve** [kánsəːrv]
동 보호하다, 절약하다
conserve the historical sites 역사 유적지를 보호하다

297 □ **caution** [kɔ́ːʃən]
명 주의, 신중함
treat the dog with caution 강아지를 조심해서 다루다

298 □ **profound** [prəfáund]
형 깊은, 심오한, 엄청난
profound happiness 깊은 행복감　　profound success 엄청난 성공

299 □ **logic** [ládʒik]
명 논리, 타당성
apply logic 논리를 적용하다

300 □ **tone** [toun]
명 어조, 말투
a tone of surprise 놀란 어조

Daily Test

| 월 일 |

A 우리말에 맞게 빈 칸에 알맞은 단어를 쓰세요.

1 We discussed the company's expenses and dwindling ______________.
우리는 회사의 지출과 줄어드는 매출에 대해 토론했다. 2012 수능

2 Water is the most important ______________ for all living things.
물은 살아있는 모든 것들을 위한 가장 중요한 필수조건이다.

3 Isaac Newton discovered ______________.
Isaac Newton은 중력을 발견했다. 15 고2학평 변형

4 In my experience, most people are far more ______________ in the morning.
내 경험상, 대부분의 사람들은 아침에 훨씬 더 생산적이다. 12 평가원

5 The medical volunteers ______________ poor people in Africa.
의료 자원봉사자들은 아프리카의 가난한 사람들을 도왔다.

6 Your ______________ is your most valuable asset.
당신의 평판은 당신의 가장 귀중한 재산이다. 12 평가원

7 The penguin ______________ heat through contact with its fellows in large groups.
펭귄은 그들의 동료와 큰 무리를 이루며 접촉하여 열을 보존한다. 10 고3학평 변형

8 As we mature, we know that we must balance courage with ______________.
우리가 성숙해지면서, 우리는 신중함과 용기의 균형을 맞춰야 함을 안다. 14 고2학평 변형

9 Her new novel was full of creative and ______________ insights.
그녀의 새 소설은 창의적이고 심오한 통찰력으로 가득 차 있었다.

10 ______________ is the set of rules for valid reasoning.
논리는 타당한 추론을 위한 규칙들의 집합이다. 10 고2학평 변형

A 우리말에 맞게 빈 칸에 알맞은 단어를 쓰시오.

1 meet a ______________ 약속을 지키다

2 ______________ a new Smartphone 새 스마트폰을 출시하다

3 the ______________ classes 상위 계층

4 consider the ______________ environment 주변 환경을 고려하다

5 ______________ his accusation 그의 혐의를 부인하다

6 a large ______________ of money 많은 양의 돈

7 restrict ______________ access 원격 접근을 제한하다

8 the law of ______________ 중력의 법칙

9 treat the dog with ______________ 강아지를 조심해서 다루다

10 a ______________ of surprise 놀란 어조

B 영어에 맞게 빈 칸에 알맞은 우리말을 쓰시오.

1 enroll in a basic class 초급 반에 ______________

2 mine for coal 석탄을 ______________

3 scarce in vitamins 비타민이 ______________

4 accompany my mother 어머니를 ______________

5 appoint a new chairman 새 의장을 ______________

6 the main ingredients of this medicine 이 약의 주요 ______________

7 a first-class carriage 일등 ______________

8 annual revenue 연______________

9 have a good reputation ______________이 좋다

10 profound happiness ______________ 행복감

C 다음 영어 풀이에 알맞은 어휘를 〈보기〉에서 고르시오.

보기	superior	gravity	attribute	obstacle	reputation

1 ______________ : far better than something else

2 ______________ : the good opinion or respect which people have about something

3 ______________ : the forces that pull things toward the Earth

4 ______________ : something that stands in the way or blocks progress

5 ______________ : a particular or characteristic feature of a thing

D 문맥에 맞게 다음 문장을 완성하시오.

1 Most sharks must stay in continuous motion •	• a the document right away?
2 Would you fax me •	• b poor people in Africa.
3 The medical volunteers aided •	• c in order to survive.
4 What we have overlooked •	• d for valid reasoning.
5 Logic is the set of rules •	• e is the ant's environment.

E 문장을 읽고 문맥에 적절한 단어를 고르시오.

1 Kevin is (eager/steady) to study software programming at university.

2 Getting regular (moderate/external) exercise is good for your mental health.

3 We would have had the correct answer if we didn't (attribute/overlook) the top part.

4 What Joe said (corresponds/launches) exactly with what I have seen.

5 The meeting created (mutual/approximate) trust between the two countries.

F 문장의 빈칸에 알맞은 단어를 〈보기〉에서 찾아 쓰시오. (필요하면 형태를 고치시오.)

보기 cognitive appoint vulnerable fascinate independent

1 "Exercise is good for attention, information processing, and performance of ______________ tasks," says Hillman.
"운동은 집중력과 정보처리, 인지적 과제 수행에 좋다"고 Hillman이 말한다. 11 고2학평 변형

2 Our sense of smell is particularly ______________ to outside influence.
우리의 후각은 특히 외부의 영향에 취약하다. 12 고3학평 변형

3 Children are ______________ by animals and can develop very special relationships with them.
어린이들은 동물에게 매료되고 동물과 매우 특별한 관계를 발전시켜 나갈 수 있다. 14 고1학평 변형

4 Westerners tend to admire someone who is ______________ and quick-thinking.
서양 사람들은 독립적이고 신속한 사고를 하는 사람들을 존경하는 경향이 있다. 11 고3평가원 변형

5 We have ______________ a manager responsible for personal information.
그래서 우리는 개인 정보를 담당하는 매니저를 임명했다. 11 고2학평 변형

G 다음 〈보기〉 중 두 문장에 공통으로 사용할 수 있는 어휘를 고르시오.

1 Remember that life is a game where there are ___________ winners. 2011 수능
The concept of humans doing ___________ things at one time has been studied by psychologists since the 1920s. 2015 수능 변형

① scarce ② profound ③ multiple ④ steady ⑤ enormous

2 Most people seem to be far more ___________ in the morning. 12 고3평가원
We had a ___________ day. We finished the whole report.

① reverse ② productive ③ superior ④ severe ⑤ imaginative

3 He became a successful composer as a result of his ___________ efforts. 09 고1학평 변형
Mary's father held Mary close while she cried ___________ tears. 12 고1학평 변형

① nutrition ② sufficient ③ verbal ④ endless ⑤ random

Study More

mine의 다양한 의미

- [동사] : '채굴하다, (광물질을) 캐다'
  Many workers went to California to **mine** for gold. 많은 일꾼들이 금을 캐기 위해 캘리포니아로 향했다.
- [소유대명사] : '나의 것'
  Alex is a friend of **mine.** Alex는 내 친구야.
  Your dress looks like **mine.** 네 드레스가 내 것과 비슷해 보여.

Day 11

MP3

301 □ **property** [prápərti]
명 성질
physical properties of water 물의 물리적인 성질

302 □ **specialize** [spéʃəlàiz]
동 전공하다, 전문화하다
specialize in physics 물리학을 전공하다

303 □ **plain** [plein]
형 분명한 명 평원
the plain fact 분명한 사실

304 □ **reliable** [riláiəbl]
형 믿을만한, 신뢰할만한
gain information from reliable sources 믿을만한 출처로부터 정보를 얻다

305 □ **soaked** [soʊkt]
형 흠뻑 젖은 동 soak 담그다, 적시다
soaked in sweat 땀에 흠뻑 젖은

306 □ **justify** [dʒʌ́stəfài]
동 정당화하다, 해명하다
justify aggressive behavior 공격적인 행동을 정당화하다

307 □ **probability** [prɑ̀bəbíləti]
명 가능성, 개연성
probability of winning 승리의 가능성

308 □ **widespread** [wáidspréd]
형 광범위한
widespread damage 광범위한 손해

309 □ **minor** [máinər]
명 중요하지 않은, 가벼운
minor planets 소행성들

310 □ **administration** [ədmìnistréiʃən]
명 관리, 경영
major in business administration 경영학을 전공하다

311 □ **abandon** [əbǽndən]
동 버리다
abandon her vehicle 그녀의 자동차를 버리다

312 □ **institution** [ìnstitjúːʃən]
명 기관, 제도
a financial institution 금융 기관

313 □ **commit** [kəmít]
동 저지르다, 범하다
commit a crime 범죄를 저지르다

314 □ **scholarship** [skɑ́lərʃìp]
명 장학금
win a scholarship 장학금을 받다

315 □ **spell out** [spel aʊt]
~을 간결하게 설명하다
need to spell out the problem 그 문제를 설명할 필요가 있다

Daily Test

| 월 일 |

Ⓐ 우리말에 맞게 빈 칸에 알맞은 단어를 쓰세요.

1 This is a new Italian restaurant which ______________ in seafood.
이곳은 해산물 음식을 전문적으로 하는 새로운 이태리 음식점이다.

2 I want my children to become responsible and ______________.
나는 내 아이들이 책임감 있고 신뢰할 수 있게 되기를 바란다. 16 고3학평 변형

3 His shirt was ______________ in sweat because of the game.
그의 셔츠는 경기로 인해 땀에 젖었다.

4 The ______________ of an earthquake is much higher in this place than anywhere else.
이 장소에서 지진의 가능성은 다른 곳들 보다 훨씬 더 높다.

5 ______________ conflicts help our relationships develop defense capabilities.
가벼운 갈등은 우리의 관계가 방어력을 구축하도록 돕는다. 14 고1학평 변형

6 Government leaders should be humane and honest rather than being experts in ______________.
정부 지도자들은 행정 전문가이기보다는 인간적이며 정직해야 한다. 10 고1학평 변형

7 Jimmy and Dwight ______________ their toys and came inside.
Jimmy와 Dwight는 그들의 장난감을 버리고 안으로 들어왔다. 15 고2학평 변형

8 Harry was elected Principal Librarian at the newly founded London ______________.
Harry는 새로 설립된 런던 협회에 수석 사서로 임명되었다. 16 평가원

9 Susan got a full ______________ and studied without any concern about school expenses.
Susan은 전액 장학금을 받았고, 학비 걱정 없이 공부했다.

10 Brenda ______________ everything we needed to know.
Brenda는 우리가 알아야 할 모든 세부사항을 설명해 주었다.

Day 11

MP3

316 charity
[tʃǽrəti]
명 자선, 자선단체
a charity for refugees 난민을 위한 자선단체

317 screw
[skruː]
명 나사 동 나사로 고정시키다
tighten the screw 나사를 조이다

318 assemble
[əsémbl]
동 모으다, 조립하다
easy to assemble 조립하기 쉬운

319 accessible
[əksésəbl]
형 접근 할 수 있는, 접근 가능한, 다가가기 쉬운
accessible information 접근 할 수 있는 정보

320 comprehend
[kɑ̀mprihénd]
동 이해하다
comprehend the question 문제를 이해하다

321 bury
[béri]
동 묻다, 매장하다
bury a bone in the ground 땅에 뼈를 묻다

322 hop
[hɑp]
동 깡총깡총 뛰다
hop on your left foot 왼발로 깡총깡총 뛰다

323 cooperation
[kouɑ̀pəréiʃən]
명 협력, 협동
promote beneficial cooperation 서로에게 도움이 되는 협력을 증진하다

324 underlying
[ʌ́ndərlàiiŋ]
형 근본적인, 기초를 이루는
underlying principles of life 인생의 기본 원칙

325 mood
[muːd]
명 분위기, 기분
in a positive mood 긍정적인 분위기에서

326 notion
[nóuʃən]
명 개념, 생각
notion of liberty 자유라는 개념

327 capture
[kǽptʃər]
동 포로로 잡다, 포착하다
capture a thief 도둑을 잡다

328 reserve
[rizə́ːrv]
동 예약하다, 보유하다 명 비축(물)
reserve a hotel room for parents 부모님을 위해 호텔방을 예약하다

329 deserve
[dizə́ːrv]
동 ~받을 만 하다
deserve to be praised 칭찬 받을 만 하다

330 Pacific
[pəsífik]
형 태평양의 명 태평양
the Pacific coast 태평양 연안

Daily Test

| 월 일 |

A 우리말에 맞게 빈 칸에 알맞은 단어를 쓰세요.

1 Ms. Green, the ______________ president, was preparing the monthly event by herself.
자선단체 장인 Ms. Green은 이번 달 행사를 그녀 혼자서 준비하는 중이었다. 2014 수능

2 She tightened the ______________ on the wall to hang up a picture.
그녀는 그림을 걸기 위해 벽에 나사를 조였다.

3 The toy train is easily ______________ and taken apart.
그 장난감 기차는 쉽게 조립되고 분리된다. 06 고3학평 변형

4 Gyeongbokgung Palace is easily ______________ to the general public.
경복궁은 일반인들이 쉽게 접근할 수 있다.

5 To learn how to read and ______________, we need to practice making our own meaning in response to text.
읽고 이해하는 법을 배우기 위해서, 우리는 읽는 글에 대응하여 우리만의 의미를 만드는 걸 연습할 필요가 있다. 10 고3학평 변형

6 Healthy competition can't happen without ______________.
건강한 경쟁은 협동 없이는 이뤄지지 않는다. 15 고2학평 변형

7 One of the ______________ principles of investing is based upon the relationship between risk and return.
투자에 기본을 이루는 원칙 중 하나는 위험과 수익 간의 관계에 에 근거하고 있다. 15 고2학평 변형

8 There is now considerable controversy surrounding the ______________ of general intelligence.
현재 일반적인 지능의 개념을 둘러싼 상당한 논쟁이 있다. 15 고2학평 변형

9 She ______________ to have a long vacation after all her hard work.
그녀는 모든 힘든 일 끝에 긴 휴가를 받을 만 했다.

10 Sharks live in the warm waters of the Eastern ______________ region.
상어들은 동태평양 지역의 따뜻한 물 속에서 산다. 15 고1학평 변형

Day 12

MP3

331 **expertise** [èkspəːrtíːz]
명 전문적 기술
require considerable expertise 상당한 전문적 기술을 요구하다

332 **automobile** [ɔ́ːtəməbìːl]
명 자동차
the automobile accident 자동차 사고

333 **outer** [áutər]
형 외부의
build an outer wall 외벽을 세우다

334 **ratio** [réiʃiou]
명 비율, 비
golden ratio 황금 비율

335 **psychology** [saikáləʤi]
명 심리학, 심리
major in child psychology 아동 심리학을 전공하다

336 **suburb** [sʌ́bəːrb]
형 교외
live in a suburb 교외에 살다

337 **flip** [flip]
동 휙 뒤집다, ~을 튀기다 명 툭 던지기
flip a coin 동전을 뒤집다

338 **facial** [féiʃəl]
형 얼굴의
his facial expression 그의 얼굴 표정

339 **altitude** [ǽltitjùːd]
명 고도
at high altitudes 높은 고도에서

340 **commute** [kəmjúːt]
동 통근하다
commute by subway 지하철로 통근하다

341 **squeeze** [skwiːz]
동 짜다, 짜내다 명 (손으로) 꼭 짜기
squeeze juice from oranges 오렌지 주스를 짜다

342 **abstract** [ǽbstrækt]
형 추상적인
an abstract concept 추상적인 개념

343 **meanwhile** [míːnhwàil]
부 한편, 그 동안에
in the meanwhile 그 동안에

344 **violate** [váiəlèit]
동 위반하다, 침해하다
violate traffic regulations 교통규칙을 위반하다

345 **Renaissance** [rènəsáːns]
명 문예 부흥기, 르네상스
Renaissance painters 르네상스 화가들

Daily Test

| 월 일 |

A **우리말에 맞게 빈 칸에 알맞은 단어를 쓰세요.**

1 ______________ expression and body movement play an important part in conveying information.
얼굴 표정과 몸짓은 정보를 전달하는 중요한 부분이다. 06 고1학평 변형

2 The ancient Greeks believed that all beautiful things share the same ______________.
고대 그리스인들은 모든 아름다운 것들은 같은 비율을 공유한다고 믿었다. 04 평가원

3 Mathematics definitely influenced ______________ art.
수학은 분명히 르네상스 예술에 영향을 주었다. 2005 수능

4 Cities in Western Europe tend to be economically healthy compared with their ______________.
서유럽의 도시들은 그들의 교외지방과 비교했을 때 경제적으로 부유한 경향이 있다. 2009 수능

5 CCTV can ______________ people's privacy.
CCTV는 사람들의 사생활을 침해할 수 있다. 15 고1학평 변형

6 A lot of people ______________ long distances these days.
요즘에는 많은 사람들이 먼 거리를 통근한다.

7 Scientists can see some mountains and valleys on the ______________ layers of the Moon.
과학자들은 달의 바깥 층에 있는 산들과 계곡들을 볼 수 있다.

8 Louise is very interested in the human mind and wants to study ______________ at university.
Louise는 인간의 마음에 매우 관심이 많아서 대학에서 심리학을 공부하고 싶어 한다.

9 For a coin to really ______________ perfectly during a coin toss, it needs to spin in just the right way.
동전이 동전던지기에서 완벽하게 뒤집히기 위해서, 동전은 올바른 방향으로 회전해야 한다.

10 Red pandas have adapted to living at high ______________ in the mountains.
너구리 판다들은 산의 높은 고도에서 살아가는 것에 적응되었다.

Day 12

MP3

346 **license** [láisəns]
명 면허, 허가 동 (공적으로) 허가하다
a driver's license 면허증

347 **permit** [pə́:rmit]
동 허용하다 명 허가
permit to take photographs 사진 찍는 것을 허용하다

348 **procedure** [prəsí:dʒər]
명 절차, 과정
safety procedures 안전 절차

349 **elaborate** [ilǽbərit]
형 정교한, 공들인 동 자세히 설명하다
elaborate design of the dress 드레스의 정교한 디자인

350 **solitary** [sálitèri]
형 혼자 하는, 단독의, 혼자 사는
go on a solitary walk 혼자 산책하다

351 **offend** [əfénd]
동 기분 상하게 하다, (법규를) 위반하다
be offended by her remark 그녀의 발언에 불쾌해지다

352 **fulfill** [fulfíl]
동 이루다, 이행하다
fulfill Jane's hope Jane의 소망을 이루다

353 **paw** [pɔ:]
명 (동물의) 발
a cat's paw 고양이의 발

354 **cattle** [kǽtl]
명 (집합적으로) 소
a herd of cattle 소 떼

355 **innocence** [ínəsəns]
명 결백, 무죄
prove her innocence 그녀의 결백을 증명하다

356 **invisible** [invízəbl]
형 보이지 않는, 볼 수 없는
invisible hands 보이지 않는 손

357 **addict** [ǽdikt]
명 (약물, 오락거리 등의) 중독자
a baseball addict 야구 광 be addicted to ~에 중독되다(빠지다)

358 **botanical** [bətǽnikəl]
형 식물(학)의
read botanical books 식물학 책을 읽다

359 **genre** [ʒá:ŋrə]
명 장르, 유형
a genre of Korean traditional music 한국 전통 음악의 한 장르

360 **stroke** [strouk]
명 발작, 타법, (수영등의) 스트로크 동 쓰다듬다
a fatal stroke 치명적인 발작

Daily Test

| 월 일 |

A **우리말에 맞게 빈 칸에 알맞은 단어를 쓰세요.**

1 Most young men ______________ their military duty by serving about two years in the army.
대부분의 젊은 남자들은 입대해서 약 2년 동안 군 복무를 이행한다.

2 Eric offered photos as proof of his ______________.
Eric은 그의 결백함의 증거로 사진을 제시했다. 12 고1학평 변형

3 Tigers and foxes are ______________ animals.
호랑이와 여우는 혼자 사는 동물들이다.

4 Certain animals can see things that are ______________ to the human eye.
어떤 동물들은 인간의 눈에는 보이지 않는 것들을 볼 수 있다.

5 For driving a big truck or a bus, you need to get a special driver's ______________.
대형 트럭이나 버스를 운전하려면, 특별한 운전 면허증을 따야 한다.

6 Peter and James are ______________ to playing soccer.
Peter와 James는 축구에 중독되었다. 10 평가원

7 Adventure stories were the most popular ______________ of literature for both males and females in the 80's.
모험 이야기는 80년대 남녀 모두에게 가장 인기 있는 장르였다. 07 고3학평 변형

8 They might refer to these substances as ______________ extracts.
그들은 이 물질들을 식물성 추출물로 지칭할 수도 있을 것이다. 14 고3평가원 변형

9 As the night sets in, the leopards began to attack dogs and ______________ in the village.
밤이 되자 그 표범들은 마을에 있는 개들과 소들을 공격하기 시작했다. 2016 수능 변형

10 I'll ask my teacher if entering the room is ______________.
나는 선생님께 그 방의 출입이 허가 되는지 물어볼 것이다. 2014 수능

Review Test 06

Day 11 + Day 12 | 월 일 |

A 우리말에 맞게 빈 칸에 알맞은 단어를 쓰시오.

1 physical ________________ of water 물의 물리적인 성질

2 ________________ in sweat 땀에 젖다

3 major in business ________________ 경영학을 전공하다

4 ________________ a bone in the ground 땅에 뼈를 묻다

5 ________________ a thief 도둑을 잡다

6 require considerable ________________ 상당한 전문적 기술을 요구하다

7 build an ________________ wall 외벽을 세우다

8 at high ________________ 높은 고도에서

9 go on a ________________ walk 혼자 산책하다

10 prove her ________________ 그녀의 결백을 증명하다

B 영어에 맞게 빈 칸에 알맞은 우리말을 쓰시오.

1 specialize in physics 물리학을 ________________

2 probability of winning 승리의 ________________

3 commit a crime 범죄를 ________________

4 comprehend the question 문제를 ________________

5 in a positive mood 긍정적인 ________________에서

6 major in child psychology 아동 ________________을 전공하다

7 commute by subway 지하철로 ________________

8 safety procedures 안전 ________________

9 be offended by her remark 그녀의 발언에 ________________

10 a baseball addict 야구 ________________

C 다음 영어 풀이에 알맞은 어휘를 〈보기〉에서 고르시오.

보기	commute	altitude	soaked	stroke	hop

1 _______________ : to move by jumping

2 _______________ : the height of something above the level of earth or sea

3 _______________ : to touch something gently with your hand

4 _______________ : to get very wet

5 _______________ : to travel regularly to your work or school

D 문맥에 맞게 다음 문장을 완성하시오.

1 I want my children to become •	• a responsible and reliable.
2 Brenda spelled out everything •	• b without cooperation.
3 She tightened the screw on the wall •	• c of his innocence.
4 Healthy competition can't happen •	• d that we needed to know.
5 Eric offered photos as proof •	• e to hang up a picture.

E 문장을 읽고 문맥에 적절한 단어를 고르시오.

1 Joan's essay is well written and deserves (attention/license).

2 Now, (squeeze/offend) the orange to extract the juice.

3 It is illegal to drive without a(n) (altitude/license).

4 Lucy has a (botanical/flexible) way of thinking.

5 The reporter said that he gained the information from (solitary/reliable) sources.

F 문장의 빈칸에 알맞은 단어를 〈보기〉에서 찾아 쓰시오. (필요하면 형태를 고치시오.)

보기					
보기	underlying	permit	specialize	widespread	fulfill

1 Are visitors ______________ to take photographs inside this museum?
박물관 내에서 방문객들이 사진 찍은 것이 허용되나요?

2 They ______________ in creating extremely realistic effects on very low budgets.
그들은 아주 적은 예산으로 매우 사실적인 효과를 만들어내는 것을 전문으로 했다. 14 고2학평 변형

3 Many students sign up for his classes because of his ______________ reputation.
많은 학생들이 널리 알려진 명성 때문에 그의 수업을 신청한다. 05 고2평가원

4 Sports help us learn how to set a goal and ______________ it.
스포츠는 목표를 설정하고 이루는 방식을 가르쳐 줄 수 있다. 10 고2학평 변형

5 The ______________ message of his new book is "Don't Believe Everything You Think."
그의 새 책에서 바탕이 되는 메시지는 "당신이 보는 것을 모두 믿지는 마시오."이다. 12 고3평가원 변형

G 다음 〈보기〉 중 두 문장에 공통으로 사용할 수 있는 어휘를 고르시오.

1 He got a fine because he ___________ the speed limit.
The students who ___________ the rules got a warning from the school.

① reserved ② addicted ③ commuted ④ violated ⑤ soaked

2 You should not try to ___________ your failure by making excuses.
It is hard to ___________ your decision without enough data.

① stroke ② abandon ③ capture ④ commit ⑤ justify

3 They ___________ their original plan due to lack of money.
Art in ancient societies was frequently ___________ after serving its purpose. 2010 수능 변형

① comprehended ② captured ③ commuted
④ abandoned ⑤ offended

Study More

'-able(-ble)' : [형용사에서] '~ 수 있는'의 뜻을 나타낸다.

- [reliable] 형 믿을 수 있는
Helen was a **reliable** witness. Helen은 믿을만한 목격자였다.
- [accessible] 형 접근 가능한
This site is not **accessible** to the public. 이 사이트는 일반인은 접근 할 수 없다.
- [invisible] 형 볼 수 있는
There was an **invisible** barrier between the two countries. 두 나라간에 보이지 않는 장벽이 있었다.

Day 13

MP3

361 **aroma** [əróumə]
명 향기, 방향
unique aroma 독특한 향

362 **crew** [kruː]
명 선원, 승무원
a crew member 승무원

363 **vague** [veig]
형 희미한, 막연한, 모호한
have a vague impression 희미한 인상을 갖다

364 **toxic** [tάksik]
형 유독성의
eliminate toxic substances 독성 물질을 제거하다

365 **reminder** [rimáindər]
명 상기시키는 것, 독촉장, 기념품
reminder of the accident 그 사고를 생각나게 하는 것

366 **spark** [spɑːrk]
명 불꽃, 불똥 동 촉발시키다, 유발하다
spark of electricity 전기의 불꽃

367 **molecule** [málәkjùːl]
명 분자
a model of molecule 분자 모형

368 **depth** [depθ]
명 깊이
the depth of the river 강의 깊이

369 **misunderstanding** [mìsʌndərstǽndiŋ]
명 오해
a misunderstanding between family members 가족 간의 오해

370 **hesitate** [hézitèit]
동 망설이다, 주저하다
hesitate to call 부르길 망설이다

371 **opponent** [əpóunənt]
형 반대의 명 상대, 적수, 반대자
a tough opponent 힘든 상대

372 **nevertheless** [nèvərðəlés]
부 그럼에도 불구하고
a small but nevertheless important change 작지만 중요한 변화

373 **possession** [pəzéʃən]
명 소유, 재산
a man of great possessions 위대한 재산가

374 **military** [mílitèri]
명 군대 형 군대의
wear a military uniform 군복을 입다

375 **hormone** [hɔ́ːrmòun]
명 호르몬
a hormone imbalance 호르몬 불균형

Daily Test

| 월 일 |

A 우리말에 맞게 빈 칸에 알맞은 단어를 쓰세요.

1 The picture became a regular ______________ of my dream.
그 그림은 내 꿈을 정기적으로 상기시키는 것이 되었다. 12 고1학평 변형

2 Even an ill-formed idea can ______________ a great idea in someone else.
심지어 이상한 생각들도 다른이에게는 위대한 생각의 불씨가 될 수 있다. 12 고1학평 변형

3 Many of the ship's ______________ survived the huge waves and were rescued.
그 배의 많은 선원들이 거대한 파도로부터 살아 남았고 구조 되었다.

4 We must be careful of eating ______________ mushrooms from mountains.
우리는 산에서 가져 온 독성 버섯을 먹는 것을 주의해야 한다.

5 Sandra is surprised by the delicious ______________ of the dinner her son has prepared.
Sandra는 그녀의 아들이 준비한 맛있는 저녁식사 냄새를 맡고 놀랐다. 15 고1학평 변형

6 Nick ______________ to tell his friends about the news.
Nick은 그의 친구들에게 그 소식을 전하는 것을 머뭇거렸다. 14 고3평가원 변형

7 During deep sleep, a lot of growth ______________ secretion occurs.
숙면 동안 많은 성장 호르몬 분비가 발생한다.

8 Cultural difference may lead to ______________ in language classes.
문화적 차이는 언어 수업에서 오해로 이끌 수 있다. 08 평가원

9 ______________, the kind of help that computers can provide is very limited.
그럼에도 불구하고, 컴퓨터가 제공할 수 있는 도움의 종류는 한정적이다. 10 평가원

10 Both ______________ have to cooperate on the rules: there's a mutual agreement of cooperation.
양쪽 상대 모두 상호간 협동의 동의가 있다는 규칙에 협력해야 한다. 15 고1학평 변형

Day 13

MP3

376 **broad** [brɔ:d]
형 넓은
a broad window 넓은 창문

377 **compliment** [kámpləmənt]
명 칭찬 동 칭찬하다
compliment each other 서로 칭찬하다

378 **respectively** [rispéktivli]
부 각자, 제각기
use French and English respectively 각각 불어와 영어를 사용하다

379 **heal** [hi:l]
동 치유되다, 치유하다
use the herb to heal the sick 환자를 치료하기 위해 허브를 사용하다

380 **scout** [skaut]
동 정찰하다, 찾아내다 명 정찰
scout for firewood 땔감을 찾아 정찰하다

381 **approve** [əprú:v]
동 찬성하다, 승인하다
approve a new plan 새로운 계획을 승인하다

382 **credit** [krédit]
명 신용, 학점
a credit card 신용카드 pay by credit card 신용카드로 지불하다

383 **lifestyle** [laifstail]
명 생활 방식, 습관
a healthy lifestyle 건강한 생활 방식

384 **endure** [indjúər]
동 견디다
endure pain 고통을 견디다

385 **thorough** [θə́:rou]
형 철저한, 완전한
make a thorough preparation 철저한 준비를 하다

386 **browse** [brauz]
동 둘러보다, 훑어보다
browse a bookstore 서점을 둘러보다

387 **flexible** [fléksəbl]
형 유연한, 융통성 있는
a flexible way of thinking 융통성 있는 사고방식

388 **identical** [aidéntikəl]
형 동일한, 똑같은
an identical signature 똑같은 싸인

389 **bounce** [bauns]
동 튀다, 튀기다
bounce a ball off the wall 벽에 공을 튀기다

390 **useless** [jú:slis]
형 소용없는, 쓸모 없는
useless advice 쓸모 없는 충고

Daily Test

| 월 일 |

A **우리말에 맞게 빈 칸에 알맞은 단어를 쓰세요.**

1 One of the easiest ways to be likeable is to offer a sincere ______________.
호감을 주는 가장 쉬운 방법 중에 하나는 진실한 칭찬을 하는 것이다. 14 고1학평 변형

2 Can I pay by ______________ card?
신용카드로 지불해도 되나요? 2006 수능

3 They don't have enough time to ______________ water in the desert.
그들은 사막에서 물을 찾아낼 충분한 시간이 없다.

4 Take a ______________ attitude toward career choices.
직업 선택에 있어 유연한 태도를 취하세요. 12 고1학평 변형

5 Some animals may also know the secret ______________ powers of herbs.
몇몇 동물들은 이미 허브의 비밀스러운 치유 능력을 알고 있을지도 모른다. 05 평가원

6 Because of the huge earthquake, the land became ______________.
거대한 지진으로 인하여 그 땅은 쓸모 없게 되었다.

7 Recently, the city decided to ______________ construction of a new central library.
최근에 시는 새로운 중앙 도서관의 건축을 허가하기로 결심했다. 07 고2학평 변형

8 The first step in solving a sleep problem is to examine your ______________.
수면 문제를 해결하기 위한 첫 번째 단계는 당신의 생활 방식을 점검하는 것이다.

9 When light from an object hits a person, only some of it ______________ off.
물체의 빛이 사람에게 닿았을 때, 그것 중 일부만이 튕겨 나간다. 2010 수능

10 Although the town was very small, it was a nice place to ______________ around.
그 마을은 매우 작았지만 이곳 저곳을 둘러보기엔 좋았다.

Day 14

MP3

391 ☐ **religious** [rilídʒəs]
형 종교의
read a religious book 종교 서적을 읽다

392 ☐ **bush** [buʃ]
명 덤불, 관목
a rose bush 장미 덤불

393 ☐ **romantic** [roumǽntik]
형 낭만적인, 공상적인
a romantic holiday 낭만적인 휴일 romantic thoughts 낭만적인 생각

394 ☐ **evident** [évidənt]
형 분명한, 명백한
evident proof 명백한 증거 self-evident 자명한

395 ☐ **roast** [roust]
동 굽다, 볶다
roast coffee beans 커피콩을 볶다

396 ☐ **bunch** [bʌntʃ]
명 다발, 송이
a bunch of flowers 꽃다발 한 묶음

397 ☐ **sour** [sauər]
형 신, 시큼한
a sour flavor 신맛

398 ☐ **oral** [ɔ́(:)rəl]
형 구두의, 입의
follow oral directions 구두 지시를 따르다

399 ☐ **distraction** [distrǽkʃən]
명 집중을 방해하는 것, 주의 산만
study without any distraction 주의 산만 없이 공부하다

400 ☐ **scatter** [skǽtər]
동 흩뿌리다, 흩어지다
scatter potato seeds 감자 씨를 뿌리다

401 ☐ **faith** [feiθ]
명 믿음, 신념, 신앙(심)
have strong faith 강한 신념을 가지다

402 ☐ **drown** [draun]
동 익사하다, 물에 빠지다
drown at sea 바다에서 익사하다

403 ☐ **crime** [kraim]
명 범죄
crime prevention 범죄 예방

404 ☐ **counter** [káuntər]
명 계산대, 판매대
sit behind the counter 계산대 뒤에 앉다

405 ☐ **pesticide** [péstisàid]
명 살충제, 농약
spray agricultural pesticide 농약을 뿌리다

Daily Test

| 월 일 |

A **우리말에 맞게 빈 칸에 알맞은 단어를 쓰세요.**

1 Thomas dropped a ______________ of coins and pencils.
Thomas는 한 다발의 동전과 연필을 떨어뜨렸다. 16 고2학평 변형

2 Many Koreans like to ______________ chestnuts and eat them on winter nights.
많은 한국인들은 겨울 밤에 밤을 구워서 먹는 것을 좋아한다.

3 The ______________ garden justifies its reputation as 'the place where poets go to die.'
그 낭만적인 정원은 '시인들이 죽으러 가는 공간'으로서 그것의 명성을 정당화한다. 2008 수능

4 For ______________ prevention in this area, the police patrol every night.
이 지역의 범죄 예방을 위해 경찰들이 매일 밤 순찰을 한다.

5 To study effectively, get rid of ______________: the TV, the Internet, and e-mail.
효율적으로 공부하기 위해서 TV, 인터넷, e-mail과 같은 집중을 방해하는 것들을 치워라. 15 고1학평 변형

6 If we build a hydroelectric dam, entire forests will ______________.
우리가 수력 전기댐을 짓는다면, 숲 전체가 물에 잠길 것이다. 16 고1학평 변형

7 Traces of the painter's pleasure and happiness are ______________ in this paint.
이 그림에는 화가의 기쁨과 행복함의 흔적이 명백하다.

8 Sometimes promises made in good ______________ can't be kept.
때때로 좋은 신념으로 한 약속은 지켜지지 않을 수 있다. 08 평가원

9 After Beethoven's death his sketchbooks were ______________ and in many cases broken up.
베토벤이 죽은 후에 그의 스케치북은 흩어졌고 그 중 대다수가 부서졌다. 11 평가원

10 A bird in the hand is worth two in the ______________.
손 안에 새 한 마리가 덤불 속 새 두 마리보다 가치 있다. 2010 수능

Day 14

MP3

406 **conform**
[kənfɔ́ːrm]
동 순응하다, 일치하다
conform to social norms 사회적 규범에 순응하다

407 **nerve**
[nəːrv]
명 신경
autonomic nerves 자율 신경

408 **persistent**
[pərsístənt]
형 끊임없는, 끈질긴
persistent attempts 끈질긴 시도

409 **session**
[séʃən]
명 기간, 회의, 개정
a training session 훈련 기간

410 **portray**
[pɔːrtréi]
동 묘사하다
portray himself as a winner 자기자신을 승자로 묘사하다

411 **beverage**
[bévəridʒ]
명 음료
a beverage with caffeine 카페인 음료

412 **innate**
[inéit]
형 타고난, 선천적인
an innate instinct 타고난 본능

413 **rectangular**
[rektǽŋgjələr]
형 직사각형의
a rectangular table 직사각형 탁자

414 **rear**
[riər]
명 뒤쪽
a rear attack 배후 공격

415 **inferior**
[infí(ː)əriər]
형 하급의, 질 낮은
an inferior official 하급 공무원

416 **manual**
[mǽnjuəl]
명 사용 설명서 형 수동의
a computer manual 컴퓨터 사용 설명서 manual art 수공예

417 **conference**
[kánfərəns]
명 회의, 회견, 학회
hold a press conference 기자 회견을 열다

418 **adversity**
[ædvə́ːrsəti]
명 역경, 재난
face terrible economic adversity 심각한 경제적 역경에 직면하다

419 **cease**
[siːs]
동 중단하다, 그치다
cease mass production 대량 생산을 중지하다

420 **transaction**
[trænsǽkʃən]
명 거래, 매매
a commercial transaction 상거래

Daily Test

| 월 일 |

A 우리말에 맞게 빈 칸에 알맞은 단어를 쓰세요.

1 We tend to perceive the door of a classroom as _______________ no matter which angle it is viewed from.
우리는 교실의 문이 어떤 각도에서 보이는지 상관없이 직사각형으로 인지하는 경향이 있다. 2014 수능

2 The camcorder suddenly _______________ to function.
그 캠코더가 갑자기 작동을 멈추었다.

3 President Obama spoke about the nuclear test ban in a news _______________.
오바마 대통령은 기자 회견에서 핵 실험 금지에 대해 이야기 했다.

4 The doctor concluded that Sam suffered _______________ damage and that he might never regain the full use of his right arm.
의사는 Sam이 신경 손상으로 고통 받았고 다시는 그의 오른팔을 완전히 쓰지 못할 것이라고 결론지었다. 15 평가원

5 The chosen volunteers will participate in a two-day training _______________ run by the Volunteer Coordinator.
선택 받은 봉사자는 봉사 담당자들이 운영하는 이틀의 훈련 기간에 참여할 것이다. 15 고2학평 변형

6 Neither side disclosed details of the _______________ at the meeting.
그 회의에서 어느 쪽도 거래의 세부사항에 대해 공개하지 않았다.

7 Life becomes a process of finding ways to become less _______________.
인생은 열등감을 줄이는 방법을 찾는 과정이다. 09 고3학평 변형

8 Acting against _______________ means cultivating positivity in whatever way you can.
역경에 맞서는 행동은 우리가 할 수 있는 모든 방법에서 적극성을 끌어내는 것이다. 14 고2학평 변형

9 Virtual water is present in dairy products, soups, _______________, and liquid medicines.
가상수는 일상품과 수프, 음료수, 물약에 존재한다. 16 고1학평 변형

10 The team members' _______________ efforts were involved in completing the project.
그 프로젝트를 완수 하는데 있어서 팀원들의 끊임 없는 노력이 수반되었다.

Review Test 07

Day 13 + Day 14 | 월 일 |

A 우리말에 맞게 빈 칸에 알맞은 단어를 쓰시오.

1 unique ______________ 독특한 향

2 ______________ of the accident 그 사고를 생각나게 하는 것

3 a ______________ between family members 가족간의 오해

4 ______________ pain 고통을 견디다

5 ______________ a ball off the wall 공을 벽에 튀기다

6 a ______________ holiday 낭만적인 휴일

7 follow ______________ directions 구두 지시를 따르다

8 ______________ potato seeds 감자 씨를 뿌리다

9 ______________ to social norms 사회적 규범에 순응하다

10 a ______________ table 직사각형 탁자

B 영어에 맞게 빈 칸에 알맞은 우리말을 쓰시오.

1 eliminate toxic substances ______________ 물질을 제거하다

2 the depth of the river 강의 ______________

3 a man of great possessions 위대한 ______________

4 pay by credit card ______________ 카드로 지불하다

5 make a thorough preparation ______________ 준비를 하다

6 study without any distraction ______________ 없이 공부하다

7 drown at sea 바다에서 ______________

8 a beverage with caffeine 카페인 ______________

9 an inferior official ______________ 공무원

10 a commercial transaction ______________

C 다음 영어 풀이에 알맞은 어휘를 〈보기〉에서 고르시오.

보기	roast	heal	inferior	toxic	oral

1 ______________ : to get healthy or well again

2 ______________ : to bake something over a fire

3 ______________ : or of relating to the mouth; spoken rather than written

4 ______________ : something that is made of poison or related to poison

5 ______________ : not as good as something else in quality or rank

D 문맥에 맞게 다음 문장을 완성하시오.

1 Nick hesitated to tell •	• a a great idea in someone else.
2 Nevertheless, the kind of help that •	• b his friends about the news.
3 Even an ill-formed idea can spark •	• c good faith can't be kept.
4 Thomas dropped a bunch •	• d of coins and pencils.
5 Sometimes promises made in •	• e computers can provide is very limited.

E 문장을 읽고 문맥에 적절한 단어를 고르시오.

1 I bought a (bunch/crew) of flowers for my mother's birthday.

2 The machine suddenly (bounced/ceased) to work.

3 The three brothers look almost (identical/broad).

4 We didn't have much time. (Nevertheless/Therefore) we were able to finish the report on time.

5 I like the (botanical/sour) taste of lemon.

F 문장의 빈칸에 알맞은 단어를 〈보기〉에서 찾아 쓰시오. (필요하면 형태를 고치시오.)

보기	flexible	opponent	hesitate	evident	persistent

1 The teacher advised us to take a ______________ attitude toward career choices.
선생님께서는 우리에게 직업 선택에 대해서 융통성 있는 태도를 취하라고 조언해 주셨다. 12 고1학평 변형

2 For a fair competition, both ______________ have to respect the rules of the game.
공정한 경쟁을 위해서 양쪽 상대 모두 규칙을 존중해야 한다. 15 고2학평 변형

3 "I ______________ a lot, but once I undertook it, it just felt so right," he said.
"나는 많이 망설였지만 일단 그것을 시작하고 보니 매우 옳다고 느껴졌다."라고 그는 말했다. 10 고1학평

4 It is ______________ from his face that he must have done something wrong.
그의 얼굴을 보니 무언가 잘못을 했음이 명백하다.

5 His ______________ efforts have finally paid off.
그의 지속적인 노력은 마침내 보답을 받았다.

G 다음 〈보기〉 중 두 문장에 공통으로 사용할 수 있는 어휘를 고르시오.

1 There is a powerful, 17-ton telescope in the ____________ section of the aircraft. 11 고2학평 변형

His office is in the ____________ of the building.

① endure ② oral ③ manual ④ rear ⑤ vague

2 A map must distort reality in order to ____________ a complex, three-dimensional world on a flat sheet of paper. 4 고2학평 변형

She used her paintings to ____________ the harsh reality of life in Romania. 13 고3학평 변형

① spark ② heal ③ portray ④ roast ⑤ scatter

3 Recently, the city ____________ construction of a new central library. 07 고2학평 변형

We are happy to tell you that we have ____________ your request. 09 고2학평 변형

① browsed ② conformed ③ drowned ④ approved ⑤ scouted

Study More

혼동하기 쉬운 단어 compliment vs. complement

- [compliment] 명 칭찬 동 칭찬하다
  His behavior deserved a handsome **compliment.** 그의 행동은 후한 칭찬을 받을 만했다.
- [complement] 명 보완, 보어 동 보완하다
  The boys had different writing styles that **complemented** each other well.
  그 소년들은 글 쓰는 성향이 달라서 서로를 잘 보완해 주었다.

Day 15

MP3

421 □ **craft** [kræft]
명 수공예, 기술
arts and crafts 미술 공예

422 □ **console** [kánsoul]
동 위로하다, 위안을 주다
console oneself 스스로를 위로하다

423 □ **modify** [mádəfài]
동 수정하다
modify the errors 오류를 수정하다

424 □ **naked** [néikid]
형 벌거벗은
invisible to the naked eye 육안으로 보이지 않는

425 □ **fragile** [frǽdʒəl]
형 깨지기 쉬운, 취약한
a fragile vase 깨지기 쉬운 화병

426 □ **maintenance** [méintənəns]
명 유지, 보수
the building maintenance 건물 보수

427 □ **on behalf of** [ən bihǽf əv]
~을 대신(대표)하여
on behalf of our school 우리 학교를 대표하여

428 □ **infer** [infə́ːr]
동 추론하다, 뜻하다
infer from the context 문맥에서 추론하다

429 □ **incorrect** [ìnkərékt]
형 부정확한, 틀린
incorrect spelling 부정확한 철자

430 □ **persuasive** [pərswéisiv]
형 설득력 있는
make a persuasive argument 설득력 있는 주장을 하다

431 □ **plot** [plɑt]
명 줄거리, 계략 동 ~을 계획하다, 모의하다
the plot of the play 그 연극의 줄거리

432 □ **orchard** [ɔ́ːrtʃərd]
명 과수원
an apple orchard 사과 과수원

433 □ **passionate** [pǽʃənit]
형 열정적인
passionate love 열정적인 사랑

434 □ **delicate** [délәkit]
형 정교한, 섬세한, 미묘한
the delicate mechanism of the car 자동차의 정교한 장치

435 □ **container** [kəntéinər]
명 용기, 그릇
a container made of metal 금속으로 만들어진 용기

Daily Test

| 월 일 |

A 우리말에 맞게 빈 칸에 알맞은 단어를 쓰세요.

1 Certain species are more crucial to the ______________ of their ecosystem than others.
특정한 종은 다른 종보다 생태계의 유지에 더 결정적이다. 16 평가원

2 Kafka was determined to write a new letter every day-just to ______________ the little girl.
카프카는 오직 그 여자 아이를 위로하기 위하여 매일 새로운 편지를 쓰기로 단단히 결심했다. 11 고2학평

3 The old teapot which lost its lid became an ideal ______________ for a bunch of roses.
뚜껑이 없어진 오래된 차주전자는 장미 한 다발의 꽃을 꽂을 수 있는 유일한 화분이 되었다. 2009 수능

4 In the second room, you can create or ______________ folk craft articles with some materials.
두 번째 방에서는, 약간의 재료들을 이용하여 민속 공예품을 만들거나 수정할 수 있다.

5 The company was faced with the ______________ task of removing Charles from the head of a department.
회사는 부서장 직에서 Charles를 해고시켜야 하는 미묘한 일에 직면했다. 15 고2학평 변형

6 ______________ the school, I would like to extend an invitation to you and your family.
학교를 대표해서, 나는 당신과 당신 가족들을 모두 초대하고 싶습니다. 2008 수능

7 With your donation, we can preserve ______________ coral reefs around the world.
당신의 기부로 우리는 전 세계의 약한 산호초들을 보호할 수 있습니다. 16 평가원

8 If there is a ring on a man's finger one can ______________ that he is married or has lover.
남자의 손가락에 반지가 있다면 그가 결혼을 했거나, 연인이 있다는 것을 추론할 수 있다.

9 We are more ______________ when we express ourselves through stories.
우리는 이야기를 통해 스스로를 표현 할 때 더 설득력 있게 된다. 15 고3학평 변형

10 If you look at the sun with a ______________ eye often, you could go blind.
맨 눈으로 태양을 자주 보게 된다면 실명할 수도 있다.

Day 15

MP3

436 □ **pitch** [pitʃ]
명 소리의 높이
rhythm and pitch 리듬과 음의 높이

437 □ **overwhelm** [òuvərhwélm]
동 압도하다
be overwhelmed by her beauty 그녀의 아름다움에 압도당하다

438 □ **certainty** [sə́:rtənti]
명 확실(성), 확신
the certainty of morality 도덕적 확실성

439 □ **groom** [gru(:)m]
명 신랑
the bride and groom 신랑 신부

440 □ **hook** [huk]
명 갈고리, 걸이 동 연결하다
a hat hook 모자걸이 hook a rope to a sled 썰매에 줄을 연결하다

441 □ **multiply** [mʌ́ltəplài]
동 곱하다
multiply 3 by 20 3에 20을 곱하다

442 □ **deadline** [dédlàin]
명 마감일, 최종 기한
set a deadline for the report 보고서에 최종 기한을 정하다

443 □ **freshman** [fréʃmən]
명 신입생, 1학년
a college freshman 대학 신입생

444 □ **currency** [kə́:rənsi]
명 통화, 화폐
pay in Japanese currency 일본 화폐로 지불하다

445 □ **limitation** [lìmətéiʃən]
명 한계, 제한
inherent limitation 본질적인 한계

446 □ **measurable** [méʒərəbl]
형 잴 수 있는, 주목할 만한
measurable distance 측정 가능한 거리

447 □ **fairly** [fɛ́ərli]
부 꽤, 공정하게
speak French fairly well 불어를 상당히 잘하다

448 □ **forehead** [fɔ́(:)rid]
명 이마
her broad forehead 그녀의 넓은 이마

449 □ **exaggerate** [igzǽdʒərèit]
동 과장하다
tend to exaggerate the truth 진실을 과장하는 경향이 있다

450 □ **immune** [imjú:n]
형 면역의, 면역이 된
strengthen the immune system 면역 체계를 강화하다

Daily Test

| 월 일 |

A 우리말에 맞게 빈 칸에 알맞은 단어를 쓰세요.

1 While predictions about the future are always difficult, some can be made with ________________.
미래에 대한 예측은 항상 어려운 반면에, 그 중에 몇몇은 확실해 질 수 있다. 11 평가원

2 Can you tell me when the ________________ for applications?
지원 마감일이 언제인지 말해주실래요? 2016 수능

3 A rich man donated his property, and the money from its sale will be dealt out ________________ to the poor.
한 부자가 그의 재산을 기부하였고, 그 돈은 가난한 사람들에게 공평하게 분배될 것이다.

4 Don Quixote ignores reality and ________________ everything.
돈키호테는 현실을 무시하고 모든 것들을 과장한다.

5 The word '________________' meaning 'man' is seldom used outside the context of a wedding.
남성'을 의미하는 '신랑'이라는 단어는 결혼식의 맥락 밖에서는 거의 쓰이지 않는다. 10 고1학평 변형

6 This company has an age ________________ policy.
이 회사는 연령 제한 정책이 있다.

7 When there is a long pause in a conversation, people feel an ________________ need to fill it.
대화 도중 긴 침묵이 생길 때, 사람들은 그것을 매워야 한다는 압도적인 필요성을 느낀다. 2010 수능

8 Achievement is something tangible, clearly defined and ________________.
성취는 실체가 있고 명확하게 정의되며 측정할 수 있다. 16 고2학평 변형

9 Clients send massages through facial expression, body movement, and voice ________________.
고객들은 그들의 표정, 몸짓, 그리고 목소리 높낮이를 통해서 메시지를 전한다. 10 평가원

10 Sleep deprivation has an influence on the ________________ system.
수면 부족은 면역 체계에 큰 영향을 미친다. 10 고3학평 변형

Day 16

MP3

451 **deposit** [dipázit]
명 예금, 보증금 동 예금(예치) 하다
make a deposit 예금하다

452 **compassion** [kəmpǽʃən]
명 연민, 동정심
compassion for the poor 가난한 사람들에 대한 동정심

453 **costly** [kɔ́(:)stli]
형 값이 비싼
wear a costly dress 값비싼 드레스를 입다

454 **shrink** [ʃriŋk]
동 줄다, 줄어들게 하다
The sweater will shrink in the wash. 그 스웨터는 세탁 중에 줄어들 거야.

455 **dwell** [dwel]
동 살다, 거주하다
dwell in a remote place 멀리 떨어져 살다

456 **eclipse** [iklíps]
명 (일식, 월식의) 식
the first solar eclipse of the year 올해 첫 개기월식

457 **democratic** [dèməkrǽtik]
형 민주적인
a democratic solution 민주적인 해결책

458 **concentration** [kànsəntréiʃən]
명 집중, 농축
interfere with concentration 집중을 방해하다

459 **carve** [kɑːrv]
동 조각하다, 깎아서 만들다
carve your name on a cup 컵 위에 이름을 새기다

460 **candidate** [kǽndidèit]
명 후보자
become a presidential candidate 대통령 후보가 되다

461 **shore** [ʃɔːr]
명 해안, 호숫가
swim to the shore 해안까지 수영해서 가다

462 **embrace** [imbréis]
동 포용하다, 받아들이다
embrace tightly 꼭 껴안다

463 **thread** [θred]
명 실 동 실을 꿰다
thread the needle 바늘에 실을 꿰다

464 **subjective** [səbdʒéktiv]
형 주관적인
give a subjective evaluation 주관적 평가를 내리다

465 **breakdown** [bréikdàun]
명 고장, 쇠약, (기계, 차 등의) 고장
a breakdown repair service 고장 수리 서비스

Daily Test

| 월 일 |

A 우리말에 맞게 빈 칸에 알맞은 단어를 쓰세요.

1 Some young workers ______________ up to half of their salaries.
일부 젊은 직장인들은 그들의 월급의 절반까지를 예금한다.

2 Arranging things in advance will enable you to avoid ______________ and possibly dangerous mistakes.
물건을 미리 정리해 두는 것은 당신이 값 비싸고 어쩌면 위험할 수 있는 실수를 하는 것을 막아준다. 10 고1학평 변형

3 Moisture is stored in the root of a plant, and during droughts that root ______________, dragging the stem underground.
수분은 식물의 뿌리에 저장되고 가뭄 동안에 뿌리는 수축되고 줄기를 땅 속으로 끌어당기게 된다. 15 평가원

4 A solar ______________ is when the moon blocks out the sun's light.
일식이란 달이 태양의 빛을 가릴 때 이다.

5 Whenever Ann is losing ______________, she gathers her belongings and moves to another place.
Ann이 집중력이 흩어질 때 마다, 그녀는 소지품을 챙겨서 다른 장소로 이동한다. 2015 수능

6 They ______________ lanterns from vegetables such as potatoes.
그들은 감자와 같은 채소로 등불을 조각했다. 04 평가원

7 I tried to paddle back to ______________ but my arms and legs were paralyzed.
다시 해안가로 돌아가려고 노를 저었지만 내 팔과 다리가 마비되었다. 2012 수능

8 You need to ______________ innovation; otherwise you will not stay on top.
당신은 혁신을 받아들일 필요가 있다. 다시 말해서, 그렇지 않으면 정상에서 머물지 못할 것이다. 06 평가원

9 The ______________ approach to probability is based mostly on opinions, feelings, or hopes.
가능성에 대한 주관적 접근은 대개 의견과 감정, 또는 희망에 기반을 둔다. 15 고2학평 변형

10 Jeremy is under a lot of stress, so he's on the verge of a nervous ______________ now.
Jeremy는 너무 많은 스트레스를 받았고, 그는 지금 신경쇠약 직전이다.

Day 16

MP3

466 despair [dispέər]
명 절망, 좌절 동 절망하다, 체념하다
a deep sense of despair 깊은 절망감

467 grumble [grʌ́mbl]
동 투덜거리다
grumble about the test result 시험 결과에 대해 투덜거리다

468 economics [ìːkənɑ́miks]
명 경제학
major in economics 경제학을 전공하다

469 priority [praiɔ́(ː)rəti]
명 우선 순위 , 우선권
give priority 우선순위를 두다

470 coax [kouks]
동 구슬리다, 달래다
coax her dog into coming closer 그녀의 강아지가 가까이 오도록 구슬리다

471 cushion [kúʃən]
명 등 받침, 방석
sit on a cushion 방석을 깔고 앉다

472 dental [déntəl]
형 치과의
a dental appointment 치과 진료 예약

473 circuit [sə́ːrkit]
명 순환, 순회
a city center circuit 도시 중심 순환로

474 cheek [tʃiːk]
명 볼, 뺨
the baby's chubby cheek 아기의 통통한 볼

475 dynamic [dainǽmik]
형 역동적인, 활발한
her dynamic movement 그녀의 역동적인 움직임

476 privilege [prívəlidʒ]
명 특권, 특혜
give up his privileges 그의 특권을 포기하다

477 yawn [jɔːn]
동 하품하다 명 하품
with a yawn 하품을 하면서

478 consonant [kɑ́nsənənt]
명 자음
memorize English consonants 영어 자음을 암기하다

479 render [ˈrendə(r)]
동 (어떤 상태가 되게) 만들다
render our plan useless 우리의 계획을 쓸모 없게 만들다

480 dye [dai]
동 염색하다
dye your hair black 머리를 검게 염색하다

Daily Test

| 월 일 |

A 우리말에 맞게 빈 칸에 알맞은 단어를 쓰세요.

1 Daniel Brown, professor of ______________, is retiring this month.
경제학 교수인 Daniel Brown은 이번 달에 은퇴할 예정이다. 16 고3학평 변형

2 Staying healthy should be the number one ______________ in your life.
건강하게 지내는 것이 네 삶에 최우선순위가 되어야 한다.

3 My son hates taking medicine so much, I have to ______________ him into it.
나의 아들은 약 먹는 것을 정말 싫어하기 때문에, 난 그가 그걸 먹게끔 달래야만 한다.

4 Each bag is wrapped in a ______________ and then placed inside a shipping box.
각각의 가방은 쿠션으로 포장되어서 운송 상자 안에 보관된다. 2014 수능

5 His ______________ surgery is scheduled for the morning.
그의 치아 수술이 아침에 예정되어 있어요. 2016 수능 변형

6 The electrons move along a ______________ and produce electricity.
전자는 회로를 따라 함께 움직여서 전기를 생산한다. 09 고2평가원 변형

7 Judy's puppies run to her and lick her ______________ when she comes home.
Judy가 집에 오면 그녀의 강아지들은 그녀에게 달려가 그녀의 양 볼을 핥는다.

8 Our mind is strengthened by contact with ______________ and well-ordered minds.
우리의 정신은 역동적이고 질서가 잡힌 마음과 접촉할 때 강해진다. 08 평가원

9 When people ______________, they instinctively increase blood flow, bringing in low temperature air.
사람들이 하품 할 때는, 낮은 온도의 공기를 들여오고 본능적으로 혈액의 흐름을 증가시킨다. 12 고1학평 변형

10 The inventor's innovations ______________ useless the enormous alternators used for generating power in early radio transmitters.
그 발명가의 혁신은 초기 라디오 전송장치에서 동력을 발생시키기 위해 사용했던 거대한 교류발전기를 쓸모 없게 만들었다. 12 평가원

A 우리말에 맞게 빈 칸에 알맞은 단어를 쓰시오.

1 ______________ oneself 스스로를 위로하다

2 make a ______________ argument 설득력 있는 주장을 하다

3 ______________ love 열정적인 사랑

4 the ______________ of morality 도덕적 확실성

5 a college ______________ 대학 신입생

6 speak French ______________ well 불어를 상당히 잘하다

7 make a ______________ 예금하다

8 The sweater will ______________ in the wash. 그 스웨터는 세탁 중에 줄어들 거야.

9 ______________ in a remote place 멀리 떨어져 살다

10 ______________ tightly 꼭 껴안다

B 영어에 맞게 빈 칸에 알맞은 우리말을 쓰시오.

1 the plot of the play 그 연극의 ______________

2 an apple orchard 사과 ______________

3 hook a rope to a sled 썰매에 줄을 ______________

4 pay in Japanese currency 일본 ______________로 지불하다

5 inherent limitation 본질적인 ______________

6 compassion for the poor 가난한 사람들에 대한 ______________

7 the first solar eclipse of the year 올해 첫 ______________

8 carve your name on a cup 컵 위에 이름을 ______________

9 a dental appointment ______________ 진료 예약

10 memorize English consonants 영어 ______________을 암기하다

C 다음 영어 풀이에 알맞은 어휘를 〈보기〉에서 고르시오.

보기	shore	dwell	dental	modify	orchard

1 ______________ : to change some parts of something, usually to improve or change it

2 ______________ : of or relating to teeth or the dentist

3 ______________ : an area of land where fruits are grown

4 ______________ : to live or stay in a place

5 ______________ : the land on the edge of a sea or lake

D 문맥에 맞게 다음 문장을 완성하시오.

1 Your motivation to console •	• a but my arms and legs were paralyzed.
2 With your donation, we can preserve fragile •	• b may influence the alternative you imagine.
3 Can you tell me when •	• c coral reefs around the world.
4 I tried to paddle back to shore •	• d is retiring this month.
5 Daniel Brown, professor of economics, •	• e the deadline for applications?

E 문장을 읽고 문맥에 적절한 단어를 고르시오.

1 Remember that the (deadline/thread) for the scholarship application is next Friday.

2 He (exaggerated/coaxed) her to run for school president.

3 You need to (modify/infer) the errors in your application form as soon as possible.

4 I attended the meeting on (top/behalf) of my brother.

5 He is (sorry/passionate) about learning foreign languages.

F 문장의 빈칸에 알맞은 단어를 〈보기〉에서 찾아 쓰시오. (필요하면 형태를 고치시오.)

보기 subjective dynamic immune measurable overwhelm

1 The ______________ approach to probability is based mostly on opinions, feelings, and hopes.
확률에 대한 주관적인 접근법은 대체로 사람들의 의견, 감정, 희망을 기초로 한다. 15 고2학평 변형

2 Double Dutch is a ______________ form of jumping rope that kids really love.
Double Dutch는 아이들이 매우 좋아하는 역동적인 형태의 줄넘기이다. 12 고3학평 변형

3 Lack of sleep has a bad effect on the ______________ system.
수면 부족은 면역 체계에 안 좋은 영향을 미친다. 10 고3학평 변형

4 Valid experiments also must have ______________ data.
타당한 실험은 또한 측정할 수 있는 자료를 가지고 있어야 한다. 2013 수능

5 Shay's father looked at his son, ______________ with pity.
Shay의 아버지는 연민의 감정에 휩싸여 아들을 쳐다 보았다. 11 고1학평 변형

G 다음 〈보기〉 중 두 문장에 공통으로 사용할 수 있는 어휘를 고르시오.

1 The trunk of a banana tree is so ____________ that even moderate winds can blow it down. 08 고3 평가원 변형

Peter was working like some high-geared, ____________, strong machine. 08 고3 학평 변형

① costly ② dynamic ③ delicate ④ naked ⑤ passionate

2 We are often flooded by ____________ information on the Internet. 2005 수능 변형

Their analysis was criticized for using ____________ data.

① dental ② persuasive ③ fragile ④ incorrect ⑤ evident

3 The study of math needs lots of ____________ and practice, but it isn't really hard. 06 고1 평가원

Learning the arts can also improve motivation, ____________, confidence, and teamwork. 12 고1 학평 변형

① concentration ② consonant ③ eclipse ④ priority ⑤ deposit

Study More

학년을 지칭하는 여러 가지 단어 Junior, Senior, Freshman, Sophomore

- Andy is college **freshman** this year. Andy는 올해 대학 신입생이다.
- I spent my **junior** year in Vietnam. 나는 2학년 때 베트남에 있었다.
- There will be the **senior** prom next week. 다음주에 졸업 무도회가 있을 예정이다.
- When I was a **sophomore**, the 2002 World Cup was held in Korea.
  내가 고2 였을 때, 2002년 월드컵이 한국에서 개최되었다.

Day 17

MP3

481 □ **glow** [glou]
동 (은은히)빛나다, 타다 명 부드러운 빛
glow in the dark 어둠 속에서 빛나다

482 □ **legitimate** [lidʒítəmit]
형 타당한, 정당한
make a legitimate investment 합법적인 투자를 하다

483 □ **motor** [móutər]
명 모터, 전동기, 발동기 형 자동차의
an electric motor 전기 모터

484 □ **explicit** [iksplísit]
형 노골적인, 명백한
explicit strategy 노골적인 전략

485 □ **loose** [lu:s]
형 느슨해진, 헐렁한, (흙 등이) 단단하지 않은
loose-fitting cotton pants 헐렁한 면 바지

486 □ **medieval** [mì:diíːvəl]
형 중세의
in medieval days 중세 시대에

487 □ **illuminate** [iljúːmənèit]
동 조명하다, 밝게 비추다
illuminate the dining room 거실에 등불을 켜다

488 □ **masterpiece** [mǽstərpìːs]
명 걸작, 명작
an immortal masterpiece 불후의 명작

489 □ **initiative** [iníʃiətiv]
명 (목적 달성을 위한 새로운) 계획
an initiative to increase the rice demand 쌀 수요를 늘리려는 계획

490 □ **knot** [nɑt]
명 매듭, 무리
untie a knot 매듭을 풀다

491 □ **glorious** [glɔ́ːriəs]
형 영광스러운
a glorious triumph 영광스러운 승리

492 □ **mount** [maunt]
동 오르다, 시작하다 명 산
mount a hill 언덕을 오르다

493 □ **laundry** [lɔ́ːndri]
명 세탁물, 세탁, 빨래
a pile of dirty laundry 더러운 세탁물 더미

494 □ **merit** [mérit]
명 장점, 이점, 가치 동 (칭찬, 관심 등을) 받을 만 하다
merits and demerits 장점과 단점

495 □ **miserable** [mízərəbl]
형 비참한, 고달픈
feel miserable 비참함을 느끼다

Daily Test

| 월 일 |

A 우리말에 맞게 빈 칸에 알맞은 단어를 쓰세요.

1 Light from the candle ______________ in the dark room.
초에서 나오는 빛이 어두운 방에서 은은히 빛난다.

2 These ______________ distinctions are often ignored in statistics that merely count cases.
이러한 타당한 구분이 단순히 사례의 수를 계산하는 통계에서는 무시 된다. 12 고3학평 변형

3 When we visited the British Museum, we could see relics from ______________ life.
대영박물관에 방문했을 때 우리는 중세 시대의 유적들을 볼 수 있었다.

4 On a stormy day, the beautiful building was suddenly ______________ by a shaft of light.
폭풍우가 치던 날, 그 아름다운 건물은 갑자기 한줄기 서광에 의해 빛났다. 15 고2학평 변형

5 No sooner had he completed his ______________, Lily stepped into the cafe.
그가 자신의 대작을 완성하자마자, Lily는 카페에 들어섰다. 17 평가원

6 Taking the ______________ means recognizing our responsibility to make things happen.
주도권을 잡는다는 것은 어떤 일이 일어나게 하는 우리의 책임감을 인정하는 것을 의미한다. 07 평가원

7 Jason knew exactly how to tie a ______________.
Jason은 어떻게 매듭을 매는 지 정확하게 알고 있었다. 16 고3 평가원 변형

8 Harsh necessity can be the mother of ______________ invention.
가혹한 필요가 영광스런 발명의 어머니가 될 수 있다. 15 고1학평 변형

9 We tend to consider water consumption in strictly immediate terms, such as taking a shower or doing the ______________.
우리는 물 소비를 샤워를 하거나 세탁을 하는 것처럼 엄격하게 직접적인 측면에서 생각하는 경향이 있다. 11 고3학평 변형

10 His speech about war and peace seemed to have considerable ______________.
전쟁과 평화에 대한 그의 연설은 상당히 가치가 있는 것으로 보였다.

Day 17

MP3

496 optimist [ɑ́ptəmist]
명 낙관론, 낙천주의자
a born optimist 타고난 낙천주의자

497 framework [fréimwə̀ːrk]
명 틀, 구조, 체계
English grammatical framework 영어 문법적 구조

498 gum [gʌm]
명 껌, 잇몸
chew gum 껌을 씹다

499 execute [éksəkjùːt]
동 실시하다, 처형하다
execute projects simultaneously 프로젝트를 동시에 실행하다

500 garage [gərɑ́ːdʒ]
명 차고, 주차장
clean the garage 차고를 청소하다

501 fierce [fiərs]
형 치열한, 사나운
be tired of the fierce competition 치열한 경쟁에 지치다

502 interrupt [ìntərʌ́pt]
동 가로막다, 중단시키다
be interrupted by an injury 부상 때문에 중단되다

503 mad [mæd]
형 미친, 몹시 화가난
go mad 미치다, 아주 화가 나다

504 homeless [hóumlis]
형 집이 없는
help the homeless children 집이 없는 아이들을 돕다

505 inward [ínwərd]
부 안쪽으로 형 내부의
slope inward 안쪽으로 경사지다

506 orbit [ɔ́ːrbit]
명 (천체, 인공 위성 등의) 궤도
the Earth's orbit around the sun 태양 주위 지구의 궤도

507 mimic [mímik]
동 흉내 내다 형 모방의, 모의의
mimic a monkey 원숭이 흉내를 내다

508 intimate [íntəmit]
형 친밀한
intimate relationship 친밀한 관계

509 empathy [émpəθi]
명 감정이입, 공감
empathy for his poor situation 그의 안 좋은 상황에 대한 공감

510 hay [hei]
명 건초
a pile of hay 건초 더미

Daily Test

| 월 일 |

A 우리말에 맞게 빈 칸에 알맞은 단어를 쓰세요.

1 I definitely think the words '_______________' and 'garbage' must be related.
나는 확실히 '차고'와 '쓰레기'의 단어들이 관련되어 있다고 생각한다. 12 고1학평 변형

2 When I sit down to read, I read only for a few minutes because Cindy _______________ me.
내가 독서를 하기 위해 앉을 때, Cindy가 날 방해해서 난 고작 몇 분밖에 읽지 못한다. 04 평가원

3 Sue said that the woman sitting on the bench is _______________.
Sue는 벤치에 앉아있는 저 여자가 미쳤다고 말했다. 14 고2학평 변형

4 We are collecting shoes for _______________ children.
우리는 집이 없는 아이들을 위해 신발을 모으는 중이다. 15 고1학평 변형

5 The boy's smile expressed his _______________ happiness.
그 소년의 미소는 그의 내적 행복을 드러내었다.

6 America's National Aeronautics and Space Administration put chimpanzees into _______________ in 1959.
1959년에 미항공우주국은 챔팬지들을 우주(궤도)에 보냈다. 10 고2학평

7 It is well known that parrots _______________ the words they hear.
앵무새가 그들이 들은 단어들을 흉내내는 것은 잘 알려져 있다.

8 Few people have _______________ knowledge of the new product.
새로운 상품에 대해 정통한 지식을 갖고 있는 사람은 거의 드물다. 10 평가원

9 The capacity for _______________ is crucial to moral imagination.
공감할 수 있는 능력은 도덕적 상상에 있어 아주 중요하다. 13 고1학평 변형

10 The farmer had to haul away a full load of _______________ three times a day.
그 농부는 하루에 세 번 차로 건초 더미를 운반해야 했다.

Day 18

MP3

511 **trustworthy** [trʌ́stwə̀ːrði]
형 신뢰할 수 있는
a trustworthy source of information 믿을만한 정보의 출처

512 **install** [instɔ́ːl]
동 설치하다
install new software 새로운 소프트웨어를 설치하다

513 **packet** [pǽkit]
명 통, 소포, 꾸러미
a packet of letters 편지 꾸러미

514 **toll** [toul]
명 통행료 동 종을 울리다
a toll free highway 통행료 무료 고속도로

515 **complaint** [kəmpléint]
명 불평, 불만
deal with consumer complaints 소비자 불만을 처리하다

516 **anniversary** [æ̀nəvə́ːrsəri]
명 기념일
our 22nd wedding anniversary 우리의 결혼 22주년 기념일

517 **democracy** [dimɑ́krəsi]
명 민주주의
strengthen democracy 민주주의를 강화하다

518 **beloved** [bilʌ́vid]
형 가장 사랑하는, 소중한
a beloved pet 사랑 받는 애완동물

519 **comet** [kɑ́mit]
명 혜성
discover a new comet 새로운 혜성을 발견하다

520 **timing** [taimiŋ]
명 (특정한 일, 계획이 있는) 시기
the exact timing of production 정확한 생산 시기

521 **canal** [kənǽl]
명 운하, 수로
build a canal 운하를 만들다

522 **catalogue** [kǽtəlɔ̀(ː)g]
명 목록, 카탈로그
make a catalogue 카탈로그를 만들다

523 **classify** [klǽsəfài]
동 분류하다
classify movies by genre 장르별로 영화를 분류하다

524 **barren** [bǽrən]
형 척박한, 황량한
a barren wasteland 불모지

525 **constructive** [kənstrʌ́ktiv]
형 건설적인
give constructive advice 건설적인 충고를 하다

Daily Test

| 월 일 |

Ⓐ 우리말에 맞게 빈 칸에 알맞은 단어를 쓰세요.

1 According to ancient superstitions, a mole on one's nose means that he or she is strong-willed and ______________.
고대 미신에 따르면, 코에 난 점은 그 사람이 의지가 강하고 신뢰할 수 있음을 의미한다. 2005 수능

2 In the mid 1800s, the first passenger elevator was ______________ in a New York department store.
1800년대 중반에, 최초의 고객용 승강기가 뉴욕 백화점에 설치되었다.

3 The biggest ______________ of kids who don't read is that they can't find anything to read that interests them.
독서를 하지 않는 아이들의 가장 큰 불만은 그들이 흥미를 느낄만한 책들을 찾지 못한다는 것이다. 14 고1학평 변형

4 I want 'Happy Wedding ______________' written on the cheese cake.
저는 치즈 케이크 위에 '행복한 결혼 기념일'이라고 적고 싶어요. 16 고3학평 변형

5 Competition is the engine of evolution and the foundation of ___________.
경쟁은 발전의 엔진 역할을 하고 민주주의의 근간이다. 15 고2학평 변형

6 Bibimbab is ______________ by many people all over the world.
비빔밥은 전 세계의 많은 사람들에게 사랑 받고 있다.

7 When ______________ pass from the Outer Solar System to the Inner Solar System, a big change occurs.
혜성이 외부 태양계로부터 내부 태양계를 지날 때, 큰 변화가 일어난다.

8 A representative of the ______________ city said that Venice was formed by the historical and cultural environment.
대표적인 운하 도시인 베니스의 대표자는 Venice가 역사적, 문화적 환경에 의해 형성되었다고 말했다.

9 Wind blew across the ______________ landscapes and water ran down from the mountaintops and slopes.
바람은 황량한 풍경을 가로지르며 불었고 물은 산 꼭대기와 산비탈을 타고 흘러 내렸다. 2012 수능

10 Teenagers can do something ______________ like visiting orphanages.
십대들은 고아원 방문 같은 건설적인 일을 할 수 있다.

Day 18

MP3

526 **anchor** [ǽŋkər]
명 닻 동 닻을 내리다, 정박하다
drop anchor 닻을 내리다

527 **chin** [tʃin]
명 턱
pull in your chin 턱을 당기다

528 **prejudice** [prédʒədis]
명 편견
racial prejudice 인종적 편견

529 **realm** [relm]
명 영역, 범위
the realm of nature 자연계

530 **physiological** [fìziəládʒikəl]
형 생리학의, 생리적인
a physiological reaction 생리적인 반응

531 **shortly** [ʃɔ́:rtli]
부 곧, 즉시
shortly after her arrival in Seoul 그녀가 서울에 도착한 즉시

532 **apt** [æpt]
형 ~하기 쉬운
be apt to remember 기억하기 쉽다

533 **tariff** [tǽrif]
명 관세
impose import tariffs 수입 관세를 부과하다

534 **cone** [koun]
명 원뿔, 솔방울
a cone-shaped hat 원뿔 모양 모자

535 **dedicate** [dédəkèit]
동 헌신하다, 바치다
dedicate his life to the experiment 그의 삶을 그 실험에 바치다

536 **convict** [kánvikt]
동 유죄를 선고하다
be wrongfully convicted 부당하게 유죄 판결을 받다

537 **cope with** [koup wið]
동 ~에 대처하다, 대응하다
cope with pain 고통에 대처하다

538 **detach** [ditǽtʃ]
동 떼다, 분리하다
a two bedroom detached house 방 2개짜리 분리된 집

539 **representative** [rèprizéntətiv]
명 대표(자), 대리인 형 대표하는, 전형적인
the Korean representative 한국 대표

540 **tender** [téndər]
형 상냥한, 부드러운, 약한
a tender smile 부드러운 미소

Daily Test

| 월 일 |

A 우리말에 맞게 빈 칸에 알맞은 단어를 쓰세요.

1 It is important to treat your students without ______________.
당신의 학생들을 편견없이 대하는 것은 중요합니다.

2 Nature lies outside the urban and agricultural ______________, in regions of Earth where natural drocesses are unhindered.
자연은 도시와 농촌 지역 외부에, 다시 말해 자연의 과정이 방해받지 않는 지구의 지역에 존재한다. 11 평가원

3 As you know, farting is a natural ______________ phenomenon.
너도 알다시피, 방귀는 자연스러운 생리 현상이란다.

4 The nutcracker uses its powerful bill to twist the ______________ of pine trees and remove the nuts.
산갈가마귀는 솔방울을 비틀어 열고 견과를 빼내기 위해 자신의 강력한 부리를 사용한다. 12 고1학평 변형

5 Florence Nightingale ______________ her whole life to caring for sick people.
플로렌스 나이팅게일은 아픈 사람들을 돌보는 것에 그녀의 삶을 헌신했다.

6 Two brothers were ______________ of stealing sheep.
두 형제는 양을 훔쳤기에 유죄를 선고 받았다. 14 고2학평 변형

7 I want to know how to ______________ stress.
나는 스트레스에 어떻게 대처하는지 알고 싶습니다. 2015 수능

8 Looking through the camera lens made Smith ______________ from the scene.
카메라 렌즈를 통해 보는 것은 Smith가 현장에서 분리되도록 만들었다. 2011 수능

9 Researchers didn't know how to obtain a ______________ sample of the population.
연구원들은 인구의 대표 샘플을 얻는 방법을 알지 못했다. 09 평가원

10 What the boy needs is to find a ______________ and warm family.
그 소년에게 필요한 것은 상냥하고 따뜻한 가족을 찾아주는 것이다.

Review Test 09

Day 17 + Day 18 | 월 일 |

A 우리말에 맞게 빈 칸에 알맞은 단어를 쓰시오.

1 a pair of ______________-fitting cotton pants 헐렁한 면 바지

2 an immortal ______________ 불후의 명작

3 a ______________ triumph 영광스러운 승리

4 ______________ projects simultaneously 프로젝트를 동시에 실행하다

5 help the ______________ children 집이 없는 아이들을 돕다

6 a ______________ source of information 믿을만한 정보의 출처

7 strengthen ______________ 민주주의를 강화하다

8 give ______________ advice 건설적인 충고를 하다

9 ______________ after her arrival in Seoul 그녀가 서울에 도착한 즉시

10 impose import ______________ 수입 관세를 부과하다

B 영어에 맞게 빈 칸에 알맞은 우리말을 쓰시오.

1 glow in the dark 어둠 속에서 ______________

2 in medieval days ______________ 시대에

3 mount a hill 언덕을 ______________

4 a born optimist 타고난 ______________

5 clean the garage ______________를 청소하다

6 install new software 새로운 소프트웨어를 ______________

7 discover a new comet 새로운 ______________을 발견하다

8 build a canal ______________를 만들다

9 racial prejudice 인종적 ______________

10 a two bedroom detached house 방 2개짜리 ______________ 집

C 다음 영어 풀이에 알맞은 어휘를 〈보기〉에서 고르시오.

보기	hay	garage	mimic	barren	prejudice

1 ______________ : a judgment made without knowing exact facts

2 ______________ : to copy or imitate

3 ______________ : very dry and having few plants

4 ______________ : dry grass used for animal food

5 ______________ : a part of a building where your car is parked and kept

D 문맥에 맞게 다음 문장을 완성하시오.

1	Jason knew exactly •	• a	how to tie a knot.
2	The aircar arrived at •	• b	crucial to moral imagination.
3	The capacity for empathy is •	• c	written on the cheese cake.
4	I want 'Happy Wedding Anniversary' •	• d	the orbit of the Island of Paradise.
5	Nature lies outside the urban •	• e	and agricultural realms .

E 문장을 읽고 문맥에 적절한 단어를 고르시오.

1 I can't (dedicate/indicate) much time to writing reports for the newspaper.

2 If you are in a debate, make your intention (fierce/explicit).

3 He is (apt/proud) to remember other people's mistakes.

4 Trust is the most important element in an (intimate/delicate) relationship.

5 I don't mean to (convict/interrupt) you but can you speak more slowly?

F 문장의 빈칸에 알맞은 단어를 〈보기〉에서 찾아 쓰시오. (필요하면 형태를 고치시오.)

보기 barren classify illuminate legitimate constructive

1 The old farmer planted over 100,000 acorns in a ______________ land in the Alps.
그 늙은 농부는 알프스 산의 황량한 땅에 10만개가 넘은 도토리를 심었다. 06 고3학평 변형

2 Music has traditionally been ______________ according to the musical instrument.
음악은 전통적으로 악기에 의해 분류되었다. 15 고3평가원 변형

3 Einstein ______________ the workings of the universe with great clarity.
Einstein은 아주 명확하게 우주의 활동을 조명했다. 12 고3평가원 변형

4 We will determine soon whether any such inquiry is for ______________ reasons.
우리는 문의사항이 정당한 이유에 의한 것인지 곧 결정하겠습니다. 15 고2학평 변형

5 Some people believe that competition can be a ______________ activity.
어떤 사람들은 경쟁이 건설적인 활동이 될 수 있다고 믿는다. 15 고2학평 변형

G 다음 〈보기〉 중 두 문장에 공통으로 사용할 수 있는 어휘를 고르시오.

1 We believe that he would be able to ___________ with the problems wisely.
One of the biggest differences between men and women is how they ___________ with stress. 04 고3학평 변형

① agree ② keep up ③ break up ④ cope ⑤ put up

2 All of a sudden, he wanted to see his ___________ wife and two sons. 2008 수능 변형
This is one of the songs ___________ by all my family members.

① detached ② beloved ③ convicted ④ glowed ⑤ believed

3 Service ___________ are expected to have a great deal of produce knowledge. 17 고3평가원 변형
The ___________ of the two countries made a formal agreement after a long meeting.

① optimists ② anchors ③ realms ④ comets ⑤ representatives

Study More

혼동하기 쉬운 단어 sympathy vs. empathy

- [sympathy] 명 동정, 연민
  Many people have **sympathy** for the little girl. 많은 사람들이 그 어린 소녀에게 연민을 느낀다.
- [empathy] 명 감정이입, 공감
  When you and your friend trust each other, you can express **empathy** for his friend's situation.
  당신과 친구가 서로를 믿을 때, 당신은 친구의 상황을 공감 할 수 있게 된다.

Day 19

MP3

541 **peel** [pi:l]
동 껍질을 벗기다
peel a pear 배 껍질을 벗기다

542 **navy** [néivi]
명 해군 형 남색의
join the navy 해군에 입대하다

543 **notorious** [noutɔ́:riəs]
형 악명 높은
a notorious prisoner 악명 높은 죄수

544 **neglect** [niglékt]
동 등한시하다, ~을 무시하다
neglect your study 학업을 등한시하다

545 **dissolve** [dizálv]
동 녹이다, 해산하다
dissolve sugar in water 물에서 설탕을 녹이다

546 **outstanding** [àutstǽndiŋ]
형 두드러진, 뛰어난
an outstanding achievement 두드러진 성과

547 **poisonous** [pɔ́izənəs]
형 독이 있는, 유독의
poisonous plants 독이 있는 식물

548 **gossip** [gásəp]
명 소문, 수다
gossip about the actor 그 배우에 대한 소문

549 **liberate** [líbərèit]
동 해방시키다
liberate a colony 식민지를 해방시키다

550 **grace** [greis]
명 우아함, 품위, 예의
smiled with grace 우아하게 웃다

551 **frown** [fraun]
동 눈살을 찌푸리다
frown with concern 걱정에 눈살을 찌푸리다

552 **dismiss** [dismís]
동 무시하다, 해고하다
dismiss his opinion 그의 의견을 무시하다

553 **leftover** [léftòuvər]
명 나머지, 잔여
leftover food 남은 음식

554 **halt** [hɔ:lt]
동 멈추다 명 중단
an abrupt halt 갑작스러운 중단

555 **hydrogen** [háidrədʒən]
명 수소
combine with hydrogen 수소와 결합하다

Daily Test

| 월 일 |

A 우리말에 맞게 빈 칸에 알맞은 단어를 쓰세요.

1 ______________ the mango, take out the seed and then dice it.
망고의 껍질을 벗기고, 씨를 꺼낸 다음 주사위 모양으로 자르세요.

2 Larry's grandfather left the ______________ in 1981 with an honorable discharge.
Larry의 할아버지는 1981년에 해군을 명예 제대 했다.

3 The Rust Belt is ______________ for its poor air quality.
Rust Belt는 공기 질이 안 좋기로 악명 높다. 14 평가원

4 Because of busy schedules, many people ______________ breakfast or choose to skip it entirely.
바쁜 일정 때문에, 많은 사람들이 아침을 등한시하거나 아예 거르는 걸 선택한다. 07 고3학평 변형

5 When water is stored in plastic containers, chemicals from the plastic can ______________ into it.
물이 플라스틱 통에 들었을 때, 플라스틱의 화학적 요소가 물 속으로 용해될 수 있다. 10 고2학평 변형

6 Jim Nelson, a junior at Manti High School, was an ______________ athlete.
Manti 고등학교 2학년인 Jim Nelson은 뛰어난 운동선수였다. 15 평가원

7 The Golden poison frog is considered the most ______________ animal on earth.
황금 독화살 개구리는 지구상에서 가장 유독성의 동물로 알려져 있다. 14 고1평가원 변형

8 He fought to ______________ his nation from suppression.
그는 그의 조국을 억압 속에서 해방시키기 위해 싸웠다.

9 Though we cannot ______________ Mr. Smith's opinion completely, his argument is not persuasive.
우리가 Mr. Smith의 의견을 완전히 묵살 할 순 없지만, 그의 주장은 설득력이 없다. 2004 수능

10 Everybody knows that water, H2O, is made up of ______________ and oxygen.
모든 사람들은 물이 수소와 산소로 이루어진 것을 알고 있다. 04 평가원

Day 19

MP3

556 poetic [pouétik]
형 시의
a poetic expression 시적 표현

557 navigate [nǽvəgèit]
동 항해하다, 길을 찾다
navigate the Pacific ocean 태평양을 항해하다

558 disability [dìsəbíləti]
명 장애
people with severe mental disabilities 심각한 정신 장애를 겪는 사람들

559 fist [fist]
명 주먹
make a fist 주먹을 쥐다

560 lately [léitli]
부 요즘, 최근에
working hard lately 최근에 열심히 일하다

561 even [íːvən]
형 평평한, 고른
walk on even ground 평평한 땅을 걷다

562 harmonious [hɑːrmóuniəs]
형 조화로운, 화목한
a harmonious effect 조화로운 효과

563 faculty [fǽkəlti]
명 능력, 재능, (대학의) 학부, 교수단
the faculty of speech 언어적 능력

564 foretell [fɔːrtél]
동 예언하다
foretell the future by the stars 별로서 미래를 예언하다

565 immortal [imɔ́ːrtəl]
형 불멸의, 불후의
an immortal soul 불멸의 영혼

566 disposable [dispóuzəbl]
형 일회용의 명 일회용품
stop using disposable chopsticks 일회용 젓가락 사용을 멈추다

567 drill [dril]
명 연습, 훈련 동 연습시키다
a repetitive pronunciation drill 반복되는 발음 연습

568 fraction [frǽkʃən]
명 부분, 일부
finished a fraction of his homework 그의 숙제 중 일부를 끝냈다

569 motive [móutiv]
명 동기
an underlying motive 숨겨진 동기

570 dissatisfied [dissǽtisfàid]
형 불만스러워하는
dissatisfied customers 불만스러워하는 고객들

Daily Test

| 월 일 |

A **우리말에 맞게 빈 칸에 알맞은 단어를 쓰세요.**

1 Shakespeare hoped that ______________ greatness would grant him a kind of earthly immortality.
셰익스피어는 시적 위대함이 그에게 세속적인 불멸을 가져다 주기를 희망했다. 2016 수능

2 Henry ______________ the Congo river under the sponsorship of King Leopold of Belgium.
Henry는 벨기에의 Leopold왕의 후원을 받아 콩고강을 항해했다. 07 고3학평 변형

3 When you try to achieve a dream, ______________ cannot be a problem.
꿈을 이루기 위해 노력할 때, 장애는 문제가 될 수 없다.

4 I turned off the motor and hit the steering wheel with my ______________.
나는 자동차 시동을 끄고 내 주먹으로 핸들을 쳤다. 08 고2학평 변형

5 ______________ many people have been putting in a lot of overtime before long holidays.
최근 많은 사람들이 긴 연휴 전까지 연장 근무들을 많이 한다.

6 People from diverse backgrounds have started to live ______________, loving lives together.
다양한 배경의 사람들이 조화롭고 서로를 사랑하며 살기 시작했다. 2011 수능

7 Dreams have been regarded as a sign that enables us to ______________ the future.
꿈은 우리가 미래를 예측할 수 있게 해주는 신호로 여겨졌다. 2012 수능

8 If you want to speak English like a native speaker, do a lot of repetitive pronunciation ______________.
네가 만약 원어민처럼 영어를 말하고 싶다면 반복된 발음 연습을 많이 해라.

9 Psychoanalysts believe that understanding the unconscious ______________ is very important.
정신분석가들은 무의식적인 동기의 이해가 매우 중요하다고 믿는다. 05 고3학평 변형

10 John is felt ______________ with the way his mother treats him.
John은 그의 엄마가 그를 대하는 방식이 불만족스럽다.

Day 20

MP3

571 **spit** [spit]
동 뱉다 명 침, 침뱉기
spit gum 껌을 뱉다

572 **blast** [blæst]
명 폭발, 한 바탕 부는 바람 동 폭파하다
a bomb blast in LA LA에서의 폭탄 폭발

573 **contaminate** [kəntǽmənit]
동 오염시키다
contaminate drinking water 식수를 오염시키다

574 **bathe** [beið]
동 목욕하다, 세척하다
bathe your eyes in cold water 찬물로 눈을 씻다

575 **thoughtful** [θɔ́:tfəl]
형 사려 깊은, 생각이 깊은
thoughtful behavior 사려 깊은 행동

576 **outrageous** [autréidʒəs]
형 너무나 충격적인, 터무니없는
outrageous behavior 너무나 충격적인 행동

577 **undo** [ʌndú:]
동 풀다, 원상태로 돌리다
undo some of the damage 손상을 복구하다

578 **collide** [kəláid]
동 충돌하다, 부딪히다
collide with a big iceberg 커다란 빙하와 부딪히다

579 **caterpillar** [kǽtərpìlər]
명 애벌레
beetles and caterpillars 딱정벌레와 애벌레

580 **regulate** [régjəlèit]
동 규제하다, 조절하다
be regulated by law 법으로 규제되다

581 **pollen** [pálən]
명 꽃가루, 화분
have an allergy to pollen 꽃가루 알레르기가 있다

582 **skeptical** [sképtikəl]
형 회의적인, 의심많은
have a skeptical view 회의적 관점을 가지다

583 **comprehensive** [kàmprihénsiv]
형 포괄적인, 종합적인
make a comprehensive plan 포괄적인 계획을 세우다

584 **commonplace** [kámənplèis]
형 아주 흔한, 평범한
commonplace people 평범한 사람들

585 **compatible** [kəmpǽtəbl]
형 호환이 되는, 양립 될 수 있는
compatible with the computer 컴퓨터와 호환이 되는

Daily Test

| 월 일 |

A 우리말에 맞게 빈 칸에 알맞은 단어를 쓰세요.

1 If you are concerned about fine dust, ______________ your eyes twice a day.
만약 미세먼지가 걱정 된다면, 하루에 두 번 눈을 씻으세요.

2 It was really ______________ of you to say that.
그렇게 말해주시다니 당신은 정말 사려 깊군요.

3 The more ______________ a rumor, the faster it travels.
소문이 더 충격적일수록, 빠르게 전달된다. 12 고1학평 변형

4 Tie two strings on the stick some distance apart so the strings don't ______________.
두 끈을 어느 정도 거리를 두고 막대기에 묶어서 서로 부딪히지 않도록 하여라. 08 고2학평 변형

5 ______________ won't eat the bad tasting leaves.
애벌레는 맛이 없는 잎은 먹지 않을 것이다.

6 The human body changes in order to ______________ body temperature more efficiently.
인간의 몸은 보다 더 효율적으로 체온을 조절하기 위해 변화한다. 09 고3학평 변형

7 Many children are allergic to the ______________ in the air in spring.
많은 어린이들이 봄에 공기 중에 있는 꽃가루에 알레르기가 있다.

8 Many doctors are ______________ about the helpfulness of online medical information.
많은 의사들이 인터넷 의학 정보의 유용성에 대해 회의적이다. 10 고3학평 변형

9 It is difficult for children to have a ______________ understanding of gravity.
아이들이 중력에 대해 종합적인 이해를 하는 것은 어렵다.

10 Contentment is thoroughly ______________ with wanting the future to be quite different.
만족감은 미래가 완전히 다르길 바라는 것과 완전히 양립될 수 있다. 13 고3학평 변형

Day 20

MP3

586 **suspect** [sʌ́spekt]
동 의심하다 명 혐의자, 용의자
suspect her motives 그녀의 동기를 의심하다

587 **workout** [wə́ːrkàut]
명 운동, 연습
regular workout 규칙적인 운동

588 **progressive** [prəgrésiv]
형 진보적인, 점진적인
progressive ideas 진보적 사상

589 **vibrate** [váibreit]
동 떨리다, 흔들리다
Julia's lips vibrated. Julia의 입술이 떨렸다.

590 **coverage** [kʌ́vəridʒ]
명 보도(방송), 범위, 보급(률)
newspaper coverage 신문 보도

591 **province** [právins]
명 지방, 분야
Western provinces of Japan 일본의 서쪽 지방

592 **steep** [stiːp]
형 가파른
climb steep hills 가파른 언덕을 오르다

593 **deadly** [dédli]
형 치명적인 부 극도로
a deadly wound 치명적인 상처

594 **stroll** [stroul]
동 거닐다, 산책하다 명 산책
take a stroll in the park 공원에서 산책하다

595 **descend** [disénd]
동 내려오다, 내려가다
descend from a tree 나무에서 내려오다

596 **tutor** [tjúːtər]
명 가정교사
hire a tutor 가정교사를 고용하다

597 **storage** [stɔ́ːridʒ]
명 저장(소), 보관(소)
storage space 저장 공간

598 **bilingual** [bailíŋgwəl]
형 두 나라 말을 사용하는
be bilingual in English and Japanese 영어와 일본어 2개 국어를 구사하는

599 **span** [spæn]
명 기간, 전 범위
a specific time span 특정한 기간 이내에

600 **profession** [prəféʃən]
명 직업, 직종
the medical profession 의료직

Daily Test

A 우리말에 맞게 빈 칸에 알맞은 단어를 쓰세요.

1 While a good ______________ should offer pressure and challenges, it should absolutely should never be painful.
좋은 운동은 압박과 도전을 제공해야 하지만 반면에, 절대 고통스러우면 안된다. 12 고1학평 변형

2 The RPC, founded in1996, describes itself as a ______________ organization fighting for social change.
1996년에 설립된 RPC는 그 스스로를 사회적 변화에 맞서는 진보적 단체로서 설명한다. 2009 수능

3 The snake swells up, hisses loudly, ______________ its tail, and even bites.
그 뱀은 부풀어 오르고, 쉭쉭 소리를 내고, 꼬리를 흔들며 심지어 물기까지 한다. 05 평가원

4 Live ______________ of tonight's soccer game will be on channel 7.
7번 채널에서 오늘밤 그 축구 경기의 생중계 방송이 있을 것이다.

5 For the early mountanieers, knowledge of the ______________ effects of extreme altitude was limited, and their equipment was poor.
초기 등산가들에게 있어서, 극한 고도의 치명적 영향에 대한 지식은 한정적이었고, 그들의 장비는 열악했다. 2012 수능

6 My family and my puppies like to ______________ in the park on summer nights.
나의 가족과 강아지들은 여름 밤 공원을 산책하는 것을 좋아한다.

7 He did not attend school till he was nine, but he was taught at home by a British ______________.
그는 9살이 될 때까지 학교에 나가지 않았지만 집에서 영국인 가정교사에게 교육을 받았다. 09 평가원

8 Roy's possessions will go into ______________.
Roy의 소장품들은 보관소에 들어 갈 거에요.

9 A mother wants to increase the length of her child's attention ______________.
엄마들은 주의 집중 시간의 길이를 늘이고 싶어한다. 14 고2학평 변형

10 A person's potential can be fully realized only if he is involved in the right ______________.
개인의 잠재력은 오직 그가 알맞은 직업에 종사하고 있을때 전적으로 실현될 수 있다. 10 고2학평 변형

Review Test 10

Day 19 + Day 20 | 월 일 |

A 우리말에 맞게 빈 칸에 알맞은 단어를 쓰시오.

1 join the ________________ 해군에 입대하다

2 ________________ sugar in water 물에서 설탕을 녹이다

3 an abrupt ________________ 갑작스러운 중단

4 a ________________ expression 시적 표현

5 a ________________ effect 조화로운 효과

6 ________________ drinking water 식수를 오염시키다

7 ________________ behavior 사려 깊은 행동

8 ________________ behavior 너무나 충격적인 행동

9 ________________ with the computer 컴퓨터와 호환이 되는

10 climb ________________ hills 가파른 언덕을 오르다

B 영어에 맞게 빈 칸에 알맞은 우리말을 쓰시오.

1 poisonous plants ________________ 식물

2 liberate a colony 식민지를 ________________

3 working hard lately ________________ 열심히 일하다

4 finished a fraction of his homework 그의 숙제 중 ________________를 끝냈다

5 dissatisfied customers ________________ 고객들

6 spit gum 껌을 ________________

7 be regulated by law 법으로 ________________

8 Julia's lips vibrated. Julia의 입술이 ________________.

9 a deadly wound ________________ 상처

10 the medical profession 의료 ________________

C 다음 영어 풀이에 알맞은 어휘를 〈보기〉에서 고르시오.

보기	gossip	descend	motive	collide	disposable

1 ______________ : made to be used once and thrown away

2 ______________ : talk about other people or their secrets when they are not with you

3 ______________ : a reason or emotion for doing something

4 ______________ : to strike or hit against something

5 ______________ : to go down from a higher place

D 문맥에 맞게 다음 문장을 완성하시오.

1 The Rust Belt is notorious for •		• a was an outstanding athlete.
2 Jim Nelson, a junior at Manti High School, •		• b all of the pollen in the air in spring.
3 I turned off the motor and hit •		• c its poor air quality.
4 Caterpillars couldn't eat •		• d the badtasting leaves.
5 Many children are allergic to •		• e the steering wheel with my fist.

E 문장을 읽고 문맥에 적절한 단어를 고르시오.

1 Johnny (peeled/bathed) the oranges to make orange juice.

2 My grandparents like to take a (fist/stroll) in the park in the morning.

3 The new software was not (compatible/chanted) with my old computer.

4 Elisa (descends/frowns) upon children behaving badly in a restaurant.

5 Harry (dismissed/dissolved) comments from his friends on his essay.

F 문장의 빈칸에 알맞은 단어를 〈보기〉에서 찾아 쓰시오. (필요하면 형태를 고치시오.)

보기 pollen immortal progressive notorious commonplace

1 Honey bees collect and spread ______________ so that flowers can grow.
꿀벌들은 꽃이 자랄 수 있도록 꽃가루를 모으고 퍼뜨린다.

2 The organization was founded by people with ______________ ideas about art.
그 단체는 예술에 대해 진보적인 사상을 가진 사람들에 의해 설립되었다. 2009 수능 변형

3 What devices will become ______________ that nobody has yet imagined?
아무도 상상하지 못했던 장치들 중 아주 일반적인 것이 될 것은 무엇일까요? 06 고3평가원

4 The novelist believes that he could write an ______________ classic like Shakespeare.
그 소설가는 자신이 Shakespeare처럼 불멸의 명작을 쓸 수 있다고 믿는다.

5 The region is ______________ for extreme weather conditions.
그 지역은 극심한 기상 조건으로 악명 높다.

G 다음 〈보기〉 중 두 문장에 공통으로 사용할 수 있는 어휘를 고르시오.

1 Using ___________ medical items will help to fight this growing health security issue. 12 고1학평 변형
We will buy some ___________ cups and plates for the outside lunch.

① progressive ② disposable ③ harmonious ④ even ⑤ deadly

2 Until my practice period was completed, I deliberately ___________ everything else. 07 고3평가원
The empty house over there has been ___________ for many years.

① neglected ② liberated ③ strolled ④ vibrated ⑤ bathed

3 As a scientist, he made an ___________ achievement.
He has become an ___________ speaker because he knows what people want to hear.

① fierce ② outstanding ③ dissatisfied ④ bilingual ⑤ comprehensive

Study More

'dis-' : [형용사, 명사, 동사, 부사에서] '반대', '부정'의 뜻을 나타낸다.

- [dissatisfied] 형 불만족스러운
  She was **dissatisfied** with the test result. 그녀는 시험 결과가 불만족스러웠다.
- [disadvantage] 명 불리한 점, 약점
  What's the **disadvantage** of travelling alone? 혼자 여행하는 것에 안 좋은 점은 무엇인가요?
- [dishonest] 형 정직하지 않은
  There are some **dishonest** traders in the tourist areas. 여행지에는 몇몇 정직하지 않은 상인들이 있다.

Day 21

MP3

601 **fertilize** [fə́ːrtəlàiz]
동 수정시키다, 땅을 비옥하게 하다
fertilize the soil 땅에 거름을 주다

602 **ivory** [áivəri]
명 상아, 상아색 형 상아로 만든
artificial ivory 인조 상아

603 **funeral** [fjúːnərəl]
명 장례식
attend a funeral 장례식에 참석하다

604 **fraud** [frɔːd]
명 사기
financial fraud 금융 사기

605 **insurance** [inʃú(ː)ərəns]
명 보험
take out life insurance 생명 보험에 가입하다

606 **drought** [draut]
명 가뭄
a severe drought 심각한 가뭄

607 **excel** [iksél]
동 뛰어나다, 두드러지다
excel in baking 제빵에 뛰어나다

608 **exotic** [igzátik]
형 이국적인
an exotic atmosphere 이국적인 분위기

609 **fasten** [fǽsən]
동 매다, 고정시키다
fasten a seat belt 안전벨트를 매다

610 **disrupt** [dìsrʌ́pt]
동 ~을 혼란시키다, 해치다
disrupt fair competition 공정한 경쟁을 해치다

611 **germ** [dʒəːrm]
명 세균
a germ phobia 세균 공포증

612 **encyclopedia** [ensàiklәpíːdiə]
명 백과사전
a forty-volume encyclopedia 40권짜리 백과사전

613 **flatter** [flǽtər]
동 아첨하다
Don't flatter yourself. 너 자신에게 아첨하지 마라

614 **effortless** [éfərtlis]
형 쉬운, 노력이 필요 없는
make playing the violin look effortless 바이올린 연주가 쉽게 보이게 하는

615 **irony** [áiərəni]
명 모순, 예상외의 결과
by the irony of fate 운명의 장난

Daily Test

| 월 일 |

A 우리말에 맞게 빈 칸에 알맞은 단어를 쓰세요.

1 The doll was made of ______________ and lay beside a girl.
인형은 상아로 만들어졌고 소녀 옆에 놓여 있었다. 2009 수능

2 Formal wear is required at weddings and ______________, or any other religious events.
결혼식이나 장례식 또는 다른 종교적 행사에서는 격식을 차린 복장을 갖춰야 한다. 06 고2학평 변형

3 Some ______________ endanger the health and even the lives of citizens.
몇몇 사기는 건강과 심지어 시민의 삶까지 위태롭게 한다. 09 평가원

4 On May 6, I applied for car ______________ with your company by phone.
5월 6일에 나는 전화로 당신 회사의 자동차 보험에 가입했습니다. 06 고3학평 변형

5 There has been a decrease in the water level because of years of ____________.
수년 간의 가뭄 때문에 수위가 감소하고 있다. 15 고2학평 변형

6 I had a dream about meeting new people from ______________ places.
나는 이국적인 장소에서 새로운 사람들을 만나고자 하는 꿈이 있었다. 2010 수능

7 It's easy for a ______________ on your hand to enter your mouth, so wash your hands vigorously.
손에 있는 세균은 입으로 들어가기 쉬우니 손을 깨끗이 씻어라.

8 Why don't you find some information from the ______________ over there?
저기 있는 백과사전에서 정보를 좀 찾아보는 건 어떻니? 2010 수능

9 It looks so ______________ when she sings this song.
그녀가 그 노래를 부를 때 정말 쉬워보인다.

10 Cupid shot the arrow wrong by the ______________ of fate and he fell in love.
큐피드는 운명의 장난으로 화살을 잘못 쐈고, 사랑에 빠졌다.

Day 21

MP3

616 **fabulous** [fǽbjələs]
형 (아주) 멋진, 재미있는
Jason's fabulous exhibition Jason의 멋진 전시회

617 **forbid** [fərbíd]
동 금지하다
forbid students to enter the room 그 방에 학생들의 출입을 금지하다

618 **glamorous** [glǽmərəs]
형 매력적인, 화려한
a glamorous job 매력적인 직업

619 **fossil** [fásl]
명 화석
discover a dinosaur fossil 공룡 화석을 발견하다

620 **fiance** [fiːɑːnséi]
명 약혼자
travel with his fiance 그의 약혼자와 함께 여행을 가다

621 **edible** [édəbl]
형 식용의, 먹을 수 있는
buy edible coconut oil 식용 코코넛 오일을 사다

622 **grind** [graind]
동 갈다, 빻다
grind wheat into powder 밀가루를 잘게 갈아 가루를 내다

623 **entail** [intéil]
동 수반하다, 필요로 하다, 의미하다
entail risky work 위험한 일을 수반하다

624 **ethnic** [éθnik]
형 민족의, 인종의
an ethnic leader 민족의 지도자

625 **gloomy** [glúːmi]
형 우울한, 비관적인
her gloomy expression 그녀의 우울한 표정

626 **imaginary** [imǽdʒənèri]
형 상상의, 가상적인
an imaginary animal 상상의 동물

627 **blockbuster** [blákbʌ̀stər]
명 블록버스터, 대작
the latest Hollywood blockbuster movie 최신 헐리웃 블록버스터 영화

628 **blackout** [blǽkàut]
명 정전, 소등
sudden blackout 갑작스러운 정전

629 **explosion** [iklsplouʒn]
명 폭발, 급증
a nuclear explosion 핵폭발

630 **feast** [fiːst]
명 축제, 연회, 진수성찬
prepare a huge feast 성대한 연회를 준비하다

Daily Test

| 월 일 |

A 우리말에 맞게 빈 칸에 알맞은 단어를 쓰세요.

1 Come and enjoy the ______________ drawings, sculptures, and great music!
오셔서 아주 멋진 그림, 신나는 음악을 즐기세요! 2016 수능

2 You should remember that smoking is ______________ in the hall.
당신은 흡연은 홀안에서 금지된다는걸 기억해야 합니다.

3 ______________ fuels have given us global warming and resulted in extreme weather.
화석 연료는 지구 온난화를 초래했고 극한 기후를 야기했다. 09 평가원

4 He wrote the story about his ______________ and himself for a magazine.
그는 약혼자와 자신에 대한 이야기를 잡지에 투고했다. 15 고1학평 변형

5 Flowers are not ______________, but some of them, like azaleas, can be tasted.
꽃들은 먹을 수 없지만 진달래 같은 몇몇 꽃들은 맛을 볼 수 있다.

6 When my uncle saw I was ______________, he bought beautiful flowers.
삼촌이 내가 우울해 하는 걸 보았을 때, 그는 아름다운 꽃을 사주었다. 15 고2학평 변형

7 A lot of children have an ______________ land and friends who live there.
많은 어린이들에게는 상상 속 나라와 그곳에 사는 친구들이 있다.

8 Because of a sudden earthquake, there was a ______________ for a while.
갑작스런 지진 때문에 잠깐 동안 정전이 있었다.

9 Since the engine runs on the air that we breathe, there is no risk of ______________ or pollution.
우리가 호흡하는 공기로 엔진이 작동했기 때문에, 폭발이나 오염에 대한 위험은 없다. 07 고2학평 변형

10 He would certainly bring home a great ______________ for his wife and son.
그는 아내와 아들을 위해 집으로 진수성찬을 틀림없이 가져 올 것이다. 07 고2학평 변형

Day 22

MP3

631 **reign** [rein]
동 군림하다, 통치하다 명 통치(기간)
a successful reign 성공적인 통치

632 **quarrel** [kwɔ́(:)rəl]
명 다툼, 언쟁 동 다투다
quarrel with her sister 그녀의 여동생과 다투다

633 **telescope** [téləskòup]
명 망원경
look at the stars through a telescope 망원경을 통해 별을 보다

634 **recollect** [rèkəlékt]
동 기억하다, 회상하다
recollect details of the letter 그 편지의 상세한 내용을 회상하다

635 **literate** [lítərit]
형 글을 읽고 쓸 줄 아는
literate population 읽고 쓸 줄 아는 인구

636 **shallow** [ʃǽlou]
형 얕은
play in shallow water 얕은 물에서 놀다

637 **meditation** [mèditéiʃən]
명 명상, 묵상
yoga and meditation 요가와 명상

638 **trade** [treid]
동 거래하다, 무역하다
secretly trade in arms 비밀리에 무기를 거래하다

639 **monotonous** [mənɑ́tənəs]
형 단조로운
live a monotonous life 단조로운 삶을 살다

640 **priceless** [práislis]
형 값을 매길 수 없는, 귀중한, 대단히 귀중한
gain priceless experience 값을 매길 수 없는 경험을 하다

641 **propel** [prəpél]
동 나아가게 하다, 추진하다
propel the boat 배가 나아가게 하다

642 **prohibit** [prouhíbit]
동 금하다, 금지하다
prohibit the sales of beverages 음료 판매를 금하다

643 **port** [pɔːrt]
명 항구 유 harbour 항구, 항만
enter a port 입항하다

644 **resign** [rizáin]
동 물러나다, 사임하다 명 resignation 사임, 퇴임
resign as the director 감독에서 물러나다

645 **crunch** [krʌntʃ]
동 아작아작 씹다
crunch his candies noisily 그의 사탕을 시끄럽게 아작아작 씹다

Daily Test

| 월 일 |

A **우리말에 맞게 빈 칸에 알맞은 단어를 쓰세요.**

1 The country was under the ______________ of the tyrant for many years.
그 나라는 수년 동안 폭군의 치세 하에 있었다.

2 Sometimes, political issues can cause family ______________.
가끔은 정치적 이슈가 가족간의 언쟁을 야기할 수 있다.

3 When you observe the night sky with a ______________, you must be patient.
당신이 망원경으로 밤하늘을 관찰 할 때, 반드시 인내심을 가져야 한다. 04 고3학평 변형

4 No one could ______________ the entire song.
아무도 그 노래 전체를 기억하지 못했다. 16 고3학평 변형

5 The beach at dawn provides the perfect place for ______________.
동이 틀 무렵에 바다는 명상을 위한 완벽한 장소를 제공한다. 14 고3학평 변형

6 The grave was very ______________; only about three feet deep.
그 무덤은 단지 3피트 정도의 깊이로 매우 얕았다.

7 A ______________ collection of antiques was stolen last night in China.
지난 밤 중국에서 대단히 귀중한 골동품 수집품이 도둑 맞았다.

8 As one player returns to the board, the other is ______________ into the air.
한 선수가 보드에 돌아오면, 다른 선수가 공기 중으로 솟아 오른다. 09 평가원

9 Smoking is ______________ in all Smithsonian facilities.
담배는 모든 Smithsonian 시설에서 금지됩니다. 05 평가원

10 He ______________ as governor of Texas last month.
그는 지난 달에 Texas주 지사직을 사임했다. 12 평가원

Day 22

MP3

646 □ **qualification** [kwɑ̀ləfəkéiʃən]
명 (주로 복수형으로) 자격(증), 자질　동 qualify 자격(증)을 얻다
have good qualifications for the position 직위에 맞는 훌륭한 자질을 갖추다

647 □ **lantern** [lǽntərn]
명 초롱, 호롱불, 손전등
light a lantern 초롱을 밝히다

648 □ **pendulum** [péndʒələm]
명 (시계의) 추, 진자
swing a pendulum 추가 흔들리다

649 □ **noble** [nóubl]
형 고귀한, 숭고한
noble birth 고귀한 태생　a noble mission 숭고한 사명

650 □ **resume** [rizjúːm]
동 다시 시작하다, 재개하다
resume conversation 대화를 다시 시작하다

651 □ **pod** [pɑd]
명 꼬투리　동 껍질을 벗기다
a pea pod 완두콩 꼬투리

652 □ **portion** [pɔ́ːrʃən]
명 부분, 일부
the last portion of the movie 영화의 마지막 부분

653 □ **kindergarten** [kíndərgɑ̀ːrtən]
명 유치원
go to a kindergarten 유치원에 가다

654 □ **ladder** [lǽdər]
명 사다리
climb up the ladder 사다리를 오르다

655 □ **prospective** [prəspéktiv]
형 장래의, 유망한　명 prospect 가능성
a prospective actress 유망한 배우 지망생

656 □ **marvelous** [mάːrvələs]
형 놀라운, 믿기 어려운
a marvelous story 놀라운 이야기

657 □ **refresh** [rifréʃ]
동 상쾌하게하다, 재충전하다
refresh herself with travel 여행으로 그녀 스스로 재충전하다

658 □ **memorable** [mémərəbl]
형 기억할만한, 주목할 만한
Tom's memorable summer vacation Tom의 기억에 남는 여름 방학

659 □ **leather** [léðər]
명 가죽, 가죽상품
glossy leather 윤이 나는 가죽　a man in leather 가죽자켓을 입은 남자

660 □ **resemble** [rizémbl]
동 닮다
Cindy closely resembles her father. Cindy는 그녀의 아빠를 많이 닮았다.

Daily Test

| 월 일 |

A 우리말에 맞게 빈 칸에 알맞은 단어를 쓰세요.

1 Be sure to describe your ______________ and tell them what kind of job you'd like.
너의 자격을 설명하고 그들에게 어떤 종류의 직업을 네가 원하는지 말하는 걸 명심해. 04 평가원

2 Chris constructed the first ______________ clock, revolutionizing timekeeping.
Chris는 시간기록에 혁명을 일으킨 최초의 추시계를 만들었다. 2005 수능

3 When the first miners and hunters returned from the Rocky Mountains, they brought back ______________ tales of natural beauty.
최초의 광부와 사냥꾼들이 록키산에서 돌아왔을 때, 그들은 자연의 아름다움에 대한 믿기 어려운 얘기를 가져왔다. 06 고2학평 변형

4 If our situation changes, we will call you to ______________ delivery.
우리의 상황이 변한다면, 우리는 배달을 재개하기 위해 당신께 연락 할게요. 2011 수능

5 Clusters of white flowers are produced from this tree, which then develop into long narrow seed ______________.
이 나무로부터 흰 꽃이 무리를 지어 피고 난 후 길고 가느다란 모양의 씨앗 꼬투리로 발달한다. 14 고1평가원 변형

6 You probably know only a small ______________ of the total vocabulary of English.
아마 당신은 영어의 전체 단어 중 아주 작은 부분만을 알고 있을 것이다. 10 고1학평 변형

7 If you are getting sufficient sleep, you should feel ______________ in the morning.
만약 충분한 잠을 잔다면, 당신은 아침에 상쾌함을 느낄 것이다.

8 The most ______________ place for my parents is Hawaii where they went on their honeymoon.
나의 부모님에게 가장 기억에 남을 장소는 신혼여행을 갔던 하와이다.

9 What type of cover would you like? We have fur, paper, and ______________ cover diaries.
어떤 종류의 커버를 좋아하세요? 우리는 털, 종이, 가죽 커버의 다이어리들이 있습니다. 16 고3학평 변형

10 Actually, John doesn't ______________ his parents in appearance at all.
솔직히 John은 외모상으로 그의 부모님을 전혀 닮지 않았다.

Review Test 11

Day 21 + Day 22 | 월 일 |

A 우리말에 맞게 빈 칸에 알맞은 단어를 쓰시오.

1 take out life ______________ 생명 보험에 가입하다

2 ______________ a seat belt 안전벨트를 매다

3 discover a dinosaur ______________ 공룡 화석을 발견하다

4 buy ______________ coconut oil 식용 코코넛 오일을 사다

5 an ______________ animal 상상의 동물

6 a nuclear ______________ 핵폭발

7 play in ______________ water 얕은 물에서 놀다

8 yoga and ______________ 요가와 명상

9 swing a ______________ 추가 흔들리다

10 ______________ conversation 대화를 다시 시작하다

B 영어에 맞게 빈 칸에 알맞은 우리말을 쓰시오.

1 attend a funeral ______________에 참석하다

2 a severe drought 심각한 ______________

3 excel in baking 제빵에 ______________

4 travel with his fiance 그의 ______________와 함께 여행을 가다

5 sudden blackout 갑작스러운 ______________

6 prepare a huge feast 성대한 ______________를 준비하다

7 quarrel with her sister 그녀의 여동생과 ______________

8 live a monotonous life ______________ 삶을 살다

9 a noble mission ______________ 사명

10 go to a kindergarten ______________ 가다

C 다음 영어 풀이에 알맞은 어휘를 〈보기〉에서 고르시오.

보기	drought	propel	edible	resemble	exotic

1 ______________ : a long period of time with no rain

2 ______________ : safe to eat or things that can be eaten

3 ______________ : very unusual and interesting

4 ______________ : to push or move something forward

5 ______________ : to look like something or someone

D 문맥에 맞게 다음 문장을 완성하시오.

1 The doll was made of ivory •	• a with a telescope, you must be patient.
2 Why don't you find some information •	• b the other is propelled into the air.
3 You should remember that •	• c smoking is forbidden in the hall.
4 When you observe the night sky •	• d and lay beside a girl.
5 As one player returns to the board, •	• e from the encyclopedia over there?

E 문장을 읽고 문맥에 적절한 단어를 고르시오.

1 The peaceful ceremony was (disrupted/entailed) by a group of noisy children.

2 The boat was (flattered/propelled) by a steam engine.

3 During the (reign/lantern) of the kind king, people enjoyed great freedom.

4 John was amazed by the (impersonal/marvelous) paintings at the museum.

5 Rogan (resembled/resigned) his father very much.

F 문장의 빈칸에 알맞은 단어를 〈보기〉에서 찾아 쓰시오. (필요하면 형태를 고치시오.)

보기 qualification ethnic germ exotic gloomy

1 Be sure to describe your ______________ clearly at the interview.
인터뷰에서 당신의 자격사항들을 명확하게 기술할 것을 명심하세요. 04 고2평가원 변형

2 Tourists had the opportunity to see the ______________ birds and plants in the forest park.
관광객들은 그 산림공원에서 이국적인 새들과 식물들을 볼 기회를 가졌다.

3 In big cities like New York or London, many different ______________ groups live together.
뉴욕이나 런던 같은 대도시에는 많고 다양한 민족 집단이 함께 살아간다.

4 Hades had a dark and ______________ character.
Hades신은 어둡고 음울한 성격을 가지고 있었다. 09 고1학평 변형

5 Dr. Levy says that : trying to protect ourselves from every ______________ is not possible.
Levy박사는 모든 세균으로부터 우리를 보호하려고 시도하는 것은 가능하지 않다고 말한다. 05 평가원 변형

G 다음 〈보기〉 중 두 문장에 공통으로 사용할 수 있는 어휘를 고르시오.

1 There was a time when women were strictly __________ from joining scientific societies. 05 고2 평가원 변형

Smoking is __________ in all Smithsonian facilities. 05 고3 평가원

① excelled ② fastened ③ quarreled ④ resumed ⑤ prohibited

2 It is strictly __________ to flash photographs with flash in the exhibition hall.

In many countries, the fishing of endangered species is __________ by law. 08 고1 평가원

① recollected ② forbidden ③ foretold ④ crunched ⑤ crunched

3 She interviewed a group of people from various __________ backgrounds. 12 고3 학평 변형

At the Asian Food Festival, we could try a variety of __________ foods.

① memorable ② ethnic ③ monotonous ④ shallow ⑤ glamorous

Study More

혼동하기 쉬운 단어 edible vs. audible

- [edible] 형 먹을 수 있는
  The fruits are **edible.** 그 과일은 먹을 수 있다.
  I want to buy some **edible** fungi. 전 식용 버섯을 좀 사고 싶은데요.
- [audible] 형 들을 수 있는
  His song was barely **audible.** 그의 노래는 거의 들리지 않았다.
  There was an **audible** whisper in the air. 공기 중에서 들리는 속삭임이 있었다.

Day 23

MP3

661 **affair** [əfɛ́ər]
명 일, 문제
international affairs 국제적인 문제

662 **spine** [spain]
명 척추, 등뼈 — 형 spinal 척추의
stretch your spine 등뼈를 고르게 피다

663 **divorce** [divɔ́:rs]
명 이혼 동 이혼하다
a high divorce rate 높은 이혼률

664 **treatment** [trí:tmənt]
명 치료, 처치, 대우
a new treatment for lung cancer 폐암의 새로운 치료법

665 **stationary** [stéiʃənèri]
형 움직이지 않는, 고정된
remain stationary 제자리에 있다

666 **alley** [ǽli]
명 골목, 통로
walk in a narrow alley 좁은 골목길을 걷다

667 **shortcut** [ʃɔ́:rtkʌ̀t]
명 지름길
shortcut to defeat and ruin 패배와 파멸의 지름길

668 **applause** [əplɔ́:z]
명 박수 갈채
greet her with applause 박수갈채로 그녀를 맞이하다

669 **decode** [di:kóud]
동 번역하다, 해독하다, 이해하다
decode a secret message 비밀 메시지를 해독하다

670 **drainage** [dréinidʒ]
명 배수(시설)
rainwater drainage 빗물 배수 시설

671 **shed** [ʃed]
동 없애다, 떨구다, 비추다
shed weight 살을 빼다 shed tears 눈물을 떨구다

672 **ubiquitous** [ju:bíkwitəs]
형 어디에나 있는, 아주 흔한 — 명 ubiquity 도처에 있음
ubiquitous in societies 사회 속 어디에나 있는

673 **bundle** [bʌ́ndl]
명 꾸러미, 보따리
a bundle of firewood 장작 한 꾸러미

674 **considerable** [kənsídərəbl]
형 상당한, 많은
considerable damage 상당한 손상

675 **disclose** [disklóuz]
동 폭로하다, 공개하다 — 명 disclosure 폭로
disclose the secret 비밀을 폭로하다

Daily Test

| 월 일 |

A **우리말에 맞게 빈 칸에 알맞은 단어를 쓰세요.**

1 This exercise puts tremendous pressure on the ______________.
이 운동은 척추에 엄청난 압력을 가한다. 06 고3학평 변형

2 ______________ rates have been rising in many countries around the world.
전 세계 많은 나라에서 이혼률이 오르고 있다. 08 고2학평 변형

3 Proper and early ______________ is essential.
적절하고 이른 치료는 필수적이다. 05 고3학평 변형

4 I place ______________ folders to use easily on my desktop.
나는 컴퓨터 바탕화면에 쉽게 사용하기 위해 바로 가기 폴더들을 놓아 둔다.

5 The ______________ grew louder and he kept dancing.
박수갈채가 점점 커졌고 그는 계속해서 춤을 췄다. 06 고3학평 변형

6 If you do not speak Japanese, you will be faced with a world that is difficult to ______________.
만약 당신이 일본어를 못 한다면, 당신은 이해하기 어려운 세상을 마주할 것이다. 11 고2학평 변형

7 The view of riding bicycles is so ______________ in Vietnam.
자전거를 타는 풍경은 베트남에서 어디에서나 아주 흔히 볼 수 있는 것이다.

8 Mother gave me a ______________ of lilies and roses and a big hug.
엄마는 내게 한 다발의 백합과 장미를 주셨고 크게 안아주셨다. 2016 수능

9 A ______________ amount of effort is required to change your bad habit.
당신의 나쁜 습관을 바꾸기 위해서는 상당한 노력이 필요하다. 05 고3학평 변형

10 The chairman refused to ______________ details of the takeover bid for the company.
회장은 그 회사에 대한 기업 인수 작업에 대한 자세한 내용을 밝히기를 거부했다.

Day 23

MP3

676 □ **supernatural** [sjùːpərnǽtʃərəl]
형 초자연적인
have supernatural power 초자연적인 힘이 있다

677 □ **crush** [krʌʃ]
동 으깨다, 짉다
crush oranges for juice 주스를 만들기 위해 오렌지를 짉다

678 □ **combat** [kάmbæt]
명 전투 동 싸우다, 맞서다
armed combat 무장 전투 combat poverty 가난과 싸우다

679 □ **vice** [vais]
명 악덕, 부도덕, 비행
vice and virtue 악덕과 미덕

680 □ **boast** [boust]
동 자랑하다, 뽐내다
boast of your ability 재능을 뽐내다

681 □ **uncertain** [ʌnsə́ːrtən]
형 불확실한, 불투명한
uncertain where to go 어디로 갈지 불확실한

682 □ **swift** [swift]
형 신속한, 재빠른
make a swift decision 신속한 결정을 하다

683 □ **cucumber** [kjúːkʌmbər]
명 오이
peel a cucumber 오이 껍질을 깎다

684 □ **debris** [dəbríː]
명 잔해, 파편
flying debris from the storm 폭풍으로부터 날라온 파편

685 □ **therapy** [θérəpi]
명 치료, 요법
get shock therapy 충격 요법을 받다

686 □ **suspicious** [səspíʃəs]
형 의심스러운 명 suspicion 혐의, 의혹
a suspicious death 의심스러운 죽음

687 □ **clerk** [kləːrk]
명 점원, 사무원
ask a clerk for help 점원에게 도움을 청하다

688 □ **summit** [sʌ́mit]
명 산 꼭대기, 정상회담
reach the summit 산 꼭대기에 다다르다

689 □ **antique** [æntíːk]
명 골동품 형 옛날의
an antique shop 골동품 상점

690 □ **straightforward** [strèitfɔ́ːrwərd]
형 간단한, 솔직한
a straightforward process 간단한 과정

Daily Test

| 월 일 |

A 우리말에 맞게 빈 칸에 알맞은 단어를 쓰세요.

1 Rowling's books do contain ______________ creatures.
Rowling의 책은 초자연적인 존재를 포함한다. 05 고3학평 변형

2 The car was completely ______________ under the dump truck in the accident.
그 자동차는 그 사고에서 덤프 트럭에 깔려 완전히 찌그러졌다.

3 Strength training can help ______________ depression and risk factors for heart disease and diabetes.
근력 운동은 우울증과 심장병과 당뇨의 위험요소에 맞설 수 있도록 돕는다. 2012 수능

4 We live in difficult and ______________ times.
우리는 어렵고 불확실한 시대에 살고 있다. 2012 수능

5 Salad vegetables like ______________ and tomatoes have a very high water content.
오이, 토마토와 같은 샐러드 야채들은 수분 함유량이 매우 높다. 16 고3학평 변형

6 He recommended us to use music for emotional ______________.
그는 우리에게 감정 치료법으로 음악의 사용을 추천했다. 09 평가원

7 After hearing the strange sound, Mrs. Smith became ______________ and called the police.
이상한 소리가 들려오자 Smith부인은 의혹을 갖고 경찰을 불렀다.

8 "But I must get to New York today!" an angry lady hotly told the ______________.
"하지만 난 오늘 뉴욕에 가야 한다고요!" 화가 난 여자가 점원에게 맹렬히 말했다. 2014 수능

9 Our plan was to reach the ______________ at noon, but it was impossible.
우리의 계획은 정오에 정상에 이르는 것이었는데, 그것은 불가능했다.

10 The castle is decorated with ______________ furniture.
그 성은 고풍스러운 가구들로 장식되어 있다. 06 평가원

Day 24

MP3

691 **hollow** [hálou]
형 속이 빈, 움푹 꺼진
a hollow place in the ground 땅속의 움푹 꺼진 곳

692 **duplicate** [djú:pləkit]
동 복사하다 형 복제한
duplicate a document 문서를 복사하다

693 **magnet** [mǽgnit]
명 자석
a horseshoe magnet 말굽자석

694 **ash** [æʃ]
명 재
ash from the volcanic eruption 화산재

695 **linear** [líniər]
형 직선의, 길이의, 선으로 된
linear perspective 직선 원근법

696 **enforce** [infɔ́:rs]
동 시행(집행)하다, 강요하다
enforce the law 법을 집행하다

697 **encode** [inkóud]
동 암호로 바꾸다, 부호화하다
encode important e-mails 중요한 이메일을 암호화하다

698 **limb** [lim]
명 팔다리, 수족
break a limb 팔다리가 부러지다

699 **humid** [hjú:mid]
형 습한, 눅눅한
a humid climate 습한 기후

700 **horizon** [həráizən]
명 지평선, 수평선 형 horizontal 수평(선)의, 가로의
above the horizon 지평선 위로

701 **eminent** [émənənt]
형 저명한, 탁월한 유 distinguished 유명한, 성공한
eminent as a writer 작가로서 저명한

702 **asset** [ǽset]
명 자산, 재산
asset management 자산 관리

703 **impair** [impέər]
동 손상시키다, 해치다
impair self-esteem 자존심을 손상시키다

704 **incident** [ínsidənt]
명 사건, 분쟁
an unexpected incident 예상치 못한 사건

705 **merchandise** [mə́:rtʃəndàiz]
명 상품
order merchandise 상품을 주문하다

Daily Test

| 월 일 |

Ⓐ 우리말에 맞게 빈 칸에 알맞은 단어를 쓰세요.

1 Turkeys nest in caves and ______________ trees.
칠면조들은 동굴과 속이 빈 나무에 둥지를 튼다. 15 고2학평 변형

2 Leaders with positive emotional states of mind are like human ____________.
긍정적인 마음 상태를 가진 지도자들은 인간 자석과도 같다. 16 고3학평

3 This system converts the small ______________ motion of the stretching spring into a much more visible rotary motion of the dial needle.
이 시스템은 늘어나는 용수철의 작은 선형 운동을 다이얼 비늘의 훨씬 눈에 띄는 회전 운동으로 변환한다. 2009 수능

4 Like every dangerous sport, cheerleading also needs ______________ safety regulations.
모든 위험한 운동과 같이, 치어리딩 또한 안전 규칙을 강화할 필요가 있다. 07 고2학평 변형

5 As I stood on the beach with the waves crashing onto the rocks and the sand, I looked out to the ______________.
나는 파도가 바위와 모래에 부딪히는 해변에 서서, 수평선을 바라보았다. 10 고1학평 변형

6 What made him famous was his book 'Lives of the Most ______________ Painters, Sculptors and Architects'.
그를 유명하게 만든 것은 〈가장 뛰어난 화가, 조각가, 건축가들의 생애〉라는 그의 책이었다. 2012 수능

7 Roman General Marcellus considered Archimedes a valuable scientific ______________.
로마 장군 Marcellus는 Archimedes를 가장 가치 있는 과학적 재산으로 여겼다. 11 고3학평 변형

8 Watching TV too closely or reading in the dark could ______________ your sight.
TV를 너무 가까이에서 보거나 어둠 속에서 책을 읽는 것은 당신의 시력을 손상시킬 수 있다.

9 An unexpected ______________ triggered a major conflict between the labor union members.
예상치 못한 사건이 노조원들 사이에 중대한 갈등을 촉발시켰다.

10 Those stores carry only high-priced ______________.
저 가게들은 오직 고가의 상품만을 취급한다.

Day 24

MP3

706 hazardous [hǽzərdəs]
형 위험한
hazardous bacteria 위험한 박테리아균

707 guidance [gáidəns]
명 지도, 안내
under a teacher's guidance 선생님의 안내 아래

708 goodwill [gúdwíl]
명 호의, 친선
as a gesture of goodwill 호의의 표시로써

709 harden [háːrdən]
동 단단하게 하다, 강화하다
harden metal 금속을 단단하게 하다

710 lively [láivli]
형 활기 넘치는, 활발한
lively steps 활기 넘치는 발걸음

711 infamous [ínfəməs]
형 악명 높은, 혐오할 만한 유 notorious
be infamous for its hot weather 더운 날씨로 악명 높다

712 instructive [instrʌ́ktiv]
형 유익한, 교훈적인
read an instructive article 교훈적인 글을 읽다

713 mighty [máiti]
형 강력한, 대단한 명 might 힘, 권력
high and mighty 잘난척 하는

714 lifespan [laifspæn]
명 수명
the average lifespan 평균 수명

715 glaze [gleiz]
동 광택을 내다, 창에 유리를 끼우다
a glazed door 유리를 끼운 문

716 gasp [gæsp]
동 숨이 막히다, 헐떡거리다
gasp in amazement 놀라서 숨이 막히다

717 hatred [héitrid]
명 증오, 혐오
love and hatred 사랑과 증오

718 loyalty [lɔ́iəlti]
명 충실, 충성
loyalty and devotion 충실함과 헌신

719 kidnap [kídnæp]
동 납치하다, 유괴하다
kidnap a child 아이를 유괴하다

720 drift [drift]
동 떠돌다, 표류하다
drift out to sea 바다로 떠내려가다

Daily Test

| 월 일 |

A 우리말에 맞게 빈 칸에 알맞은 단어를 쓰세요.

1 Diana has served as a ______________ ambassador worldwide.
Diana는 세계 친선 대사로서 역할을 다하고 있다. 10 고2학평 변형

2 One day at school, Judy told her ______________ counselor about her future dream-to be a teacher.
어느 날 학교에서, Judy는 그녀의 진로 상담가에게 선생님이 되고자 하는 그녀의 꿈을 말했다. 09 평가원

3 Wait for the clay mixture to ______________ and then carefully remove it from the frame and enjoy!
점토 혼합물이 단단해지기를 기다린 후 그것을 틀에서 조심스럽게 떼어낸 후 즐겨라!

4 Teams made up of diverse specialists are ______________ for their inability to get things done.
다양한 전문가들로 구성된 팀은 일처리를 못하는 것으로 악명높다. 14 고2학평 변형

5 The knight was an outstanding leader and a ______________ warrior in the kingdom.
왕국에서 그 기사는 뛰어난 지도자 이자 용맹한 전사였다.

6 Mayflies have the shortest ______________ of all animals and die after mating.
하루살이는 모든 동물들 중에서 가장 짧은 수명을 가지고 있으며 짝짓기를 한 후 죽는다.

7 Black ice refers to a thin coating of ______________ ice on a surface.
Black ice는 그 표면이 광택이 나는 얇은 코팅층을 말한다. 15 고2학평 변형

8 Mother ______________ in shock, putting a hand over her own mouth.
엄마는 충격에 그녀의 입을 손으로 막으며 숨을 헐떡였다. 15 고1학평 변형

9 As Buddha said, "______________ is never ended by ______________ but by love".
부처가 말하길, "증오는 증오로는 절대 끝날 수 없고 오직 사랑만이 끝낼 수 있다."

10 If you believe that ______________ goes hand in hand with friendship, you are probably a loyal friend yourself.
만약 당신이 충성이 우정과 관련 있다고 믿는다면, 당신은 아마 스스로의 충실한 친구이다.

Review Test 12

A 우리말에 맞게 빈 칸에 알맞은 단어를 쓰시오.

1 remain ________________ 제자리에 있다

2 walk in a narrow ________________ 좁은 골목길을 걷다

3 greet her with ________________ 박수갈채로 그녀를 맞이하다

4 ________________ in societies 사회 속 어디에나 있는

5 a ________________ of firewood 장작 한 꾸러미

6 have ________________ power 초자연적인 힘이 있다

7 ________________ and virtue 악덕과 미덕

8 peel a ________________ 오이 껍질을 깎다

9 an ________________ shop 골동품 상점

10 ________________ the law 법을 집행하다

B 영어에 맞게 빈 칸에 알맞은 우리말을 쓰시오.

1 boast of your ability 재능을 ________________

2 flying debris from the storm 폭풍으로부터 날라온 ________________

3 a humid climate ________________ 기후

4 above the horizon ________________ 위로

5 impair self-esteem 자존심을 ________________

6 an unexpected incident 예상치 못한 ________________

7 as a gesture of goodwill ________________의 표시로써

8 harden metal 금속을 ________________

9 the average lifespan 평균 ________________

10 gasp in amazement 놀라서 ________________

C 다음 영어 풀이에 알맞은 어휘를 〈보기〉에서 고르시오.

보기	antique	spine	drift	boast	duplicate

1 ______________ : the line of connected bones down the middle of your back

2 ______________ : old in style or fashion but valuable

3 ______________ : to make a copy of something

4 ______________ : to speak or behave with much pride in yourself

5 ______________ : to move from one place to another with no control

D 문맥에 맞게 다음 문장을 완성하시오.

1 This exercise puts tremendous •	• a is required to change your bad habit.
2 A considerable amount of effort •	• b and hollow trees.
3 He recommended us to use of music •	• c for emotional therapy.
4 Turkeys nest in caves •	• d pressure on the spine.
5 Black ice refers to a thin coating •	• e of glazed ice on a surface.

E 문장을 읽고 문맥에 적절한 단어를 고르시오.

1 We need to hurry. Do you know a (disclose/shortcut) to the station?

2 It is still (uncertain/uncertainly) whether he will run for mayor.

3 The reporter refused to (disclose/boast) who sent him the information.

4 The programmer succeeded in (combating/decoding) the strange symbols in the computer file.

5 He made a (swift/debris) decision to accept the invitation.

F 문장의 빈칸에 알맞은 단어를 〈보기〉에서 찾아 쓰시오. (필요하면 형태를 고치시오.)

보기	suspicious	shed	asset	instructive	eminent

1 If you see people acting in a ______________ manner near cars, please call 616-300-3200.
자동차 주변에서 수상스러운 행동을 하는 사람을 보면 616-300-3200으로 전화해주십시오. 09 고1 평가원 변형

2 In early autumn, the trees began to ______________ their leaves.
이른 가을에 나무들이 나뭇잎들을 떨구기 시작했다. 05 고3 평가원

3 Remember, your family is your greatest ______________.
기억해, 네 가족은 너의 가장 중요한 자산이야. 2015 수능

4 Trying to be ______________, the father explained to his son how the automobile was invented.
교훈적이 되고자 아버지는 아들에게 자동차가 어떻게 발명되었는지를 설명했다. 15 고1 학평 변형

5 The hypothesis was put forward by two ______________ biologists.
그 가설은 두 저명한 생물학자들에 의해 제안되었다.

G 다음 〈보기〉 중 두 문장에 공통으로 사용할 수 있는 어휘를 고르시오.

1 It was once considered an amazing achievement to reach the ____________ of Mount Everest. 14 고2학평 변형
The leaders of both countries met at the international ____________ on health and environment.

① asset ② summit ③ bundle ④ horizon ⑤ disclose

2 Several developing countries adopted the attractive idea to ____________ climate change. 12 고3학평 변형
The general organized all his soldiers into several ____________ units.

① combat ② divorce ③ shortcut ④ duplicate ⑤ clerk

3 The role of computers in music and the performing arts has been ____________. 2004 수능 변형
A ____________ amount of effort is required to change the way you think and act. 05 고3학평 변형

① considerable ② humid ③ suspicious ④ drift ⑤ kidnap

Study More

혼동하기 쉬운 단어 loyalty vs. royalty

- [loyalty] 명 충실, 충성
  The soldiers swore their **loyalty** to the king. 병사들은 왕에게 그들의 충성을 맹세했다.
- [royalty] 명 왕족
  Jina and I were treated like **royalty.** 지나와 나는 왕족처럼 대접을 받았다.

Day 25

MP3

721 **reconsider** [rìːkənsídər]
동 재고하다
reconsider the plan 계획을 재고하다

722 **treaty** [tríːti]
명 조약, 협정, 의정서
peace treaty 평화 조약

723 **spacecraft** [spéiskræ̀ft]
명 우주선
launch spacecraft 우주선을 발사하다

724 **pulse** [pʌls]
명 맥박, 맥
a normal pulse 정상 맥박

725 **soothing** [súːðiŋ]
형 달래는, 위로하는
a soothing and relaxing sound 위로가 되고 편안한 소리

726 **staple** [stéipl]
형 주된, 주요한
staple crop of Korea 한국의 주된 곡물

727 **outgoing** [áutgòuiŋ]
형 외향적인, 떠나가는
an outgoing personality 외향적인 성격

728 **scoop** [skuːp]
명 한 숟갈의 양 동 뜨다, 파다
scoop ice cream 아이스크림을 뜨다

729 **miniature** [míniətʃər]
형 소형의, 아주 작은
a miniature airplane 소형 비행기

730 **timid** [tímid]
형 소심한, 자신이 없는
timid or sensitive 소심하거나 예민하거나

731 **purity** [pjú(ː)ərəti]
명 순수성, 깨끗함
the purity of the water 물의 순도

732 **mummy** [mʌ́mi]
명 미라
an Egyptian mummy 이집트 미라

733 **sew** [sou]
동 바느질하다, 꿰매다
sew a button on a shirt 셔츠 위에 단추를 꿰매다

734 **sprain** [sprein]
동 삐다, 접지르다
sprain his ankle badly 심하게 그의 발목을 삐다

735 **ripe** [raip]
형 익은, ~에 적합한
ripe fruit 익은 과일

Daily Test

| 월 일 |

A 우리말에 맞게 빈 칸에 알맞은 단어를 쓰세요.

1 The first manned ______________ made a soft landing successfully on the moon.
그 최초의 유인 우주선은 달에 성공적으로 연착륙했다.

2 Lie detector tests base judgments of honesty on blood pressure, ______________, respiration, and vocal pitch.
거짓말 탐지기는 혈압, 맥박, 호흡, 그리고 목소리 높낮이를 기반으로 정직성을 시험한다. 15 고3학평 변형

3 Doing this simple movement for a few minutes can be ______________ for your gloomy mind.
몇 분 동안 이 간단한 동작을 하는 것이 너의 우울한 마음을 달래 줄 수 있을 것이다.

4 He was a happy, ______________ man who made friends easily.
그는 친구를 쉽게 사귀는 행복하고 외향적인 사람이었다. 15 고2학평 변형

5 Mom rolled up a waffle and put a ______________ of ice cream on top.
엄마는 와플을 말아서 그 위에 아이스크림을 한 숟갈 올렸다. 16 고1학평 변형

6 Mia got unusual ______________ tea sets and pretty tea accessories for her birthday.
Mia는 특이한 미니 티 세트와, 예쁜 티 액세서리를 생일선물로 받았다.

7 If you tend to be shy or ______________, give yourself a push to be more aggressive when taking photos of people.
비록 당신이 소심하고 부끄러운 경향이 있더라도, 사람들의 사진을 찍을때는 당신 스스로를 좀 더 적극적으로 밀어붙여라. 10 고3학평 변형

8 The ______________ wasn't a king or a male warrior; it was a young woman.
그 미라는 왕이나 남성 전사가 아니었다. 그것은 어린 여성이었다. 08 고3학평 변형

9 Elias Howe thought of the idea of a ______________ machine after waking up.
Elias Howe는 잠에서 깬 후 재봉틀을 생각해냈다. 08 평가원

10 Andy got a chance to play in the last 10 seconds of the championship game when a starting player ______________ his ankle.
Andy는 선발선수가 그의 발목을 삐었을 때 챔피언십 경기의 마지막 10초 동안 경기를 할 기회를 얻었다. 15 평가원

Day 25

MP3

736 **milestone** [máilstòun]
명 획기적인 사건, 이정표
a milestone in Korean history 한국사에서 있어 획기적인 사건

737 **superstition** [sjù:pərstíʃən]
명 미신
the number thirteen superstition 13의 수를 불길하다고 믿는 미신

738 **prime** [praim]
형 주요한, 뛰어난
his prime concern 그의 주요 관심사

739 **poll** [pɑl]
명 여론 조사
public opinion poll 여론 조사

740 **tournament** [túərnəmənt]
명 토너먼트, 경연대회
enter a golf tournament 골프 선수권 대회에 나가다

741 **sensible** [sénsəbl]
형 분별 있는, 합리적인
a sensible investment 분별 있는 투자

742 **nap** [næp]
명 낮잠
best place to take a nap 낮잠 자기 최적의 장소

743 **multicultural** [mʌltilkʌltʃərəl]
형 다문화의
live in a multicultural family 다문화 가정에서 살다

744 **attain** [ətéin]
동 달성하다, 얻다
attain economic stability 경제적 안정을 달성하다

745 **thermometer** [θərmɑ́mitər]
명 온도계
a centigrade thermometer 섭씨 온도계

746 **twinkle** [twíŋkl]
동 반짝거리다, 반짝반짝 빛나다
twinkle like a star 별처럼 빛나다

747 **resolution** [rèzəljú:ʃən]
명 결의안, 해결, 결심
pass a resolution 결의안을 통과시키다

748 **sympathy** [símpəθi]
명 동정, 공감
sympathy and recognition 공감과 인정

749 **needle** [ní:dl]
명 바늘
thread a needle 바늘에 실을 꿰다

750 **syndrome** [síndroum]
명 증후군
suffer from dry eye syndrome 안구 건조증으로 고통 받다

Daily Test

| 월 일 |

A **우리말에 맞게 빈 칸에 알맞은 단어를 쓰세요.**

1 To win an Oscar was the best ______________ in his movie life.
오스카 상을 받은 것은 그의 영화 인생에 획기적인 사건이었다.

2 According to ancient ______________, moles reveal a person's character.
고대 미신에 따르면, 점은 그 사람의 성격을 나타낸다. 2005 수능

3 Since the ______________ is only one month away, we are practicing hard.
밴드 경연대회가 한 달 정도 남았기 때문에 우리는 열심히 연습하는 중이다 16 고2학평 변형

4 The little girl showed ______________ attitude at the press conference.
그 작은 소녀는 기자회견에서 분별력 있는 태도를 보였다.

5 You feel like taking a ______________ after a heavy meal.
밥을 많이 먹은 뒤에 당신은 낮잠을 자고 싶을 것이다. 15 고1학평 변형

6 Stars ______________ because their light has to pass through several miles of Earth's atmosphere before it reaches the eye of an observer.
별들은 그들의 빛이 관찰자의 눈에 닿기 전에 수 마일의 지구 대기를 통과해야 하기 때문에 빛난다. 11 고1학평 변형

7 All independent organizations disagreed with the ______________ passing.
모든 독립적 기관들은 그 결의안의 통과에 대해 동의하지 않았다.

8 In the meantime, I send you my love and ______________.
그 동안에, 나는 당신에게 사랑과 동정을 보냅니다.

9 We actually feel pain before the ______________ even touches the skin!
우리는 사실 바늘이 피부에 닿기도 전에 고통을 느낀다! 14 고1학평 변형

10 Harry had Down ______________ and participated in the Special Olympics.
Harry는 다운 증후군을 앓고 있었고 스페셜 올림픽에 출전했다. 14 고2학평 변형

Day 26

MP3

751 □ **ethical** [éθikəl]
형 윤리적인, 도덕적인
ethical standards 윤리적 기준

752 □ **ascend** [əsénd]
동 오르다, 상승하다
ascend a hill 언덕을 오르다

753 □ **audible** [ɔ́:dəbl]
형 잘 들리는 , 들을 수 있는
clearly audible voice 생생히 잘 들리는 목소리

754 □ **by chance** [bai tʃæns]
우연히, 혹시
win by chance 우연히 이기다

755 □ **compelling** [kəmpéliŋ]
형 강제적인, 강력한, 설득력 있는
compelling parents 강제적인 부모님

756 □ **unbelievable** [ʌ̀nbilí:vəbl]
형 믿기 어려운, 믿기 힘든
unbelievable stories 믿기 어려운 이야기들

757 □ **blink** [bliŋk]
동 눈을 깜박이다
blink in the bright sunlight 밝은 햇살에 눈을 깜박이다

758 □ **unforgettable** [ʌ̀nfərgétəbl]
형 잊을 수 없는
share unforgettable moments 잊을 수 없는 순간을 나누다

759 □ **ambassador** [æmbǽsədər]
명 대사
the Korean ambassador to France 주 프랑스 한국대사

760 □ **combination** [kɑ̀mbənéiʃən]
명 조합, 결합
chemical combination 화학적 결합

761 □ **blizzard** [blizərd]
명 눈보라
A blizzard rages. 눈보라가 몰아치다.

762 □ **bomb** [bɑm]
명 폭탄
place a bomb 폭탄을 설치하다

763 □ **worship** [wə́:rʃip]
명 예배, 숭배 동 숭배하다, 흠모하다
nature worship 자연 숭배

764 □ **warfare** [wɔ́:rfὲər]
명 전쟁, 전투
psychological warfare 심리전

765 □ **aptitude** [ǽptitjù:d]
명 소질, 적성
take an aptitude test 적성 검사를 하다

Daily Test

| 월 일 |

A 우리말에 맞게 빈 칸에 알맞은 단어를 쓰세요.

1 While there are aesthetic and ______________ reasons for preserving biodiversity, there are practical considerations as well.
생물학적 다양성을 보존하는데 심미적이고 윤리적인 이유가 있던 반면에, 실질적인 숙고 역시 있다. 13 평가원

2 Steven fell from the back of a wagon during a ______________.
눈보라가 치는 동안에 Steven은 마차 뒤에서 떨어졌다. 15 고3학평 변형

3 One day, I saw my grandmother on the street ______________.
어느 날, 거리에서 우연히 나는 할머니를 만났다. 2014 수능

4 Your eyelids protect you only when you ______________ your eyes to keep them wet.
당신의 눈꺼풀은 눈을 촉촉하게 유지하기 위해서 눈을 깜빡일 때만 당신을 보호한다. 06 고2학평 변형

5 We'll make the last ______________ memories of our high school life.
우리는 우리의 고등학교 생활에서 마지막으로 잊을 수 없는 기억을 만들 거에요. 16 평가원

6 Many TV terms come from the ______________ of two words.
많은 TV 용어들이 두 단어의 결합에서 왔다.

7 During the war, a ______________ exploded in the council building.
전쟁 중에 폭탄이 의회 건물 안에서 폭발했다.

8 There were many kinds of gods in ancient Egypt and people ______________ gods in their own way.
고대 이집트에는 다양한 신들이 있었고, 그들 각자 방식대로 신을 숭배했었다.

9 Some countries in Asia were devastated by constant ______________ at that time.
그 당시 아시아의 몇몇의 나라들이 계속된 전쟁으로 국토가 피폐해졌다.

10 ______________ things often happen all around the world.
세계 곳곳에서 믿기지 않는 일들이 종종 일어나기도 한다.

Day 26

MP3

766 **committee** [kəmíti]
명 위원회
assemble a committee 위원회를 소집하다

767 **boycott** [bɔ́ikɑt]
동 구매, 참여를 거부하다 명 (구매, 사용 등의) 거부 운동
a boycott on the use of plastic cups 플라스틱 컵 사용에 대한 거부

768 **aggressive** [əgrésiv]
형 공격적인, 적극적인
aggressive behavior 공격적인 행동

769 **destructive** [distrʌ́ktiv]
형 파괴적인
the destructive power of nuclear bombs 핵폭탄의 파괴적인 힘

770 **division** [divíʒən]
명 분할, 분배
the division of labor 노동력의 분배

771 **deliberately** [dilíbəritli]
형 의도적으로
deliberately ignoring her 그녀를 의도적으로 무시하는

772 **discourage** [diskə́:ridʒ]
동 좌절시키다, (반대하며) 막다, 단념시키다
be discouraged by the failure 실패에 의해 좌절하다

773 **be due to** [bi dju: tu:]
~할 예정이다
be due to graduate in August 8월에 졸업 예정이다

774 **wrinkle** [ríŋkl]
명 주름
wrinkles on her neck 그녀 목의 주름

775 **bold** [bould]
형 용감한, 대담한
bold behavior 대담한 행동

776 **critic** [kritik]
명 비평가
a famous movie critic 유명한 영화 평론가

777 **seemingly** [sí:miŋli]
부 겉보기에는
a seemingly healthy boy 겉보기에는 건강한 소년

778 **arbitrary** [a:rbətreri]
형 임의적인, 제멋대로인
arbitrary and unfair 독단적이고 불공평한

779 **adore** [ədɔ́:r]
동 아주 좋아하다, 숭배하다
adore his new movie 그의 새 영화를 아주 좋아하다

780 **bald** [bɔ:ld]
형 대머리의, 머리가 벗겨진
go bald 머리가 벗겨지다

Daily Test

| 월 일 |

A 우리말에 맞게 빈 칸에 알맞은 단어를 쓰세요.

1 Jack's team handed in an outstanding proposal to the ______________, and it was chosen as the best.
Jack의 팀은 위원회에 우수한 기획 안을 제출했고, 그것은 최고로 선정되었다.

2 Companies need to respond to the pressure of what customers are voicing their concerns by ______________ stores.
회사는 고객이 구매를 거부하는 것으로 그들의 불만을 표하기 때문에 압박에 반응할 필요가 있다. 16 고2학평 변형

3 I was not very successful in business, because I was the youngest child and thus less ______________ than my older brothers.
나는 제일 어렸고 형제들보다 덜 적극적이었기 때문에 사업에서 아주 성공하지는 못했다. 2009 수능

4 An obsession is negative and ______________.
집착은 부정적이고 파괴적이다. 10 고1학평 변형

5 The new educational system ______________ native arts and culture.
새로운 교육 체계는 향토예술과 문화를 막았다. 06 평가원

6 The bodyguards ______________ stand in front of the gate to lead honored guests.
그 경호원들은 귀빈들을 이끌기 위해서 문 앞에 서 있을 예정이다.

7 Do you see ______________ on my forehead?
내 이마에 주름이 보이니? 12 고1학평 변형

8 For decades, ______________ have been predicting the death of classical music.
수십 년 동안 비평가들은 클래식 음악의 몰락을 예견해왔다. 09 평가원

9 Max's decision was entirely ______________.
Max의 결정은 전적으로 제멋대로였다. 2012 수능

10 ______________ eagles build nests out of sticks on top of tall trees.
흰머리 독수리들은 높은 나무 끝에 나뭇가지로 둥지를 짓는다.

Review Test 13

Day 25 + Day 26 | 월 일 |

A 우리말에 맞게 빈 칸에 알맞은 단어를 쓰시오.

1 launch ______________ 우주선을 발사하다

2 a normal ______________ 정상 맥박

3 ______________ crop of Korea 한국의 주된 곡물

4 a ______________ airplane 소형 비행기

5 an Egyptian ______________ 이집트 미라

6 ______________ his ankle badly 심하게 그의 발목을 삐다

7 public opinion ______________ 여론 조사

8 best place to take a ______________ 낮잠 자기 최적의 장소

9 ______________ standards 윤리적 기준

10 place a ______________ 폭탄을 설치하다

B 영어에 맞게 빈 칸에 알맞은 우리말을 쓰시오.

1 a centigrade thermometer 섭씨 ______________

2 twinkle like a star 별처럼 ______________

3 clearly audible voice 생생히 ______________ 목소리

4 win by chance ______________ 이기다

5 blink in the bright sunlight 밝은 햇살에 ______________

6 the Korean ambassador to France 주 프랑스 한국 ______________

7 assemble a committee ______________를 소집하다

8 deliberately ignoring her 그녀를 ______________ 무시하는

9 wrinkles on her neck 그녀 목의 ______________

10 a famous movie critic 유명한 영화 ______________

C 다음 영어 풀이에 알맞은 어휘를 〈보기〉에서 고르시오.

보기	bold	arbitrary	ascend	blizzard	staple

1 ______________ : to go upward or rise

2 ______________ : brave or not afraid of taking a risk

3 ______________ : a basic and important food that is eaten

4 ______________ : based on personal opinions rather than on evidence or a particular purpose

5 ______________ : a very strong winter storm lasting a long time

D 문맥에 맞게 다음 문장을 완성하시오.

1 He was a happy, outgoing man •		• a a wagon during a blizzard.
2 According to ancient superstitions, •		• b who made friends easily.
3 Steven fell from the back of •		• c my grandmother on the street by chance.
4 One day, I saw •		• d negative and destructive.
5 An obsession is •		• e moles reveal a person's character.

E 문장을 읽고 문맥에 적절한 단어를 고르시오.

1 This is a(n) (prime/outgoing) opportunity to advertise our new product.

2 It may not be (ripe/sensible) to discuss such an important issue over the phone.

3 She was deeply shocked by their (bold/staple) attempts.

4 The (treaty/syndrome) was signed by the six participating countries.

5 He (lively/seemingly) forgot about the appointment.

F 문장의 빈칸에 알맞은 단어를 〈보기〉에서 찾아 쓰시오. (필요하면 형태를 고치시오.)

보기 multicultural discourage resolution compelling aggressive

1 Your footsteps will help raise awareness for ______________ families.
당신의 발걸음은 다문화 가정에 대한 인식을 높이는 데 도움을 줄 것입니다. 2011 수능

2 Your feeding of these wild animals might lead to them being ______________ towards humans.
이 야생동물에게 먹이를 주는 것은 그들을 인간에 대해 공격적으로 만들 수 있습니다. 09 고3 평가원 변형

3 According to research, looking at a mirror ______________ children from bad behavior.
연구에 의하면 거울을 쳐다보는 것은 아이들이 나쁜 행동을 하는 것을 단념시킨다. 12 고1 학평 변형

4 The city passed a ______________ for the construction of two new high schools.
시는 새로운 고등학교 두 개를 건설하는 결의안을 통과시켰다.

5 He found a ______________ reason to get out of bed early in the morning.
그는 아침 일찍 잠자리에서 나올 설득력 있는 이유를 찾았다. 14 고1 학평 변형

G 다음 〈보기〉 중 두 문장에 공통으로 사용할 수 있는 어휘를 고르시오.

1 It's time for us all to ___________ the seriousness of the problem and to do something about it. 2007 수능
Because of the unexpected circumstances, we had to ___________ our plan.

① scoop ② reconsider ③ ascend ④ twinkle ⑤ blink

2 If your cat is shy and ___________, he or she won't want to be dressed up and displayed in cat shows. 16 고1학평 변형
He was such a ___________ boy that he would turn his face away from strangers. 05 고1평가원 변형

① soothing ② audible ③ outgoing ④ timid ⑤ bald

3 Many foot problems are ___________ to poor-fitting shoes, including narrow toes and high heels. 11 고1학평 변형
The train is ___________ to arrive at the station soon.

① due ② opposed ③ prior ④ according ⑤ partial

Study More

자연현상을 나타내는 어휘 lightning, blizzard, tornado

- [lightning] 명 번개
  Lightning can strike even on sunny days. 맑은 날에도 번개는 칠 수 있다.
- [blizzard] 명 눈보라
  He invented the super computer that can predict droughts, **blizzards** and so on.
  그는 가뭄과 눈보라 등을 예측할 수 있는 슈퍼컴퓨터를 개발했다.
- [tornado] 명 회오리바람
  A powerful **tornado** hit Ann's village last month. 강력한 회오리바람이 Ann의 마을을 지난 달 덮쳤다.

Day 27

MP3

781 □ **crocodile** [krákədàil]
명 악어, 크로커다일
buy a crocodile bag 악어 가죽 가방을 사다

782 □ **demise** [dimáiz]
명 종말, 사망
Peter's sudden demise Peter의 갑작스러운 사망

783 □ **generalize** [dʒénərəlàiz]
동 일반화하다
generalize his study's findings 그의 연구결과를 일반화하다

784 □ **tension** [ténʃən]
명 긴장(상태), 갈등
political tensions 정치적 긴장

785 □ **significantly** [signífikəntli]
부 크게, 상당히
significantly larger and stronger 상당히 크고 강한

786 □ **dampen** [dǽmpən]
동 축축하게 하다, 무디게 하다
dampen your spirit 낙담시키다

787 □ **cut down** [kʌt daun]
~을 줄이다, 베어 쓰러뜨리다
cut down your salt intake 소금 섭취량을 줄이다

788 □ **curable** [kjú(:)ərəbl]
형 치료 가능한
a curable disease 치료 가능한 질병

789 □ **fluent** [flú(:)ənt]
형 유창한, 능통한
be fluent in French 불어에 유창하다

790 □ **mobile** [móubəl]
형 이동하는, 이동식의
a mobile home 이동식 주택

791 □ **consist** [kənsíst]
동 이루어지다, 구성되다
consist of four parts 네 부분으로 구성되다

792 □ **marriage** [mǽridʒ]
명 결혼
have a happy marriage 행복한 결혼 생활을 하다

793 □ **ferment** [fəːrmént]
동 발효시키다, 발효되다
ferment Kimchi 김치를 발효시키다

794 □ **debut** [déibjuː]
명 첫 출연, 데뷔
the band's debut on stage 그 밴드의 첫 무대

795 □ **figure out** [fígjər aut]
이해하다, 해결하다, 알아내다
figure out the problem 문제를 해결하다

Daily Test

| 월 일 |

A 우리말에 맞게 빈 칸에 알맞은 단어를 쓰세요.

1 People can record, write, watch movies with _______________ phones these days.
오늘 날, 사람들은 휴대 전화기들을 가지고 녹음하고, 쓰고, 영화들도 볼 수 있다.

2 If we observe nature closely, we will discover that there is constant _______________ between change and balance.
만약 우리가 가까이 자연을 관찰한다면, 우리는 변화와 균형 사이에 꾸준한 긴장이 있음을 발견할 수 있다. 2004 수능

3 Drinking at least three cups of coffee a day _______________ improves attention and memory.
하루에 최소 세 잔의 커피를 마시는 것은 주의력과 기억력을 상당히 증진시킨다. 14 고1학평 변형

4 The movie 'The Princess Diaries' opened in 2001 and that was her film _______________.
영화 '공주의 일기'는 2001년에 개봉하였고, 그것이 그녀의 데뷔 영화였다.

5 Some people want to _______________ the trees for lumber.
몇몇 사람들은 목재용으로 쓰기 위해 나무를 베길 바란다. 15 고1학평 변형

6 If Helen was _______________ in Spanish, she could got the job.
만약 Helen이 스페인어를 유창하게 했다면, 그녀는 그 일을 할 수 있었을 것이다.

7 Her entire birthday celebration _______________ of a chocolate cake with a candle.
그녀의 생일 축하는 초가 꽂힌 초콜릿 케이크가 전부였다. 15 고2학평 변형

8 A _______________ agreement is sacred and considered binding for life.
결혼 서약은 신성하고 평생 유효한 것으로 간주 된다.

9 When sugar is _______________, it produces alcohol.
설탕이 발효 될 때, 이는 알코올을 만들어 낸다. 07 평가원

10 We couldn't _______________ how to remove the truck without damaging the freeway above.
우리는 어떻게 위쪽에 있는 고속도로에 손상을 가하지 않고 트럭을 치울 지 알아내지 못했다. 06 평가원

Day 27

MP3

796 **resident** [rézidənt]
명 거주자
a town resident 마을의 주민들

797 **carry out** [kǽri aut]
~을 수행하다, 이행하다
carry out his order 그의 명령을 수행하다

798 **geology** [dʒiɑ́lədʒi]
명 지질학
major in geology 지질학을 전공하다

799 **evacuate** [ivǽkjuèit]
동 비우다, 대피시키다
evacuate a fortress 요새를 철수하다

800 **excursion** [ikskə́ːrʒən]
명 여행, 소풍, 견학
go on an excursion to Hong Kong 홍콩으로 견학을 가다

801 **historical** [histɔ́(ː)rikəl]
형 역사적인
have historical value 역사적 가치를 지니다

802 **forensic** [fərénsik]
형 법의학적인
forensic evidence 법의학적 증거

803 **efficiency** [ifíʃənsi]
명 효율
improve energy efficiency 에너지 효율을 향상시키다

804 **famine** [fǽmin]
명 기아, 굶주림, 기근
suffer from famine 굶주림에 고통 받다

805 **congress** [kɑ́ŋgrəs]
명 의회, 국회
a member of congress 국회의원

806 **expel** [ikspél]
동 배출하다, 퇴학시키다
expel gas from lungs 폐에서 가스를 배출하다

807 **defective** [diféktiv]
형 결함 있는, 불완전한
defective sight 불완전한 시력

808 **creativity** [krìːeitívəti]
명 창조성, 창의력
creativity and originality 창의력과 독창성

809 **crater** [kréitər]
명 분화구
the crater of a volcano 화산 분화구

810 **conclude** [kənklúːd]
동 결론을 내리다, 마치다
conclude that she is guilty 그녀가 유죄라 결론을 내리다

Daily Test

| 월 일 |

Ⓐ 우리말에 맞게 빈 칸에 알맞은 단어를 쓰세요.

1 Public transportation enables us to ______________ all these activities.
대중 교통은 우리가 이 모든 활동을 수행 할 수 있게 해준다. 16 고3학평 변형

2 According to astronomy, ______________, and paleontology, humans might indeed be alone in the cosmos.
천문학, 지리학, 고생물학에 따르면, 인간은 우주에서 사실 혼자 일지도 모른다. 05 고3학평 변형

3 British activist Sally Becker ______________ many children during the war.
영국의 운동가 Sally Becker는 전쟁 중 많은 아이들을 대피시켰다. 12 고3학평 변형

4 We want not only ______________ but courtesy and consideration.
우리는 효율성뿐만 아니라 정중함과 사려 깊은 점을 원합니다. 15 평가원

5 They collected many kinds of ______________ relief to send to the poor in Africa.
그들은 아프리카의 가난한 사람들에게 보내줄 다양한 종류의 기아 구호품을 모았다.

6 ______________ passed the Homestead Act in 1862.
의회는 1862년에 Homestead 법을 통과시켰다. 06 고3학평 변형

7 Because of a ______________ part, a big accident might happen.
결함이 있는 부품하나 때문에, 큰 사고가 일어날 수도 있다.

8 The company buys your ______________, not your image.
회사는 당신의 창의력을 사는 것이지 이미지를 사는 것이 아니다. 2015 수능

9 I saw a lot of plants and water in the ______________ of RanoKu volcano in Chile.
나는 칠레의 라노카우 화산 분화구 속에 생겨난 많은 식물과 물을 보았다.

10 The critics ______________ that classical music is no longer popular.
비평가들은 클래식 음악이 더 이상 인기가 없다고 결론 내렸다. 09 평가원

Day 28

MP3

811 knight [nait]
명 기사
the Knights of the Round Table 원탁의 기사단

812 pale [peil]
형 창백한
turn pale 창백해지다 his pale face 그의 창백한 얼굴

813 insist on [insíst ən]
~을 고집하다, 주장하다
insist on a refund 환불을 고집하다

814 insecure [ìnsikjúər]
형 불안정한
financially insecure 재정적으로 불안정한

815 ingenious [indʒíːnjəs]
형 기발한, 독창적인
invent ingenious devices 기발한 장치들을 발명하다

816 gigantic [dʒaigǽntik]
형 거대한
a gigantic tower 거대한 탑

817 grief [griːf]
명 깊은 슬픔
a sigh of grief 깊은 슬픔의 탄식

818 industrious [indʌ́striəs]
형 근면한, 부지런한
an industrious worker 근면한 일꾼

819 formal [fɔ́ːrməl]
형 정중한, 공식적인
his formal manner 그의 정중한 태도 a formal process 공식적인 과정

820 have ~ in common [həv in kaːmən]
공통적으로 지니다, 공통점이 있다
We have nothing in common. 우리는 공통점이 없다.

821 lava [láːvə]
명 용암
a fossil made by lava 용암에 의해 만들어진 화석

822 hijack [háidʒæ̀k]
동 납치하다 명 납치 행위
a series of hijacks 일련의 납치 사건들

823 larva [láːrvə]
명 유충, 애벌레
the larva of a butterfly 나비의 유충

824 misguided [misgáidid]
형 잘못 이해한, 잘못 지도된
misguided information 잘못 이해된 정보

825 humble [hʌ́mbl]
형 겸손한, 초라한, 소박한
live a humble life 소박한 삶을 살다

Daily Test

| 월 일 |

A 우리말에 맞게 빈 칸에 알맞은 단어를 쓰세요.

1 The ______________ felt a great longing arise in his heart, and closed his eyes again just for a moment.
기사는 마음에 큰 갈망이 이른 것을 느꼈고 잠시 동안 눈을 다시 감았다. 07 고2학평 변형

2 If you ______________ on only your opinion, you'll end up jobless.
네가 만일 너의 의견만 고집한다면, 넌 일자리를 잃게 될 거야.

3 Many people in show business seem particularly ______________.
연예 공연 업의 많은 사람들은 특히 불안정해 보인다. 06 평가원

4 The wrong color – slightly gray or very ______________ – may be a sign of illness.
살짝 회색 빛이 돌거나 매우 창백한 것과 같은 잘못된 색들은 질병의 신호일지도 모른다. 07 고1학평 변형

5 After losing her son, she cried and cried, and her voice was husky with ______________.
아들을 잃은 후, 그녀는 계속해서 울부짖었고, 슬픔에 젖어 목이 쉬었다.

6 The word 'gargantuan' has a similar meaning to the words ______________, huge, large, etc.
'gargantuan' 이라는 단어는 거대한, 큰, 커다란 등의 단어들과 비슷한 의미를 갖고 있다. 05 평가원

7 When you are introduced, the correct ______________ greeting is "How do you do?"
당신이 소개 될 때, 올바른 공식 인사는 "안녕하세요?" 입니다. 06 고2학평 변형

8 Many people think that government policy on the issue is ______________.
많은 사람들이 그 문제에 대한 정부의 정책이 잘못 이끌어졌다고 생각한다.

9 The list for the first person had the following adjectives: 'intelligent, ______________, impulsive, critical, stubborn, and envious'.
첫 번째 사람에 대한 목록에는 다음 형용사들 '지적인, 근면한, 충동적인, 비판적인, 고집센, 그리고 질투심이 강한'이 있었다.

10 Remember this proverb, "Home is home, be it ever so ______________."
'아무리 보잘 것 없다 해도 집과 같은 곳은 없다'는 속담을 기억해라.

Day 28

MP3

826 **intentional** [inténʃənəl]
형 의도적인, 고의적인
an intentional lie 의도적인 거짓말

827 **seldom** [séldəm]
부 좀처럼 ~않다
seldom make a mistake 좀처럼 실수를 하지 않는다

828 **intercept** [ìntərsépt]
동 가로막다, 가로채다
intercept information 정보를 차단하다

829 **vendor** [véndər]
명 노점, 판매자
street vendors 노점상

830 **implicate** [ímpləkèit]
동 관련시키다, 연루시키다
be implicated in the scandal 구설수에 관련되다

831 **hub** [hʌb]
명 중심지
a hub of industry 산업의 중심지

832 **in addition to** [in ədíʃən tuː]
~에 더하여, ~일뿐 아니라
in addition to mental problems 정신 문제일 뿐 아니라

833 **inactive** [inǽktiv]
형 활발하지 않은, 소극적인
a lazy and inactive student 게으르고 소극적인 학생

834 **heir** [ɛər]
명 후계자
the heir to the throne 왕위 계승자

835 **idle** [áidl]
형 게으른, 나태한
idle habits 게으른 습관 live an idle life 나태한 삶을 살다

836 **clay** [klei]
명 점토, 찰흙
make a clay model 찰흙 모형을 만들다

837 **huddle** [hʌ́dl]
동 떼지어 몰리다, 옹기종기 모이다
huddle together 함께 옹기종기 모이다

838 **shade** [ʃeid]
명 그늘, 음영, 빛 가리개
rest in the shade of a tree 나무 그늘에서 쉬다

839 **interfere with** [intərfíər wið]
방해하다, 간섭하다
interfere with concentration 집중을 방해하다

840 **jeopardize** [dʒépərdàiz]
동 위태롭게 하다
jeopardize our survival 우리의 생존을 위태롭게 하다

Daily Test

| 월 일 |

A 우리말에 맞게 빈 칸에 알맞은 단어를 쓰세요.

1 Some people make few ______________ changes in life.
몇몇 사람들은 인생에 있어 의도적인 변화를 거의 만들지 않는다. 2016 수능

2 As soon as the actor came out, many reporters ______________ him.
그 배우가 나오자 마자, 많은 기자들이 그를 가로 막았다.

3 Bangalore is a major metropolis and the fastest growing economic ______________ in India.
Bangalore는 인도의 주요 도시고 가장 빨리 성장한 경제적 중심지이다. 10 고2학평 변형

4 ______________ writing, Conroy was an accomplished jazz pianist, winning a Grammy Award in 1986.
글쓰기 뿐만 아니라, Conroy는 1986년에 Grammy 상을 수상한 기량이 뛰어난 재즈 피아니스트였다. 14 고1학평 변형

5 When Jenny was young, she was a timid and ______________ person.
Jenny가 어렸을 때, 그녀는 소심하고 소극적인 사람이었다.

6 A ______________ in a city set up shop and sold doughnuts and coffee to passersby.
도시의 한 행상인이 가게를 차렸고 지나는 사람들에게 도넛과 커피를 팔았다. 10 평가원

7 Tim and Nick correspond regularly but ______________ meet because they live far away from each other.
Tim과 Nick은 서로 멀리 떨어져 살기에 서신왕래는 정기적으로 하지만 거의 만나지는 않는다.

8 It was so fascinating to see how ordinary ______________ could turn into a beautiful pot.
일반적인 점토가 어떻게 아름다운 항아리가 되는지 보는 것은 매우 매력적이었다. 13 평가원

9 Landscaping can help block and absorb the sun's energy by providing ______________.
조경은 그늘을 제공함으로써 태양 에너지를 막고 흡수할 수 있도록 돕는다. 05 고3학평 변형

10 Consistently second-guessing ourselves would ______________ our daily functioning.
반복적으로 뒤늦게 우리 스스로를 비판하는 것은 우리의 일상 기능을 방해할 것이다. 14 평가원

Review Test 14

A 우리말에 맞게 빈 칸에 알맞은 단어를 쓰시오.

1 buy a _______________ bag 악어 가죽 가방을 사다

2 political _______________ 정치적 긴장

3 a _______________ disease 치료 가능한 질병

4 _______________ of four parts 네 부분으로 구성되다

5 major in _______________ 지질학을 전공하다

6 suffer from _______________ 굶주림에 고통 받다

7 a member of _______________ 국회의원

8 the _______________ of a volcano 화산 분화구

9 financially _______________ 재정적으로 불안정한

10 a _______________ tower 거대한 탑

B 영어에 맞게 빈 칸에 알맞은 우리말을 쓰시오.

1 ferment Kimchi 김치를 _______________

2 forensic evidence _______________ 증거

3 improve energy efficiency 에너지 _______________ 을 향상시키다

4 invent ingenious devices _______________ 장치들을 발명하다

5 a sigh of grief _______________ 의 탄식

6 a formal process _______________ 과정

7 the larva of a butterfly 나비의 _______________

8 the heir to the throne 왕위 _______________

9 make a clay model _______________ 모형을 만들다

10 interfere with concentration 집중을 _______________

C 다음 영어 풀이에 알맞은 어휘를 〈보기〉에서 고르시오.

보기 intercept tension crater famine seldom

1 ______________ : a very large hole in the ground caused by an explosion

2 ______________ : to stop or take someone or something that is going from one place to another

3 ______________ : a great lack of food over a long period of time or over a wide area

4 ______________ : rarely, not very often

5 ______________ : a feeling of anger or nervousness between people

D 문맥에 맞게 다음 문장을 완성하시오.

1 Some people want to	• •	a cut down the trees for lumber.
2 Public transportation enables us	• •	b few intentional changes in life.
3 The company buys your creativity,	• •	c government policy on the issue is misguided.
4 Many people think that	• •	d not your image.
5 Some people make	• •	e to carry out all these activities.

E 문장을 읽고 문맥에 적절한 단어를 고르시오.

1 You use too much salt in your cooking. Why don't you (cut/shut) down on it?

2 They could not (watch/figure) out how to solve the problem.

3 When he heard the terrible news his face turned (pale/idle).

4 Despite his (defective/gigantic) eyesight, Carl finally became a film director.

5 The little girl is already (formal/fluent) in three languages.

F 문장의 빈칸에 알맞은 단어를 〈보기〉에서 찾아 쓰시오. (필요하면 형태를 고치시오.)

보기	evacuate	insist on	huddle	demise	expel

1 A sudden change in weather may have caused the ______________ of the dinosaur.
갑작스러운 기후 변화가 공룡들의 종말을 야기했다.

2 He was ______________ from the team due to his inappropriate behavior.
그는 부적절한 행동 때문에 팀에서 쫓겨났다.

3 Groups of newborn animals ______________ together to stay warm.
새로 태어난 동물 무리들은 따뜻하게 지내기 위해 떼지어 모인다. 11 고3학평 변형

4 She returned the camera to the shop and ______________ receiving a full refund.
그녀는 카메라를 가게에 돌려주고 전액 환불을 고집했다. 13 고3평가원 변형

5 The brave nurse ______________ many children from the burning building.
그 용감한 간호사는 많은 아이들을 불타는 건물로부터 대피시켰다.

G 다음 〈보기〉 중 두 문장에 공통으로 사용할 수 있는 어휘를 고르시오.

1 Sandra, don't worry. You will __________ your tasks successfully. 08 고1학평 변형

The only way to stop drink driving is to __________ random breath testing. 07 고1학평 변형

① carry out ② turn out ③ drop out ④ wipe out ⑤ cancel out

2 I can't stand George any more. He __________ keeps his word. 11 고1학평

Because he likes to eat at home, he __________ eats at restaurants.

① constantly ② seldom ③ normally ④ frequently ⑤ humble

3 The researchers wanted to determine what these high achieving people had __________. 16 고1학평 변형

Jazz and classical music have a number of things __________. 2007 수능

① in case ② in turn ③ in common ④ in advance ⑤ in terms

Study More

혼동하기 쉬운 단어 grief vs. brief

- [grief] 명 (누군가의 죽음으로 인한) 슬픔, 비통
  Jack was in deep **grief** because his grandfather passed away.
  Jack은 그의 할아버지가 돌아가셔서 깊은 슬픔에 빠져있었다.
- [brief] 형 짧은, 잠시 동안의
  After a **brief** silence, the discussion resumed. 잠깐의 침묵 후에 토론은 재개 되었다.

Day 29

MP3

841 □ **obligate** [ábləgit]
동 강요하다, ~에게 의무를 지우다
be obligated to care for their children 그들의 아이들을 돌볼 의무를 지다

842 □ **peril** [pérəl]
명 위험
face a peril 위험을 직면하다

843 □ **monk** [mʌŋk]
명 수도승
become a monk 수도승이 되다

844 □ **rubbish** [rʌ́biʃ]
명 쓰레기, 형편없는 것, 헛소리
dump rubbish 쓰레기를 버리다　household rubbish 집안 쓰레기

845 □ **prominence** [prámənəns]
명 명성, 유명함　형 prominent 유명한, 중요한
gain prominence 명성을 얻다　come to prominence 유명해지다

846 □ **maze** [meiz]
명 미로
get lost in a maze 미로에서 길을 잃다

847 □ **marine** [məríːn]
형 바다의, 해양의
the study of marine life 해양 생물 연구

848 □ **malfunction** [mælfʌ́ŋkʃən]
명 고장
equipment malfunction 기계 고장

849 □ **notify** [nóutəfài]
동 알리다, 통지하다
notify students of their exam results 학생들에게 시험 결과를 통지하다

850 □ **arrogant** [ærəgənt]
형 오만한, 거만한
her selfish and arrogant behavior 그녀의 이기적이고 오만한 행동

851 □ **railway** [réilwèi]
명 철로, 철도
build a railway 철로를 만들다

852 □ **monarchy** [mánərki]
명 군주제
set up a monarchy 군주제를 확립하다

853 □ **beneficial** [bènəfíʃəl]
형 유익한, 이로운
beneficial to health 건강에 이로운

854 □ **pitiful** [pítifəl]
형 측은한, 가련한
a pitiful situation 측은한 상황

855 □ **put off** [put ɔːf]
연기하다
put off the promise 약속을 연기하다

Daily Test

| 월 일 |

A 우리말에 맞게 빈 칸에 알맞은 단어를 쓰세요.

1 There is the ______________ of flood and falling rocks in that area, so be careful.
저 지역은 홍수와 낙석의 잦은 위험이 있으니 조심해라.

2 Everyday materials such as junk metal or ______________ are transformed into works of art.
폐 금속이나 쓰레기와 같은 생활 물질들이 예술 작품으로 바뀌게 된다. 09 고2학평 변형

3 Scientists fed the bacteria to mice and then tested the mice in a ______________.
과학자들은 쥐에게 박테리아를 먹였고 미로 속에서 그 쥐들을 실험했다. 10 고2학평 변형

4 Coral reefs are the most threatened ______________ environments on Earth.
산호초는 지구에서 가장 위협받는 해양 환경이다. 16 평가원

5 His attitude was rude and ______________.
그의 태도는 무례하고 오만했다. 12 고3학평 변형

6 If you pass the job interview, we will ______________ you of the news by text message.
당신이 입사 면접에 통과하게 되면, 우리는 문자 메시지로 그 소식을 알려 드리겠습니다.

7 One day a wise old ______________ heard an impatient pounding on the door.
어느 날 늙은 현명한 수도승은 서둘러 문을 두드리는 소리를 들었다. 15 고3학평 변형

8 It was really ______________ and stupid, watching a family in a sitcom on TV instead of being a family.
가족이 함께하는 것 대신 TV 시트콤 속 가족을 보는 것은 측은하고 어리석다. 07 고2학평 변형

9 The report revealed the ______________ effects of listening to music when we are gloomy.
그 보고서는 우리가 우울할 때 음악을 듣는 것의 이로운 효과를 밝혀냈다. 08 평가원

10 My parents always say, never ______________ till the next day what you can do that day.
나의 부모님은 항상 그날의 할 일을 다음 날로 미루지 말라고 말씀하신다.

Day 29

MP3

856 paste [peist]
동 붙이다 명 반죽
copy and paste 복사와 붙여 넣기

857 oppressive [əprésiv]
형 억압하는, 탄압하는
use oppressive tactics 탄압적인 수단을 사용하다

858 memorial [məmɔ́:riəl]
명 기념비, 기념물, 기념일
a memorial for victims of terror 테러 희생자들을 위한 기념비

859 mansion [mǽnʃən]
명 대저택
live in a stately mansion 호화로운 대저택에 살다

860 masculine [mǽskjəlin]
형 남성의, 남자다운
masculine virtue 남자의 덕(만용의 덕)

861 minister [mínistər]
명 장관, 성직자
the Minister of Education 교육부 장관

862 misty [místi]
형 안개 낀
enjoy a misty view 안개 낀 경치를 즐기다

863 occupation [àkjəpéiʃən]
명 직업, 점령
state your age and occupation 당신의 나이와 직업을 기입하다

864 pebble [pébl]
명 조약돌, 자갈
throw a pebble 조약돌을 던지다

865 open-minded [óupən máindid]
형 마음이 열린, 편견 없는
an open-minded adult 마음이 열린 어른

866 patent [pǽtənt]
명 특허권
be protected by patent 특허에 의해 보호받다

867 rifle [ráifl]
동 훔치다, 샅샅이 뒤지다
start to rifle through his drawers 그의 서랍을 뒤지기 시작하다

868 pharmacy [fɑ́:rməsi]
명 약국, 조제실
at a pharmacy 약국에서 a hospital pharmacy 병원의 조제실(약국)

869 facade [fəsɑ:d]
명 정면, 앞면
complete the facade of the cathedral 대성당의 전면을 완성하다

870 monologue [mɑ́nəlɔ̀(:)g]
명 독백, 일인극
a dramatic monologue 극적 독백

Daily Test

| 월 일 |

A 우리말에 맞게 빈 칸에 알맞은 단어를 쓰세요.

1 Leopold grew enormously rich, spending his money on yachts and ______________.
Leopold는 엄청난 부자가 되었고 자신의 돈을 요트나 대저택등에 썼다. 07 고3학평 변형

2 Joe considers rugby to be a very ______________ sport.
Joe는 럭비가 아주 남성적인 스포츠라고 생각한다.

3 The morning dawns through a ______________ fog.
희뿌연 안개와 함께 동이 텄다. 07 고3학평 변형

4 Our teacher told us to remove all the small ______________ on the playground as punishment.
우리 선생님은 벌로 운동장에 있는 모든 작은 돌들을 치우라고 말씀하셨다.

5 Being ______________ increases future opportunities.
마음이 열린 태도를 갖는 건 미래의 기회를 늘려준다. 12 고1학평 변형

6 When a firm discovers a new drug, ______________ laws give the firm a monopoly on the sale of that drug.
한 회사가 신약을 발견했을 때, 특허법은 그 회사에게 약 판매에 대한 독점권을 준다. 11 고3학평 변형

7 A sinju is a stick-shaped ______________ tablet made of wood.
신주는 막대기 모양의 나무로 된 위패이다. 07 고2학평 변형

8 Cut, ______________, and you're done.
자르고 붙이면 다 한 거에요. 10 고3학평 변형

9 The ______________ of Health and Welfare warned that smoking is harmful and may cause cancer.
보건복지부 장관은 흡연은 해롭고 암을 유발할 수 있다고 경고했다. 10 고3학평 변형

10 The old actor made a ______________ in appreciation of his wife's dedication and love.
그 나이든 배우는 그의 아내에게 그녀의 헌신과 사랑에 고마움을 전하기 위해 일인극을 만들었다.

Day 30

MP3

871 **barely**
[bέərli]

부 간신히, 빠듯하게, 거의 ~아니게
be barely able to stand 간신히 서있다

872 **regardless of**
[rigɑ́:rdlis əv]

전 ~에 상관없이, 관계없이
regardless of her social status 그녀의 사회적 지위와 관계없이

873 **stumble**
[stʌ́mbl]

동 비틀거리다, 발을 헛디디다
stumble along 비틀거리며 걷다

874 **rebel**
[rébəl]

명 반역자, 저항 세력
suppress a rebel 반역자를 처벌하다

875 **revolve**
[rivɑ́lv]

동 돌다, 회전하다
revolve on its axis 축을 중심으로 회전하다

876 **slope**
[sloup]

명 경사지, 비탈
a gentle slope 완만한 경사

877 **paddle**
[pǽdl]

명 노 동 노를 젓다
paddles of various sizes and shapes 다양한 크기와 모양의 노

878 **reptile**
[réptil]

명 파충류
protect endangered reptiles 멸종위기에 처한 파충류를 보호하다

879 **inflation**
[infléiʃən]

명 물가 인상
a high rate of inflation 높은 물가 상승률

880 **rapport**
[ræpɔ́:r]

명 (친밀한) 관계
develop rapport 친밀한 관계를 구축하다

881 **rationalize**
[rǽʃənəlàiz]

동 합리화하다
rationalize her rude behavior 그녀의 무례한 행동을 합리화하다

882 **sow**
[sau]

동 (씨를) 뿌리다, 심다
sow flower seeds 꽃씨를 뿌리다

883 **speculate**
[spékjəlèit]

동 추측하다, 짐작하다
speculate about motivation 동기를 추측하다

884 **repertoire**
[repərtwa:(r)]

명 연주곡 목록, 레퍼토리
a wide repertoire 다양한 연주곡 목록

885 **revolutionize**
[rèvəljú:ʃənàiz]

동 ~에 혁명을 일으키다
revolutionize the study of physics 물리학 연구에 혁명을 일으키다

Daily Test

| 월 일 |

A **우리말에 맞게 빈 칸에 알맞은 단어를 쓰세요.**

1 We find no evidence in Classical times of tailors: the word itself _______________ exists in Greek or Latin.
우리는 고대 시대에 재단사에 대한 어떤 증거도 찾을 수 없다. 그리스어나 라틴어에는 그 단어 자체가 거의 존재하지 않는다. 13 평가원

2 Everyone should be treated equally _______________ his or her social status.
모든 사람들은 사회적 지위에 상관없이 동등하게 대우 받아야 한다.

3 The _______________ is too steep for children to climb.
그 비탈은 아이들이 오르기에는 너무 가파르다. 2015 수능

4 Most dinosaurs were much larger than the _______________ that we have today.
대다수의 공룡은 오늘 날의 파충류들보다 훨씬 컸다. 09 고1학평 변형

5 _______________ can be a major life concern for most people.
물가 인상률은 대부분의 사람들에게 가장 큰 삶의 걱정거리이다. 16 평가원

6 Mr. Han gave his students plenty of time to build good _______________ with the new student.
한 선생님은 그의 학생들에게 새로운 친구와 좋은 관계를 쌓을 수 있도록 충분한 시간을 주었다.

7 If you want to grow some plants, you should _______________ your seeds in good soil.
네가 만약 약간의 식물들을 기르고 싶다면, 너는 좋은 토양에 씨앗을 심어야 한다.

8 Most psychics like to _______________ about when the world will end.
대부분의 심령술사들은 세계가 언제 끝날지에 대해 짐작하기를 좋아한다.

9 Her _______________ always includes medieval church music and waltz music.
그녀의 연주 목록에는 언제나 중세 교회 음악과 왈츠음악이 포함된다.

10 The invention of Braille _______________ communication for millions.
Braille점자의 발명은 수백만의 의사소통에 혁명을 일으켰다. 12 고3학평 변형

Day 30

MP3

886 **robber** [rɑ́bər]
명 강도
catch the bank robber 은행강도를 잡다

887 **scar** [skɑːr]
명 흉터
a scar on his hand 그의 손 위에 난 흉터

888 **sticky** [stíki]
형 끈적거리는, 달라붙는
sticky with glue 풀로 끈적거리는

889 **throne** [θroun]
명 왕위
take the throne 왕위에 오르다

890 **symbolize** [símbəlaiz]
동 상징하다, 기호화하다
symbolize good fortune 행운을 상징하다

891 **up-to-date** [ʌp tuː deit]
형 현대의, 최신 유행의
up-to-date equipment 현대 최신 장비

892 **sigh** [sai]
동 한숨짓다 명 한숨, 한숨소리
sigh deeply 깊게 한숨 쉬다

893 **misleading** [mislíːdiŋ]
형 오해의 소지가 있는, 오도하는
her misleading advice 그녀의 오해의 소지가 있는 조언

894 **renovate** [rénəvèit]
동 혁신하다, ~을 보수하다
renovate society 사회를 혁신하다

895 **tumble** [tʌ́mbl]
동 굴러 떨어지다, 넘어지다
tumble down the stairs 계단에서 넘어지다

896 **talkative** [tɔ́ːkətiv]
형 말하기를 좋아하는, 수다스러운
a talkative person 수다스러운 사람

897 **obesity** [oubíːsəti]
명 비만
prevent obesity 비만을 예방하다 rates of obesity 비만 율

898 **turn down** [təːrn daun]
동 거절하다, 줄이다
turn down his proposal 그의 제안을 거절하다

899 **twilight** [twáilàit]
명 석양, 황혼
in the twilight 해질녘에 the twilight years 인생의 황혼기

900 **riot** [ráiət]
명 폭동, 시위
A political riot broke out. 정치적 폭동이 발생했다.

Daily Test

| 월 일 |

A 우리말에 맞게 빈 칸에 알맞은 단어를 쓰세요.

1 Queen Elizabeth celebrated 60 years on the ______________ in 2012.
Elizabeth 여왕은 2012년 즉위 60주년을 축하 하였다.

2 White has always ______________ purity.
흰색은 항상 순수함을 상징해왔다.

3 Elementary biology textbooks help to produce a ______________ impression of what perception entails.
기초 생물학 교과서는 무엇이 인지를 수반하는지에 대한 잘못된 인상을 만들게 한다. 2013 수능

4 In times of financial trouble, beware - prices are almost certainly going to ______________.
재정적 문제에 있어서, 가격은 거의 항상 내려갈 수 있음을 알아라.

5 I find myself sitting next to someone who's quite ______________.
나는 내가 꽤 수다스러운 사람 옆에 앉았음을 깨달았다. 05 고3학평 변형

6 The decline in physical activity has contributed to ______________ and long-term health problems.
신체적 활동의 감소는 비만과 장기적인 건강 문제에 기여한다. 09 평가원

7 When I saw a ______________ on his knee, I was surprised.
내가 그의 무릎에 난 흉터를 보았을 때, 난 깜짝 놀랐다.

8 The theater income was limited since it can start the showings only at ______________.
그 극장은 땅거미가 져야만 상영을 시작할 수 있었기 때문에 극장의 수입은 한정적이었다. 07 고3학평 변형

9 The police tried to suppress the ______________ that broke out in the jail.
경찰은 감옥에서 발생한 폭동을 진압하기 위해 애썼다.

10 A lot of people join the campaign to ______________ the current online culture.
많은 사람들이 현재 온라인 문화를 혁신하기 위한 운동에 참여한다.

Review Test 15 Day 29 + Day 30 | 월 일 |

A 우리말에 맞게 빈 칸에 알맞은 단어를 쓰시오.

1 get lost in a ________________ 미로에서 길을 잃다

2 the study of ________________ life 해양 생물 연구

3 set up a ________________ 군주제를 확립하다

4 ________________ to health 건강에 이로운

5 enjoy a ________________ view 안개 낀 경치를 즐기다

6 a gentle ________________ 완만한 경사

7 protect endangered ________________ 멸종위기에 처한 파충류를 보호하다

8 ________________ flower seeds 꽃씨를 뿌리다

9 a ________________ on his hand 그의 손 위에 난 흉터

10 take the ________________ 왕위에 오르다

B 영어에 맞게 빈 칸에 알맞은 우리말을 쓰시오.

1 face a peril ________________을 직면하다

2 dump rubbish ________________를 버리다

3 a pitiful situation ________________ 상황

4 live in a stately mansion 호화로운 ________________에 살다

5 throw a pebble ________________을 던지다

6 be protected by patent ________________에 의해 보호받다

7 sticky with glue 풀로 ________________

8 up-to-date equipment ________________ 장비

9 a talkative person ________________ 사람

10 A political riot broke out. 정치적 ________________이 발생했다.

C 다음 영어 풀이에 알맞은 어휘를 〈보기〉에서 고르시오.

보기	renovate	robber	reptile	facade	marine

1 ______________ : a person who steals by using or threatening to use force

2 ______________ : of or relating to the sea

3 ______________ : cold-blooded animals with dry scales such as snakes or lizards

4 ______________ : to repair or improve a house or a building

5 ______________ : the front side of a building

D 문맥에 맞게 다음 문장을 완성하시오.

1 His attitude was •	• a	and you're done.
2 Being open-minded increases •	• b	life concern for most people.
3 Cut, paste, •	• c	about when the world will end.
4 Inflation can be a major •	• d	rude and arrogant.
5 Most psychics like to speculate •	• e	future opportunities.

E 문장을 읽고 문맥에 적절한 단어를 고르시오.

1 He treated people equally (regardless of/depending on) their job.

2 The game was (put off/put on) until next week due to the bad weather.

3 He (turned on/turned down) Gary's proposal because he did not trust him.

4 The moon (resolves/revolves) around the earth.

5 Tim, can you go to the (mansion/pharmacy) and get some medicine for my headache?

F 문장의 빈칸에 알맞은 단어를 〈보기〉에서 찾아 쓰시오. (필요하면 형태를 고치시오.)

보기 malfunction up to date rapport renovate inflation

1 Just two months ago, we ______________ our park, so all of our facilities are clean and like new.
꼭 두 달 전에, 저희는 공원을 보수해서 모든 편의 시설이 깨끗하고 새것과 같습니다. 17 고3 평가원

2 Unfortunately, we cannot work today due to an equipment ______________.
유감스럽게도 기계 고장 때문에 오늘 작업을 할 수 없습니다.

3 A leader's emotional intelligence includes self-awareness, empathy, and ______________ with others.
지도자의 감성 지능은 자기인식, 공감, 그리고 다른 이들과의 친화력을 포함한다. 13 고1 학평 변형

4 As you see in the curve of the graph, as unemployment rises, ______________ decreases.
그래프에의 곡선에서 볼 수 있듯이 실업률이 올라감에 따라 물가인상은 감소한다. 09 고1 평가원 변형

5 Students are expected to keep their contact information ______________ at all times.
학생들은 항상 연락처를 최신으로 유지해야 합니다.

G 다음 〈보기〉 중 두 문장에 공통으로 사용할 수 있는 어휘를 고르시오.

1 The researchers ___________ that there must be a close link between the two phenomena.
Because we have no information we can only ___________ about the cause of the incident.

① renovate ② obligate ③ tumble ④ notify ⑤ speculate

2 Distance learning has recently become ___________ in the field of further education. 05 고3평가원
The ___________ scholar devoted his life to the study of human psychology.

① misty ② open-minded ③ prominent ④ pitiful ⑤ marine

3 So I ___________ again and fell over the sofa when I tried to get up. 06 고1학평 변형
While browsing the Internet, I ___________ on an ad for a magazine, the Economist. 11 고2학평 변형

① stumbled ② sighed ③ sowed ④ revolutionized ⑤ pumped

Study More

'-ize' : '~으로 되다', '되게 만들다'의 의미를 나타낸다.

- [rationalize] 동 합리화하다
  Eric **rationalizes** his stupid mistake. Eric은 그의 어리석은 실수를 합리화했다.
- [symbolize] 동 상징하다
  A four leaf clover **symbolizes** good fortune. 네잎 클로버는 행운을 상징한다.

Index

D

E

Q

R

S

T

U

V

W

Y

Answer Key

정답 및 해설

Answer Key

Day 01

Daily Test 1 P. 09

A
1 accord
2 percentage
3 emotional
4 continuous
5 responses
6 employ
7 term
8 experimental
9 benefits
10 attractions

Daily Test 2 P. 11

A
1 dependent
2 pressure
3 races
4 consequences
5 Efficiently
6 female
7 instance
8 react
9 concept
10 Perhaps

Day 02

Daily Test 1 P. 13

A
1 significant
2 Throughout
3 united
4 assume
5 detailed
6 predict
7 concerns
8 outcome
9 profit
10 coexist

Daily Test 2 P. 15

A
1 invest
2 claimed
3 occasion
4 generally
5 biology
6 principles
7 seeking
8 depart
9 range
10 attitudes

Review Test 01

Day 01 + Day 02 P. 16

A
1 accord
2 plea
3 experimental
4 races
5 Perhaps
6 feature
7 further
8 limited
9 generally
10 seek

B
1 율
2 고용하다
3 운영하다
4 예
5 도덕적인
6 통합하다
7 상세한
8 이익
9 출발하다
10 태도

C
1 attraction
2 dependent
3 means
4 response
5 contribute

D
1 c
2 e
3 a
4 d
5 b

E
1 outcome
2 response
3 eventually
4 dependent
5 attraction

해석
1. 그 실험의 결과를 예측하기에는 너무 일러요.
2. 저는 제 질문에 대한 그의 답변을 아직 받지 못했습니다.
3. 수 년의 고생 후에, John은 마침내 그의 식당을 개업할 수 있었다.
4. 이 프로젝트의 성공은 전적으로 대중의 흥미에 달려 있어요.
5. 에펠탑은 파리에서 가장 유명한 관광 명소이다.

F

1 competitive
2 essential
3 consequences
4 accurate
5 claim

G

1 ④ emotional
2 ② significant
3 ④ contributed

해석

1. 사람은 그들의 감정 상태에 따라서 다른 방식으로 행동할지도 모른다.
신체적인 병과 정신적인 스트레스에는 긴밀한 관계가 있다.
2. 이 터치스크린의 가장 중요한 장점 중 하나는 사용하기 쉬운 점이다.
그들은 그 행사를 계획하는데 상당한 시간과 돈을 투자했다.
3. 많은 학생들이 그들의 재능을 그 프로젝트에 기여했다.
그는 널리 미국 음악계에 "race music"을 도입하는데 크게 기여했다.

Day 03

Daily Test 1 P. 21

A

1 contrast
2 aspect
3 entertained
4 Frequent
5 refers
6 crop
7 detected
8 explanation
9 lack
10 addition

Daily Test 2 P. 23

A

1 manufactured
2 satisfaction
3 completely
4 environmental
5 appealed
6 operate
7 yield
8 accomplish
9 classic
10 conscious

Day 04

Daily Test 1 P. 25

A

1 intelligence
2 recalling
3 replaced
4 adjust
5 contains
6 exception
7 frustrated
8 practical
9 pursue
10 academic

Daily Test 2 P. 27

A

1 exposure
2 lawyer
3 Agriculture
4 conventional
5 Innovation
6 mark
7 rural
8 deplete
9 sorts
10 acquire

Review Test 02

Day 03 + Day 04 P. 28

A

1 contrast
2 crops
3 lack
4 analysis
5 yield
6 intelligence
7 adjust
8 exposure
9 Agriculture
10 mark

B

1 즐겁게 해주다
2 승진하다
3 책임
4 호소
5 회사
6 필요성
7 현실적인
8 학업
9 혁신
10 지방

C

1 refer
2 promote
3 crop
4 factor
5 practical

D

1 a
2 e
3 c
4 b
5 d

E

1 aspect
2 frequent
3 completely
4 replaced
5 objective

해석

1. 네가 새 학교의 가장 좋아하는 면은 무엇이니?
2. Tom의 가족은 그 식당에 자주 간다.
3. 그녀는 오늘 우리의 약속을 완전히 잊고 있었다.
4. 제 신발은 닳았어요. 그들은 곧 바꿀 필요가 있어요.
5. 이 수업의 주된 주제는 물리학의 기본에 대해 학습하는 것입니다.

F

1 recalling
2 relatively
3 contained
4 inner
5 demonstrated

G

1 ④ environmental
2 ⑤ frustrated
3 ⑤ in addition to

해석

1. 환경적 문제가 국제적인 이슈가 되는 것은 분명해지고 있다.
많은 이들이 환경오염과 기후 변화의 연결성을 알고 있다.
2. 나는 그의 역사 에세이의 낮은 수준에 매우 불만스러웠다.
그는 친구들의 부정적인 논평에 좌절했다.
3. 과학자일 뿐만 아니라 그는 또한 유명한 가수였다.
그는 영어뿐만 아니라 3개 국어를 말한다.

Day 05

Daily Test 1 P. 33

A

1 decade
2 disasters
3 equipment
4 extent
5 Central
6 contents
7 Excessive
8 instructions
9 mass
10 additional

Daily Test 2 P. 35

A

1 architecture
2 convey
3 identify
4 Internal
5 relation
6 struggled
7 phenomenon
8 colleagues
9 delighted
10 fundamental

Day 06

Daily Test 1 P. 37

A

1 insights
2 persuaded
3 security
4 unexpected
5 ceremony
6 Dozens
7 nutritious
8 pounded
9 restricts
10 unpleasant

Daily Test 2 P. 39

A

1 law
2 meaningful
3 absences
4 dramatic
5 indicates
6 literature
7 pace
8 political
9 severe
10 statements

Review Test 03

Day 05 + Day 06 P. 40

A

1 disaster
2 extent
3 instructions
4 generate
5 phenomenon
6 insight

7 attach
8 nutritious
9 gradual
10 political

B
1 성
2 확장하다
3 서술법, 화법
4 관계
5 기뻐서
6 설득하다
7 개막식
8 불면증
9 문학
10 진술

C
1 decade
2 crucial
3 dozen
4 law
5 colleague

D
1 c
2 e
3 a
4 b
5 d

E
1 mass
2 identify
3 imports
4 meaningful
5 crucial

해석

1. 많은 양의 눈이 학교의 입구를 막았다.
2. 수지는 한눈에 그녀의 아들의 필체를 알아 볼 수 있었다.
3. 한국은 중동 국가들로부터 주로 기름을 수입한다.
4. 이 곰 인형은 내 딸에게 매우 의미 있는 것입니다.
5. 그의 새 앨범의 성공에 있어 중요한 요인은 무엇이었나요?

F
1 unexpected
2 indicates
3 internal
4 additional
5 central

G
1 ④ convey
2 ③ reproduce
3 ② convince

해석

1. 비행기뿐만 아니라, 배는 또한 전 세계에 상품을 전달하는데 사용된다. 언어와 같이, 표정과 몸짓은 정보를 전달 할 수 있다.
2. 바이러스가 살아있는 세포 안에 있을 때, 이는 스스로 더 많이 번식할 수 있다. 새 또는 파충류와 같은 많은 동물은 알을 낳음으로써 번식한다.
3. Jeremy는 그가 그 일을 위한 최고의 지원자라고 나를 확신시키기 위해 노력하는 중이다. 아무도 다른 사람들이 그의 코에 대해 신경 쓰지 않을 거라고 그를 확신시킬 수 없었다.

Day 07

Daily Test 1 P. 45

A
1 wandered
2 commercial
3 merely
4 badly
5 categories
6 celebration
7 childhood
8 cultivates
9 emissions
10 messes

Daily Test 2 P. 47

A
1 resistance
2 Verbal
3 burst into
4 counselor
5 devoted
6 fade
7 Hence
8 frightened
9 grabbed
10 grocery

Day 08

Daily Test 1 P. 49

A
1 releases
2 remarkable
3 reverse
4 transformed
5 translated
6 wheat
7 suffering
8 enthusiasm
9 approximately
10 brilliant

Daily Test 2 P. 51

A
1 desperate
2 disturbs

3 edit
4 exhausted
5 external
6 metaphor
7 paused
8 sequence
9 pasture
10 output

Review Test 04

Day 07 + Day 08 P. 52

A
1 wander
2 authority
3 childhood
4 fade
5 load
6 reverse
7 stimulate
8 enthusiasm
9 exhaust
10 metaphor

B
1 단지
2 경작하다
3 저항
4 조상
5 놀라다
6 봉하다
7 번역하다
8 대략
9 똑같이
10 목초지

C
1 verbal
2 category
3 chase
4 ancestor
5 translate

D
1 d
2 a
3 b
4 c
5 e

E
1 desperate
2 sufficient
3 devoted
4 remarkable
5 consulted

해석
1. 그 회사는 새로운 유형의 자동차를 개발하기 위해 필사적으로 노력했다.
2. 우리는 이번 주에 그 일을 할 충분한 시간이 없어요.
3. 그녀는 그녀의 모든 시간과 힘을 새로운 소설을 쓰는데 바쳤다.
4. 그 나라는 환경적으로 놀랄 만한 발전을 이루었다.
5. 우리는 우리의 새로운 사업에 관한 조언을 얻기 위해 교수님과 상담했다.

F
1 biological
2 emissions
3 commercial
4 suffering
5 random

G
1 ② acknowledged
2 ④ released
3 ③ settle

해석
1. Sara는 문서 작성의 모든 양상을 학습하는데는 시간이 든다고 인정했다.
좋게 생각하는 것은 시간이 드는 과정인 것이 널리 인정되었다.
2. 사람이 스트레스를 경험할 때, 스트레스 호르몬은 뇌로부터 나온다.
일 년 후, 그녀는 그녀의 첫 팝 앨범을 발매했다.
3. 새로 결혼한 부부는 근처 마을에 정착하기로 계획중이다.
특별 위원회는 학생 분쟁을 합의하기 위해 설립되었다.

Day 09

Daily Test 1 P. 57

A
1 commitment
2 multiple
3 vulnerable
4 launch
5 motion
6 passage
7 register
8 scarce
9 sensitive
10 strategy

Daily Test 2 P. 59

A
1 absolutely
2 cognitive
3 independent
4 leadership
5 instantly
6 accompanied
7 admit
8 appointed
9 denied
10 document

Day 10

Daily Test 1 P. 61

A

1 fascinated
2 depression
3 skilled
4 overlooked
5 eager
6 ingredient
7 fate
8 endless
9 resolved
10 scents

Daily Test 2 P. 63

A

1 revenue
2 requirement
3 gravity
4 productive
5 aided
6 reputation
7 conserve
8 caution
9 profound
10 Logic

Review Test 05

Day 09 + Day 10 P. 64

A

1 commitment
2 launch
3 superior
4 surrounding
5 deny
6 sum
7 remote
8 gravity
9 caution
10 tone

B

1 등록하다
2 채굴하다
3 부족한
4 동반하다
5 임명하다
6 성분
7 객차
8 매출
9 평판
10 깊은

C

1 superior
2 reputation
3 gravity
4 obstacle
5 attribute

D

1 c
2 a
3 b
4 e
5 d

E

1 eager
2 moderate
3 overlook
4 corresponds
5 mutual

해석

1. Kevin은 대학에서 소프트웨어 프로그래밍을 공부하길 열망한다.
2. 규칙적인 운동을 하는 것은 당신의 정신 건강에 좋다.
3. 우리가 윗부분을 간과하지 않았다면 정확한 답을 찾았을 것이다.
4. Joe가 말한 것은 정확하게 내가 본 것과 일치한다.
5. 그 회의는 두 국가 간에 상호적인 신뢰를 만들었다.

F

1 cognitive
2 vulnerable
3 fascinated
4 independent
5 appointed

G

1 ③ multiple
2 ② productive
3 ④ endless

해석

1. 인생은 다수의 승자가 존재하는 게임인 것을 기억하세요.
인간이 한 번에 다양한 일을 하는 것의 개념은 1920년대 이래로 심리학자들에 의해 연구되고 있다.
2. 대부분의 사람은 아침에 더 생산적인 것처럼 보인다.
우리는 생산적인 하루를 보냈어. 우리는 보고서 전체를 다 완성했다.
3. 그는 그의 끝없는 노력의 결과로 성공한 작곡가가 되었다.
Mary의 아버지는 그녀가 끝없이 우는 동안 Mary를 꼭 껴안았다.

Day 11

Daily Test 1 P. 69

A

1 specializes
2 reliable
3 soaked
4 probability

5 Minor
6 administration
7 abandoned
8 Institution
9 scholarship
10 spelled out

Daily Test 2 P. 71

A
1 charity
2 screw
3 assembled
4 accessible
5 comprehend
6 cooperation
7 underlying
8 notion
9 deserved
10 Pacific

Day 12

Daily Test 1 P. 73

A
1 Facial
2 ratio
3 Renaissance
4 suburbs
5 violate
6 commute
7 outer
8 psychology
9 flip
10 altitudes

Daily Test 2 P. 75

A
1 fulfill
2 innocence
3 solitary
4 invisible
5 license
6 addicted
7 genre
8 botanical
9 cattle
10 permitted

Review Test 06

Day 11 + Day 12 P. 76

A
1 properties
2 soaked
3 administration
4 bury
5 capture
6 expertise
7 outer
8 altitudes
9 solitary
10 innocence

B
1 전공하다
2 가능성
3 저지르다
4 이해하다
5 분위기
6 심리학
7 통근하다
8 절차
9 불쾌해지다
10 광

C
1 hop
2 altitude
3 stroke
4 soaked
5 commute

D
1 a
2 d
3 e
4 b
5 c

E
1 attention
2 squeeze
3 license
4 flexible
5 reliable

해석
1. Joan의 에세이는 잘 쓰였고 관심을 받을 만 하다.
2. 이제, 주스를 얻기 위해 오렌지를 짜세요.
3. 운전 면허증 없이 운전하는 것은 불법이다.
4. Lucy는 유연한 사고방식을 갖고 있다.
5. 기자는 그가 믿을만한 출처에서 정보를 얻었다고 말했다.

F
1 permitted
2 specialized
3 widespread
4 fulfill
5 underlying

G
1 ④ violated
2 ⑤ justify
3 ④ abandoned

해석
1. 그는 그가 속도 제한을 위반했기 때문에 벌금을 물었다.
규칙을 어긴 학생들은 학교로부터 경고를 받았다.

2. 당신은 변명을 함으로써 당신의 실패를 정당화하면 안 된다.
충분한 정보 없이 당신의 결정을 정당화하는 것은 힘들다.
3. 그들은 자금 부족 때문에 초기 계획을 포기했다.
고대 사회의 예술품들은 그들의 목적을 수행한 후에는 자주 버려졌다.

Day 13

Daily Test 1 P. 81

A
1 reminder
2 spark
3 crew
4 toxic
5 aroma
6 hesitated
7 hormone
8 misunderstandings
9 Nevertheless
10 opponents

Daily Test 2 P. 83

A
1 compliment
2 credit
3 scout
4 flexible
5 healing
6 useless
7 approve
8 lifestyle
9 bounces
10 browse

Day 14

Daily Test 1 P. 85

A
1 bunch
2 roast
3 romantic
4 crime
5 distractions
6 drown
7 evident
8 faith
9 scattered
10 bush

Daily Test 2 P. 87

A
1 rectangular
2 ceased
3 conference
4 nerve
5 session
6 transaction
7 inferior
8 adversity
9 beverages
10 persistent

Review Test 07

Day 13 + Day 14 P. 88

A
1 aroma
2 reminder
3 misunderstanding
4 endure
5 bounce
6 romantic
7 oral
8 scatter
9 conform
10 rectangular

B
1 독성
2 깊이
3 재산가
4 신용
5 철저한
6 주의 산만
7 익사하다
8 음료
9 하급
10 상거래

C
1 heal
2 roast
3 oral
4 toxic
5 inferior

D
1 b
2 e
3 a
4 d
5 c

E
1 bunch
2 ceased
3 identical
4 Nevertheless
5 sour

해석
1. 나는 엄마의 생신을 위해 꽃 한 다발을 샀다.
2. 그 기계는 갑자기 작동을 멈추었다.
3. 세 형제는 거의 비슷하게 보인다.

4. 우리는 시간이 많이 없었다. 그럼에도 불구하고 우리는 제 시간에 보고서를 완성 할 수 있었다.
5. 나는 레몬의 신 맛이 좋아요.

F
1 flexible
2 opponents
3 hesitated
4 evident
5 persistent

G
1 ④ rear
2 ③ portray
3 ④ approved

해석
1. 항공기 뒤편에는 힘이 센 17톤의 망원경이 있다.
그의 사무실은 건물 뒤편에 있어요.
2. 지도는 복잡하고 3차원적인 세계를 평평한 종이의 묘사하기 위해 실제를 왜곡한다.
그녀는 그녀의 그림을 로마니아의 삶의 가혹한 현실을 묘사하기 위해 사용했다.
3. 최근에 그 도시는 새로운 중앙 도서관의 건설을 승인했다.
우리는 우리가 당신의 요청을 승인했다고 당신께 전할 수 있어서 기쁩니다.

Day 15

Daily Test 1 P. 93

A
1 maintenance
2 console
3 container
4 modify
5 delicate
6 On behalf of
7 fragile
8 infer
9 persuasive
10 naked

Daily Test 2 P. 95

A
1 certainty
2 deadline
3 fairly
4 exaggerate
5 groom
6 limitation
7 overwhelming
8 measurable
9 pitch
10 immune

Day 16

Daily Test 1 P. 97

A
1 deposit
2 costly
3 shrinks
4 eclipse
5 concentration
6 carved
7 shore
8 embrace
9 subjective
10 breakdown

Daily Test 2 P. 99

A
1 economics
2 priority
3 coax
4 cushion
5 dental
6 circuit
7 cheeks
8 dynamic
9 yawn
10 rendered

Review Test 08

Day 15 + Day 16 P. 100

A
1 console
2 persuasive
3 passionate
4 certainty
5 freshman
6 fairly
7 deposit
8 shrink
9 dwell
10 embrace

B
1 줄거리
2 과수원
3 연결하다
4 화폐
5 한계
6 동정심
7 개기월식
8 새기다
9 치과
10 자음

C
1 modify
2 dental
3 orchard
4 dwell
5 shore

D

1 b
2 c
3 e
4 a
5 d

E

1 deadline
2 coaxed
3 modify
4 behalf
5 passionate

해석

1. 장학금 신청의 마감일이 다음주 금요일인 걸 기억하세요.
2. 그는 그녀가 학교 회장에 출마하도록 구슬렸다.
3. 넌 가능한 한 빨리 너의 지원서의 오류를 수정해야 해.
4. 나는 내 형을 대표해서 회의에 참석했다.
5. 그는 외국어를 배우는 데 열정적이다.

F

1 subjective
2 dynamic
3 immune
4 measurable
5 overwhelmed

G

1 ③ delicate
2 ④ incorrect
3 ① concentration

해석

1. 바나나 나무의 밑동이 너무 부서지기 쉬워서 미풍도 그것을 쓰러뜨릴 수 있다. Peter는 고속 기어를 넣은, 정교하고 강한 기계처럼 일하는 중이었다.
2. 우리는 종종 인터넷의 부정확한 정보에 휩쓸린다. 그들의 분석은 부정확한 정보의 사용으로 비판을 받았다.
3. 수학의 연구는 많은 집중과 연습을 필요로 하지만 그는 실제로 힘들지 않다 예술을 배우는 것은 또한 동기, 집중, 자신감, 그리고 팀워크를 향상시킨다.

Day 17

Daily Test 1 P. 105

A

1 glow
2 legitimate
3 medieval
4 illuminated
5 masterpiece
6 initiative
7 knot
8 glorious
9 laundry
10 merit

Daily Test 2 P. 107

A

1 garage
2 interrupts
3 mad
4 homeless
5 inward
6 orbit
7 mimic
8 intimate
9 empathy
10 hay

Day 18

Daily Test 1 P. 109

A

1 trustworthy
2 installed
3 complaint
4 Anniversary
5 democracy
6 beloved
7 comets
8 canal
9 barren
10 constructive

Daily Test 2 P. 110

A

1 prejudice
2 realms
3 physiological
4 cones
5 dedicated
6 convicted
7 cope with
8 detached
9 representative
10 tender

Review Test 09

Day 17 + Day 18 P. 111

A

1 loose
2 masterpiece
3 glorious
4 execute
5 homeless
6 trustworthy
7 democracy
8 constructive
9 shortly
10 tariffs

B
1 빛나다
2 중세
3 오르다
4 낙천주의자
5 차고
6 설치하다
7 혜성
8 운하
9 편견
10 분리된

C
1 prejudice
2 mimic
3 barren
4 hay
5 garage

D
1 a
2 d
3 b
4 c
5 e

E
1 dedicate
2 explicit
3 apt
4 intimate
5 interrupt

해석

1. 나는 신문에 기사를 쓰는 데 많은 시간을 할애할 수 없어요.
2. 만약 당신이 토론 중이라면, 당신의 의도를 명확하게 하세요.
3. 그는 다른 사람들의 실수를 잘 기억한다.
4. 신뢰는 친밀한 관계에 가장 중요한 요소이다.
5. 저는 당신을 방해할 생각은 없지만 더 천천히 말할 수 있나요?

F
1 barren
2 classified
3 illuminated
4 legitimate
5 constructive

G
1 ④ cope
2 ② beloved
3 ⑤ representatives

해석

1. 우리는 그가 그 문제들을 지혜롭게 다룰 수 있을 거라고 믿는다.
남자와 여자의 가장 큰 차이 중 하나는 어떻게 그들이 스트레스를 다루는가이다.
2. 갑자기, 그는 그의 사랑하는 아내와 두 명의 아들이 보고 싶어졌다.
이것은 우리 모든 가족들이 좋아하는 노래 중 하나이다.
3. 서비스 대표자들은 생산품에 대한 많은 양의 지식을 구축할 것을 기대하고 있다.
두 나라의 대표들은 긴 회의 후에 형식적 동의를 얻었다.

Day 19

Daily Test 1 P. 117

A
1 Peel
2 navy
3 notorious
4 neglect
5 dissolve
6 outstanding
7 poisonous
8 liberate
9 dismiss
10 hydrogen

Daily Test 2 P. 119

A
1 poetic
2 navigated
3 disability
4 fist
5 Lately
6 harmonious
7 foretell
8 drills
9 motives
10 dissatisfied

Day 20

Daily Test 1 P. 121

A
1 bathe
2 thoughtful
3 outrageous
4 collide
5 Caterpillars
6 regulate
7 pollen
8 skeptical
9 comprehensive
10 compatible

Daily Test 2 P. 123

A
1 workout
2 progressive
3 vibrates
4 coverage
5 deadly
6 stroll
7 tutor
8 storage
9 span
10 profession

Review Test 10

Day 19 + Day 20 P. 124

A

1 navy
2 dissolve
3 halt
4 poetic
5 harmonious
6 contaminate
7 thoughtful
8 outrageous
9 compatible
10 steep

B

1 독이 있는
2 해방시키다
3 최근에
4 일부
5 불만스러워하는
6 뱉다
7 규제되다
8 떨리다
9 치명적인
10 직종

C

1 disposable
2 gossip
3 motive
4 collide
5 descend

D

1 c
2 a
3 e
4 d
5 b

E

1 peeled
2 stroll
3 compatible
4 frowns
5 dismissed

해석

1. Johnny는 오렌지 주스를 만들기 위해 오렌지를 깎았다.
2. 우리 조부모님은 아침에 공원을 산책하는 걸 좋아하신다.
3. 새로운 소프트웨어는 내 낡은 컴퓨터에 호환되지 않았다.
4. Elisa는 식당에서 형편없이 행동하는 아이들을 향해 눈살을 찌푸렸다.
5. Harry는 그의 에세이에 대해 친구들이 남긴 지적들을 묵살시켰다.

F

1 pollen
2 progressive
3 commonplace
4 immortal
5 notorious

G

1 ② disposable
2 ① neglected
3 ② outstanding

해석

1. 일회용 의료 용품의 사용은 성장하는 건강 보장 정책 문제의 분쟁을 도와 줄 것이다.
우리는 야외 점심 식사를 위해 약간의 일회용 컵과 접시를 살 것이다.
2. 내 연습 기간이 끝나기까지, 나는 의도적으로 모든 것에서부터 해방되었다.
저기 있는 빈 집은 수년 간 비어있었다.
3. 과학자로서, 그는 놀라운 성취를 이루었다.
그는 그가 사람들이 듣고자 하는 것을 잘 알기 때문에 훌륭한 연사가 되었다.

Day 21

Daily Test 1 P. 129

A

1 ivory
2 funerals
3 frauds
4 insurance
5 drought
6 exotic
7 germ
8 encyclopedia
9 effortless
10 irony

Daily Test 2 P. 131

A

1 fabulous
2 forbidden
3 Fossil
4 fiance
5 edible
6 gloomy
7 imaginary
8 blackout
9 explosion
10 feast

Day 22

Daily Test 1 P. 133

A

1 reign
2 quarrels
3 telescope
4 recollect
5 meditation
6 shallow

7 priceless
8 propelled
9 prohibited
10 resigned

Daily Test 2 P. 135

A
1 qualifications
2 pendulum
3 marvelous
4 resume
5 pods
6 portion
7 refreshed
8 memorable
9 leather
10 resemble

Review Test 11

Day 21 + Day 22 P. 136

A
1 insurance
2 fasten
3 fossil
4 edible
5 imaginary
6 explosion
7 shallow
8 meditation
9 pendulum
10 resume

B
1 장례식
2 가뭄
3 뛰어나다
4 약혼자
5 정전
6 연회
7 다투다
8 단조로운
9 숭고한
10 유치원

C
1 drought
2 edible
3 exotic
4 propel
5 resemble

D
1 d
2 e
3 c
4 a
5 b

E
1 disrupted
2 propelled
3 reign
4 marvelous
5 resembled

해석

1. 평화로운 의식이 한 무리에 시끄러운 아이들에 의해 방해 받았다.
2. 그 배는 증기 기관에 의해 나아갔다.
3. 친절한 왕의 통치 기간 동안, 사람들은 엄청난 자유를 즐겼다.
4. John은 박물관의 경이로운 그림들에 놀랐다.
5. Rogan은 그의 아버지를 정말 많이 닮았다.

F
1 qualifications
2 exotic
3 ethnic
4 gloomy
5 germ

G
1 ⑤ prohibited
2 ② forbidden
3 ② ethnic

해석

1. 여성이 과학 단체에 가입하는 것을 엄격하게 금하던 시절이 있었다.
흡연은 모든 Smithsonian 시설에서 금지됩니다.
2. 전시장에서 플래시를 키고 사진을 찍는 것은 금지됩니다.
많은 나라에서, 멸종 위기 종들을 낚시하는 것은 법에 의해 금지된다.
3. 그녀는 다양한 민족 배경을 지닌 한 무리의 사람들을 인터뷰했다.
아시아 음식 축제에서, 우리는 다양한 민족 음식을 먹을 수 있었다.

Day 23

Daily Test 1 P. 141

A
1 spine
2 Divorce
3 treatment
4 shortcut
5 applause
6 decode
7 ubiquitous
8 bundle
9 considerable
10 disclose

Daily Test 2 P. 143

A
1 supernatural
2 crushed
3 combat

4 uncertain
5 cucumbers
6 therapy
7 suspicious
8 clerk
9 summit
10 antique

Day 24

Daily Test 1 P. 145

A
1 hollow
2 magnets
3 linear
4 enforced
5 horizon
6 Eminent
7 asset
8 impair
9 incident
10 merchandise

Daily Test 2 P. 147

A
1 goodwill
2 guidance
3 harden
4 infamous
5 mighty
6 lifespan
7 glazed
8 gasped
9 Hatred / hatred
10 loyalty

Review Test 12

Day 23 + Day 24 P. 148

A
1 stationary
2 alley
3 applause
4 ubiquitous
5 bundle
6 supernatural
7 vice
8 cucumber
9 antique
10 enforce

B
1 뽐내다
2 파편
3 습한
4 지평선
5 손상시키다
6 사건
7 호의
8 단단하게 하다
9 수명
10 숨이 막히다

C
1 spine
2 antique
3 duplicate
4 boast
5 drift

D
1 d
2 a
3 c
4 b
5 e

E
1 shortcut
2 uncertain
3 disclose
4 decoding
5 swift

해석

1. 우리는 서둘러야 해요. 당신은 역까지 가는 지름길을 알고 있나요?
2. 그가 시장에 출마할지는 아직 확실하지 않다.
3. 기자는 누가 그에게 정보를 보냈는지 밝히는 것을 거절했다.
4. 프로그래머는 컴퓨터 파일의 이상한 상징을 해독하는데 성공했다.
5. 그는 초대를 받아들인다는 빠른 결정을 내렸다.

F
1 suspicious
2 shed
3 asset
4 instructive
5 eminent

G
1 ② summit
2 ④ combat
3 ① considerable

해석

1. 에베레스트 산 정상에 닿는 것은 한 때 놀라운 성취로 여겨졌다.
두 국가의 지도자들은 건강과 환경에 대한 국제 정상회담에서 만났다.
2. 몇몇 개발도상국들은 기후 변화의 단절을 위한 매력적인 생각들을 채택했다.
그 장군은 그의 모든 병사들을 몇몇의 분리된 분대로 나누어 구성했다.
3. 음악과 예술을 행하는 데 있어 컴퓨터의 역할은 점점 상당해지고 있다.
상당한 양의 노력이 당신이 생각하고 행동하는 방식을 바꾸는 데 필요하다.

Day 25

Daily Test 1 P. 153

A
1 spacecraft
2 pulse
3 soothing
4 outgoing
5 scoop
6 miniature
7 timid
8 mummy
9 sewing
10 sprained

Daily Test 2 P. 155

A
1 milestone
2 superstitions
3 tournament
4 sensible
5 nap
6 twinkle
7 resolution's
8 sympathy
9 needle
10 syndrome

Day 26

Daily Test 1 P. 157

A
1 ethical
2 blizzard
3 by chance
4 blink
5 unforgettable
6 combination
7 bomb
8 worshipped
9 warfare
10 Unbelievable

Daily Test 2 P. 159

A
1 committee
2 boycotting
3 aggressive
4 destructive
5 discouraged
6 are due to
7 wrinkles
8 critics
9 arbitrary
10 Bald

Review Test 13

Day 25 + Day 26 P. 160

A
1 spacecraft
2 pulse
3 staple
4 miniature
5 mummy
6 sprain
7 poll
8 nap
9 ethical
10 bomb

B
1 온도계
2 빛나다
3 잘 들리는
4 우연히
5 눈을 깜박이다
6 대사
7 위원회
8 의도적으로
9 주름
10 평론가

C
1 ascend
2 bold
3 staple
4 arbitrary
5 blizzard

D
1 b
2 e
3 a
4 c
5 d

E
1 prime
2 sensible
3 bold
4 treaty
5 seemingly

해석
1. 이것은 우리의 신상품을 광고할 최선의 기회이다.
2. 전화상으로 이런 중요한 이슈에 대해 토론하는 것은 합리적이지 않을지도 몰라요.
3. 그녀는 그들의 대담한 시도에 깊은 충격을 받았다.
4. 그 조약은 6개 참여 국들에게 서명 받았다.
5. 그는 겉보기에 그 약속에 대해 잊은 것 같다.

F
1 multicultural
2 aggressive

3 discourages
4 resolution
5 compelling

G
1 ② reconsider
2 ④ timid
3 ① due

해석

1. 우리 모두가 그 문제의 심각성을 재고하고 그에 대해 무언가 해야할 때에요.
기대치 않은 상황 때문에, 우리는 우리의 계획을 재고해야 했다.
2. 만약 당신의 고양이가 부끄럽고 소심하다면, 그 또는 그녀는 차려입고 고양이 쇼에 나서는 것을 원치 않을 것이다.
그는 낯선 사람으로부터 그의 얼굴을 돌려버리는 부끄러움 많은 소년이었다.
3. 많은 발 문제는 좁은 발과 하이힐을 포함한 착용감이 좋지 않은 신발 때문이다.
기차는 곧 역에 도착할 예정입니다.

Day 27

Daily Test 1 P. 165

A
1 mobile
2 tension
3 significantly
4 debut
5 cut down
6 fluent
7 consisted
8 marriage
9 fermented
10 figure out

Daily Test 2 P. 167

A
1 carry out
2 geology
3 evacuated
4 efficiency
5 famine
6 Congress
7 defective
8 creativity
9 craters
10 concluded

Day 28

Daily Test 1 P. 169

A
1 knight
2 insist on
3 insecure
4 pale
5 grief
6 gigantic
7 formal
8 misguided
9 industrious
10 humble

Daily Test 2 P. 171

A
1 intentional
2 intercepted
3 hub
4 In addition to
5 inactive
6 vendor
7 seldom
8 clay
9 shade
10 interfere with

Review Test 14

Day 27 + Day 28 P. 172

A
1 crocodile
2 tensions
3 curable
4 consist
5 geology
6 famine
7 congress
8 crater
9 insecure
10 gigantic

B
1 발효시키다
2 법의학적
3 효율
4 기발한
5 깊은 슬픔
6 공식적인
7 유충
8 계승자
9 찰흙
10 방해하다

C
1 crater
2 intercept
3 famine
4 seldom
5 tension

D
1 a
2 e
3 d
4 c
5 b

E
1 cut
2 figure
3 pale
4 defective
5 fluent

해석
1. 당신은 요리에 너무 소금을 많이 써요. 좀 줄이는 게 어때요?
2. 그들은 그 문제를 푸는 방법을 이해하지 못했다.
3. 그가 그 끔찍한 소식을 들었을 때, 그의 얼굴은 창백해졌다.
4. 그의 불완전한 시력에도 불구하고, Carl은 마침내 영화 감독이 되었다.
5. 그 어린 소녀는 이미 3개 국어에 능통하다.

F
1 demise
2 expelled
3 huddle
4 insisted on
5 evacuated

G
1 ① carry out
2 ② seldom
3 ③ in common

해석
1. Sandra, 걱정하지 마세요. 당신은 당신의 일을 성공적으로 수행할 거예요.
음주 운전을 막는 유일한 방법은 무작위로 음주 측정을 하는 것이다.
2. 나는 George를 더 이상 견딜 수 없어요. 그는 그의 말을 거의 지키지 않아요.
그가 집에서 먹는 것을 좋아하기 때문에, 그는 거의 식당에 가지 않는다.
3. 연구원들은 이런 성취가 높은 사람들이 공통으로 갖고 있는 점에 대해 연구하길 원했다.
재즈와 클래식 음악은 많은 공통점이 있다.

Day 29

Daily Test 1 P. 177

A
1 peril
2 rubbish
3 maze
4 marine
5 arrogant
6 notify
7 monk
8 pitiful
9 beneficial
10 put off

Daily Test 2 P. 179

A
1 mansions
2 masculine
3 misty
4 pebbles
5 open-minded
6 patent
7 memorial
8 pasted
9 Minister
10 monologue

Day 30

Daily Test 1 P. 181

A
1 barely
2 regardless of
3 slope
4 reptiles
5 Inflation
6 rapport
7 sow
8 speculate
9 repertoire
10 revolutionized

Daily Test 2 P. 183

A
1 throne
2 symbolized
3 misleading
4 tumble
5 talkative
6 obesity
7 scar
8 twilight
9 riot
10 renovate

Review Test 15

Day 29 + Day 30 P. 184

A
1 maze
2 marine
3 monarchy
4 beneficial
5 misty

6 slope
7 reptiles
8 sow
9 scar
10 throne

B
1 위험
2 쓰레기
3 측은한
4 대저택
5 조약돌
6 특허
7 끈적거리는
8 현대 최신
9 수다스러운
10 폭동

C
1 robber
2 marine
3 reptile
4 renovate
5 façade

D
1 d
2 e
3 a
4 b
5 c

E
1 regardless of
2 put off
3 turned down
4 revolves
5 pharmacy

해석

1. 그는 사람들을 그들의 직업과 상관없이 동등하게 대했다.
2. 그 경기는 나쁜 날씨로 인해 다음 주까지 연기 되었다.
3. 그는 그가 Gary를 믿지 못했기 때문에 그의 제안을 거절했다.
4. 달은 지구 주변을 돈다.
5. Tim, 약국에 가서 내 두통을 위한 약을 좀 사다 줄래?

F
1 renovated
2 malfunction
3 rapport
4 inflation
5 up to date

G
1 ⑤ speculate
2 ③ prominent
3 ① stumbled

해석

1. 연구원들은 두 현상간의 긴밀한 연결이 있음에 틀림없다고 알렸다.
우리는 정보가 없기 때문에 단지 그 사건의 원인에 대해서만 알릴 수 있다.
2. 원격 교육은 최근에 보습 교육 분야에서 중요해졌다.
그 저명한 학자는 그의 삶을 인간 심리 연구에 헌신했다.
3. 내가 일어나려고 애썼을 때, 나는 다시 발에 걸렸고 소파로 떨어졌다.
인터넷을 검색하던 도중에, 나는 우연히 잡지 'the economist'의 광고를 발견했다.

WORD MAX 4 5300

Workbook

WorldCom Edu

Workbook

WORD MAX 4 5300

WorldCom Edu

Workbook

Day 01

| 월 일 |

영어 단어에 해당하는 한국어 뜻을 함께 적으세요.

accord	일치; 일치하다	accord	일치; 일치하다
percentage	백분율		
emotional	감동적인, 정서의		
plea	애원, 간청		
continuous	계속되는, 끊임없는		
response	반응, 응답		
employ	고용하다		
means	수단, 방법		
term	용어, 기간		
run	경영하다, 운영하다		
experimental	실험의		
benefit	이점, 혜택; 유익하다		
attraction	명소, 매력		
competitive	경쟁의, 경쟁력 있는		
affection	애정		
condition	상태, 조건, 상황		
personal	개인의, 개인적인		
dependent	의존하는, 의지하는		
motivate	동기를 부여하다		
pressure	압박, 압력		
race	인종		
consequence	결과, 중요성		
efficiently	효율적으로, 능률적으로		
female	여성의		
instance	예, 사례		
react	반응하다		
concept	개념		
entire	전체의, 내내		
moral	도덕의, 도덕적인		
perhaps	아마, 어쩌면		

다음 단어에 해당하는 영어 단어 또는 우리말을 쓰세요.

O____개 X____개

영어	한국어
affection	
attraction	
benefit	
competitive	
concept	
condition	
consequence	
continuous	
dependent	
efficiently	
emotional	
employ	
entire	
experimental	
female	
instance	
means	
moral	
motivate	
percentage	
perhaps	
personal	
pressure	
race	
plea	
react	
response	
run	
accord	
term	

한국어	영어
명 일치 동 일치하다	
명 상태, 조건, 상황	
형 도덕의, 도덕적인	
형 개인의, 개인적인	
형 감동적인, 정서의	
명 개념	
명 애정	
형 의존하는, 의지하는	
명 백분율	
명 애원, 간청	
명 예, 사례	
동 고용하다	
동 동기를 부여하다	
형 실험의	
명 이점, 혜택 동 유익하다	
명 인종	
형 계속되는, 끊임없는	
명 압박, 압력	
명 반응, 응답	
명 결과, 중요성	
명 수단, 방법	
부 효율적으로, 능률적으로	
명 용어, 기간	
형 여성의	
형 전체의, 내내	
동 경영하다, 운영하다	
동 반응하다	
명 명소, 매력	
형 경쟁의, 경쟁력 있는	
부 아마, 어쩌면	

Workbook

Day 02

| 월 일 |

영어 단어에 해당하는 한국어 뜻을 함께 적으세요.

feature	특징	feature	특징
significant	중요한, 상당한		
throughout	내내, ~동안		
unite	통합하다, 단결하다		
assume	추정하다, 추측하다		
detailed	상세한		
following	그 다음의		
predict	예측하다, 예견하다		
concern	관심, 우려; 걱정시키다		
eventually	마침내, 결국		
further	더, 멀리, 추가의		
outcome	결과, 성과		
profit	이익, 수익		
reward	보상; 보상하다		
coexsit	공존하다		
essential	필수적인, 본질적인		
contribute	기증하다, 기여하다		
invest	투자하다		
limited	제한된		
claim	주장; 주장하다, 요구하다		
occasion	때, 행사		
generally	일반적으로, 대개, 보통		
accurate	정확한		
biology	생물학		
principle	원리, 원칙		
seek	찾다, 추구하다		
depart	출발하다, 떠나다		
myth	신화		
range	(변화, 차이, 거리의) 범위, 다양성		
attitude	태도		

다음 단어에 해당하는 영어 단어 또는 우리말을 쓰세요.

O____개 X____개

영어	한국어
feature	
accurate	
assume	
attitude	
biology	
claim	
concern	
contribute	
depart	
detailed	
essential	
eventually	
coexsit	
following	
further	
generally	
invest	
limited	
myth	
occasion	
outcome	
predict	
principle	
profit	
range	
reward	
seek	
significant	
throughout	
unite	

한국어	영어
명 결과, 성과	
형 필수적인, 본질적인	
동 추정하다, 추측하다	
부 더, 멀리, 추가의	
명 (변화, 차이, 거리의) 범위, 다양성	
부 마침내, 결국	
형 제한된	
명 관심, 우려 동 걱정시키다	
형 중요한, 상당한	
동 기증하다, 기여하다	
동 통합하다, 단결하다	
명 때, 행사	
동 예측하다, 예견하다	
명 신화	
전 내내, ~동안	
동 출발하다, 떠나다	
형 상세한	
동 투자하다	
명 특징	
부 일반적으로, 대개, 보통	
형 그 다음의	
명 원리, 원칙	
명 이익, 수익	
명 주장 동 주장하다, 요구하다	
동 공존하다	
명 태도	
명 보상 동 보상하다	
형 정확한	
동 찾다, 추구하다	
명 생물학	

Workbook

Day 03

| 월 일 |

영어 단어에 해당하는 한국어 뜻을 함께 적으세요.

contrast	대조, 차이; 대조하다, 대비되다	contrast	대조, 차이; 대조하다, 대비되다
aspect	측면, 양상		
entertain	즐겁게 하다, 접대하다		
frequent	잦은, 빈번한		
promote	승진 시키다, 홍보하다		
refer	언급하다, 참조하다, 나타내다		
capacity	능력, 수용력		
crop	농작물, 작물		
detect	발견하다, 탐지하다		
explanation	설명, 해설		
lack	부족; 부족하다, 결핍되다		
addition	추가, 덧셈		
advanced	선진의, 상급의		
factor	요인, 요소		
goods	상품, 물건		
manufacture	제조하다; 제조		
satisfaction	만족		
responsibility	책임, 책무		
analysis	분석		
demonstrate	입증하다, 시위하다		
completely	완전히, 전적으로		
environmental	환경의		
appeal	간청, 호소; 간청하다, 호소하다		
generation	세대, 시대		
operate	가동하다, 조작하다, 작동하다		
yield	수확(량), 생산; 산출하다, 생산하다		
accomplish	성취하다, 완수하다		
classic	일류의, 전형적인, 고전적인		
conscious	의식하는, 자각하는		
firm	기업, 회사; 단단한, 확고한		

다음 단어에 해당하는 영어 단어 또는 우리말을 쓰세요.

O____개 X____개

영어	한국어
contrast	
accomplish	
addition	
advanced	
analysis	
appeal	
aspect	
capacity	
classic	
completely	
conscious	
crop	
demonstrate	
detect	
entertain	
environmental	
explanation	
factor	
firm	
frequent	
generation	
goods	
lack	
manufacture	
operate	
promote	
refer	
responsibility	
satisfaction	
yield	

한국어	영어
동 제조하다 명 제조	
형 의식하는, 자각하는	
동 승진 시키다, 홍보하다	
명 분석	
동 즐겁게 하다, 접대하다	
동 언급하다, 참조하다, 나타내다	
부 완전히, 전적으로	
명 측면, 양상	
명 요인, 요소	
명 책임, 책무	
동 가동하다, 조작하다, 작동하다	
명 상품, 물건	
형 잦은, 빈번한	
명 농작물, 작물	
명 만족	
명 능력, 수용력	
형 선진의, 상급의	
명 추가, 덧셈	
동 성취하다, 완수하다	
동 발견하다, 탐지하다	
명 간청, 호소 동 간청하다, 호소하다	
동 입증하다, 시위하다	
명 설명, 해설	
명 세대, 시대	
명 대조, 차이 동 대조하다, 대비되다	
명 수확(량), 생산 동 산출하다, 생산하다	
명 부족 동 부족하다, 결핍되다	
형 환경의	
명 기업, 회사 형 단단한, 확고한	
형 일류의, 전형적인, 고전적인	

Workbook

Day 04

| 월 일 |

영어 단어에 해당하는 한국어 뜻을 함께 적으세요.

intelligence	지능	intelligence	지능
necessity	필요성, 필수품		
recall	상기하다, 기억해내다		
replace	교체하다, 대체하다		
adjust	조절하다, 적응하다		
contain	포함하다, 함유하다		
exception	예외, 제외		
frustrated	낙담한, 좌절한		
per	~마다		
practical	현실적인, 실용적인		
pursue	추구하다, 뒤쫓다		
relatively	비교적으로, 상대적인		
setting	환경, 배경		
academic	학업의, 학문적인		
citizen	시민		
exposure	노출		
inner	내면의, 내부의		
perceive	인식하다, 인지하다		
lawyer	변호사		
agriculture	농사, 농업		
conventional	전통적인, 관습적인		
directly	곧장, 직접적으로		
innovate	혁신		
mark	자국, 흔적; 표시하다		
objective	목적; 객관적인		
overall	종합적인		
rural	시골의, 지방의		
deplete	고갈시키다, 다 써버리다		
sort	종류; 분류하다		
acquire	습득하다, 얻다		

다음 단어에 해당하는 영어 단어 또는 우리말을 쓰세요.

O____개 X____개

영어	한국어
academic	
acquire	
adjust	
agriculture	
citizen	
contain	
conventional	
directly	
exception	
exposure	
frustrated	
inner	
innovate	
intelligence	
lawyer	
mark	
necessity	
objective	
overall	
per	
perceive	
practical	
pursue	
recall	
relatively	
replace	
rural	
setting	
deplete	
sort	

한국어	영어
형 내면의, 내부의	
명 노출	
명 예외, 제외	
명 변호사	
명 시민	
동 상기하다, 기억해내다	
동 인식하다, 인지하다	
동 고갈시키다, 다 써버리다	
명 지능	
부 곧장, 직접적으로	
형 학업의, 학문적인	
형 종합적인	
동 포함하다, 함유하다	
명 농사, 농업	
명 필요성, 필수품	
부 비교적으로, 상대적인	
형 전통적인, 관습적인	
전 ~마다	
명 혁신	
명 자국, 흔적 동 표시하다	
동 교체하다, 대체하다	
형 낙담한, 좌절한	
동 조절하다, 적응하다	
명 목적 형 객관적인	
형 현실적인, 실용적인	
명 종류 동 분류하다	
동 추구하다, 뒤쫓다	
형 시골의, 지방의	
명 환경, 배경	
동 습득하다, 얻다	

Workbook

Day 05

| 월 일 |

영어 단어에 해당하는 한국어 뜻을 함께 적으세요.

decade	10년간	decade	10년간
disaster	재앙, 재해		
equipment	장비, 기기		
extent	정도, 범위		
gender	성, 성별		
central	중앙의, 중심의		
content	내용물, 목차		
excessive	과도한, 지나친		
expand	확장하다, 확대하다		
instruction	지시, 교육, 교수		
mass	덩어리, 대량		
narration	서술, 화법		
reproduce	번식하다, 복제하다		
additional	추가의		
regarding	~에 관하여		
architecture	건축학, 건축양식		
convey	전달하다		
convince	납득시키다, 설득하다		
crucial	중대한, 결정적인		
generate	발생시키다, 일으키다		
identify	확인하다, 알아보다		
internal	내부의		
relation	관계		
struggle	투쟁하다, 분투하다		
phenomenon	현상		
colleague	동료		
be engaged in	~에 종사하고 있다		
delight	기쁨; 즐겁게 하다		
destruction	파괴, 파멸		
fundamental	근본적인, 기본적인		

다음 단어에 해당하는 영어 단어 또는 우리말을 쓰세요. O____개 X____개

영어	한국어
decade	
additional	
architecture	
be engaged in	
central	
colleague	
content	
convey	
convince	
crucial	
delight	
destruction	
disaster	
equipment	
excessive	
expand	
extent	
fundamental	
gender	
generate	
identify	
instruction	
internal	
mass	
narration	
phenomenon	
regarding	
relation	
reproduce	
struggle	

한국어	영어
형 중대한, 결정적인	
전 ~에 관하여	
형 근본적인, 기본적인	
명 건축학, 건축양식	
명 재앙, 재해	
명 기쁨 동 즐겁게 하다	
명 지시, 교육, 교수	
명 10년간	
명 장비, 기기	
형 추가의	
동 납득시키다, 설득하다	
형 중앙의, 중심의	
~에 종사하고 있다	
동 전달하다	
명 정도, 범위	
동 발생시키다, 일으키다	
명 성, 성별	
명 관계	
동 확장하다, 확대하다	
형 내부의	
형 과도한, 지나친	
동 확인하다, 알아보다	
명 내용물, 목차	
명 동료	
명 덩어리, 대량	
동 투쟁하다, 분투하다	
명 현상	
명 서술, 화법	
동 번식하다, 복제하다	
명 파괴, 파멸	

Workbook

Day 06

| 월 일 |

영어 단어에 해당하는 한국어 뜻을 함께 적으세요.

insight	통찰력	insight	통찰력
persuade	설득하다		
security	보안, 안전		
truly	정말로		
unexpected	예기치 않은, 예상 밖의		
attach	붙이다, 첨부하다		
barrier	장벽, 장애물		
ceremony	의식, 식		
dozen	12개짜리, 십여 개(명)		
import	수입하다		
nutritious	영양가 있는, 영양분이 높은		
insomnia	불면증		
pound	두드리다		
restrict	제한하다		
unpleasant	불쾌한		
Greek	그리스의		
law	법, 법률, 법칙		
meaningful	의미있는, 중요한		
absence	결석, 부재		
dramatic	극적인, 인상적인		
gradual	점진적인		
indicate	나타내다, 지적하다		
literature	문학		
discrete	별개의		
pace	속도, 발걸음		
political	정치적인, 정치의		
severe	극심한, 심각한		
statement	진술, 서술		
sustain	지속하다, 지탱하다		
trap	덫; 가두다		

다음 단어에 해당하는 영어 단어 또는 우리말을 쓰세요. O____개 X____개

영어	한국어
absence	
attach	
barrier	
ceremony	
dozen	
dramatic	
gradual	
Greek	
import	
indicate	
insight	
law	
literature	
meaningful	
nutritious	
discrete	
insomnia	
pace	
persuade	
political	
pound	
restrict	
security	
severe	
statement	
sustain	
trap	
truly	
unexpected	
unpleasant	

한국어	영어
형 그리스의	
명 통찰력	
명 결석, 부재	
형 예기치 않은, 예상 밖의	
명 법, 법률, 법칙	
명 진술, 서술	
동 설득하다	
형 의미 있는, 중요한	
명 보안, 안전	
형 극심한, 심각한	
부 정말로	
형 정치적인, 정치의	
형 영양가 있는, 영양분이 높은	
명 속도, 발걸음	
형 점진적인	
동 수입하다	
형 극적인, 인상적인	
명 장벽, 장애물	
형 불쾌한	
명 문학	
동 붙이다, 첨부하다	
동 나타내다, 지적하다	
명 12개짜리, 십여 개(명)	
동 제한하다	
명 의식, 식	
형 별개의	
동 두드리다	
명 불면증	
동 지속하다, 지탱하다	
명 덫 동 가두다	

Workbook

Day 07

| 월 일 |

영어 단어에 해당하는 한국어 뜻을 함께 적으세요.

wander	거닐다, 돌아다니다	wander	거닐다, 돌아다니다
commercial	상업적인		
merely	단지, 그저		
badly	심하게, 나쁘게		
biological	생물학의		
authority	권한, 권위		
category	범주, 부문, 종류		
celebration	축하, 기념		
cell	세포		
childhood	어린 시절, 유년기		
consult	상담하다		
cultivate	경작하다, 재배하다		
defense	방어, 방위, 수비		
emission	방출, 배출		
mess	엉망; 엉망으로 만들다		
physician	(내과) 의사		
random	무작위의, 임의의		
resistance	저항(력)		
sufficient	충분한		
verbal	말의, 구두의		
ancestor	조상		
burst into	갑자기 ~을 터뜨리다, 내뿜다		
counselor	상담원		
devote	헌신하다, 바치다		
fade	바래다, 천천히 사라지다		
hence	따라서, 그러므로		
frighten	놀라게하다, 무섭게하다		
grab	붙잡다, 움켜잡다		
grocery	식료품, 잡화점		
load	짐, 화물; 짐을 싣다		

다음 단어에 해당하는 영어 단어 또는 우리말을 쓰세요. O____개 X____개

영어	한국어
wander	
ancestor	
authority	
badly	
biological	
burst into	
category	
celebration	
cell	
childhood	
commercial	
consult	
counselor	
cultivate	
defense	
devote	
emission	
fade	
frighten	
grab	
grocery	
hence	
load	
merely	
mess	
physician	
random	
resistance	
sufficient	
verbal	

한국어	영어
동 거닐다, 돌아다니다	
명 (내과) 의사	
명 식료품, 잡화점	
동 붙잡다, 움켜잡다	
명 짐, 화물 동 짐을 싣다	
부 심하게, 나쁘게	
형 생물학의	
명 방어, 방위, 수비	
형 무작위의, 임의의	
형 상업적인	
부 단지, 그저	
명 상담원	
명 세포	
명 저항(력)	
명 권한, 권위	
명 축하, 기념	
형 충분한	
명 범주, 부문, 종류	
동 경작하다, 재배하다	
동 놀라게하다, 무섭게하다	
형 말의, 구두의	
명 어린 시절, 유년기	
부 따라서, 그러므로	
명 조상	
동 상담하다	
갑자기 ~을 터뜨리다, 내뿜다	
명 엉망 동 엉망으로 만들다	
동 헌신하다, 바치다	
명 방출, 배출	
동 바래다, 천천히 사라지다	

Workbook

Day 08

| 월 일 |

영어 단어에 해당하는 한국어 뜻을 함께 적으세요.

release	방출하다, 석방하다	release	방출하다, 석방하다
remarkable	놀라운, 주목할만한		
reverse	(정)반대의; 뒤바꾸다		
ritual	의식, 절차		
seal	봉(인)하다; 도장, 봉인		
settle	해결하다, 정착하다		
stimulate	자극하다, 촉진하다		
transform	바꾸다, 변형시키다		
translate	번역하다		
wheat	밀		
suffering	고통; 고통을 겪는		
enthusiasm	열광, 열정		
acknowledge	인정하다		
approximately	대략		
brilliant	훌륭한, 빛나는		
chase	뒤쫓다, 추구하다; 추적, 추구		
contract	계약(서); 계약하다		
desperate	절망적인, 필사적인		
disturb	방해하다		
edit	편집하다, 교정하다		
enormous	거대한, 막대한		
exhaust	기진맥진하게하다, 지치다		
external	외부의, 외관의		
likewise	똑같이, 마찬가지로		
metaphor	은유, 비유		
pause	잠시 멈추다; 멈춤		
phrase	구		
sequence	연속, 순서		
pasture	목초지		
output	생산량		

다음 단어에 해당하는 영어 단어 또는 우리말을 쓰세요. O___개 X___개

영어	한국어
acknowledge	
approximately	
brilliant	
chase	
contract	
desperate	
disturb	
edit	
enormous	
enthusiasm	
exhaust	
external	
likewise	
metaphor	
output	
pause	
phrase	
release	
remarkable	
reverse	
ritual	
seal	
sequence	
settle	
stimulate	
pasture	
suffering	
transform	
translate	
wheat	

한국어	영어
동 잠시 멈추다 명 멈춤	
동 방출하다, 석방하다	
형 훌륭한, 빛나는	
동 뒤쫓다, 추구하다 명 추적, 추구	
부 대략	
명 계약(서) 동 계약하다	
동 인정하다	
형 외부의, 외관의	
명 열광, 열정	
형 절망적인, 필사적인	
형 놀라운, 주목할만한	
형 (정)반대의 동 뒤바꾸다	
동 기진맥진하게 하다, 지치다	
동 방해하다	
명 고통 형 고통을 겪는	
형 거대한, 막대한	
동 봉(인)하다 명 도장, 봉인	
동 편집하다, 교정하다	
명 의식, 절차	
명 은유, 비유	
동 자극하다, 촉진하다	
부 똑같이, 마찬가지로	
동 해결하다, 정착하다	
명 연속, 순서	
동 번역하다	
명 구	
동 바꾸다, 변형시키다	
명 생산량	
명 밀	
명 목초지	

Workbook

Day 09

| 월 일 |

영어 단어에 해당하는 한국어 뜻을 함께 적으세요.

commitment	약속, 신념	commitment	약속, 신념
multiple	많은, 다수의; 배수		
vulnerable	취약한, 연약한		
correspond	일치하다, 부합하다		
enroll	등록하다, 입학하다		
export	수출하다; 수출		
imaginative	창의적인, 상상력이 풍부한		
launch	시작하다, 출시하다		
mine	채굴하다; 광산		
motion	움직임, 행동		
passage	한 절, 통로, (시간의)흐름		
register	등록하다, 신고하다		
scarce	부족한, 드문		
sensitive	민감한, 섬세한		
strategy	전략, 계획		
absolutely	절대적으로		
cognitive	인지의		
independent	독립적인		
leadership	지도력, 지도권		
instantly	즉각, 즉시		
be concerned about	~에 대해 걱정하다		
superior	우수한, 상급의		
surrounding	인근의, 주변의		
accompany	동반하다, 동행하다		
admit	인정하다, 입장을 허락하다		
appoint	임명하다, 지명하다		
attribute	~의 탓으로 돌리다; 자질, 속성		
complicated	복잡한		
deny	부인하다, 부정하다		
document	문서, 서류		

다음 단어에 해당하는 영어 단어 또는 우리말을 쓰세요.

O____개 X____개

영어	한국어
commitment	
absolutely	
accompany	
admit	
appoint	
attribute	
be concerned about	
cognitive	
complicated	
correspond	
deny	
document	
enroll	
export	
imaginative	
independent	
instantly	
launch	
leadership	
mine	
motion	
multiple	
passage	
register	
scarce	
sensitive	
strategy	
superior	
surrounding	
vulnerable	

한국어	영어
부 즉각, 즉시	
부 절대적으로	
동 인정하다, 입장을 허락하다	
명 약속, 신념	
형 인지의	
형 독립적인	
형 많은, 다수의 명 배수	
명 문서, 서류	
동 수출하다 명 수출	
형 복잡한	
명 지도력, 지도권	
형 취약한, 연약한	
동 등록하다, 입학하다	
형 인근의, 주변의	
동 일치하다, 부합하다	
~에 대해 걱정하다	
명 움직임, 행동	
동 부인하다, 부정하다	
형 창의적인, 상상력이 풍부한	
형 우수한, 상급의	
동 시작하다, 출시하다	
명 전략, 계획	
동 채굴하다 명 광산	
동 동반하다, 동행하다	
형 민감한, 섬세한	
동 임명하다, 지명하다	
명 한 절, 통로, (시간의)흐름	
동 ~의 탓으로 돌리다 명 자질, 속성	
동 등록하다, 신고하다	
형 부족한, 드문	

Day 10

| 월 일 |

영어 단어에 해당하는 한국어 뜻을 함께 적으세요.

steady	꾸준한, 지속적인	steady	꾸준한, 지속적인
fascinate	매료시키다, 황홀하게 하다		
sum	액수, 합계		
depression	우울증, 우울함		
skilled	숙련된, 능숙한		
overlook	간과하다, 눈감아주다		
eager	열망하는, 열심인		
ingredient	재료, 성분		
fate	운명		
remote	먼, 외딴		
moderate	적당한, 중도의		
carriage	마차, 객차		
endless	끝없는, 무한한		
resolve	해결하다, 결심하다		
scent	향기, 향내		
instinct	본능		
revenue	매출, 수입		
mutual	상호간의, 서로의		
obstacle	장애, 장애물		
requirement	필요 조건, 요구		
gravity	중력		
productive	생산하는, 생산적인, 이익을 내는		
aid	원조, 지원; 돕다		
surgery	수술		
reputation	평판, 명성		
conserve	보호하다, 절약하다		
caution	주의, 신중함		
profound	깊은, 심오한, 엄청난		
logic	논리, 타당성		
tone	어조, 말투		

다음 단어에 해당하는 영어 단어 또는 우리말을 쓰세요. O___개 X___개

영어	한국어
steady	
aid	
depression	
carriage	
caution	
conserve	
eager	
endless	
fascinate	
fate	
gravity	
ingredient	
instinct	
logic	
moderate	
mutual	
obstacle	
overlook	
productive	
profound	
remote	
reputation	
requirement	
resolve	
revenue	
scent	
skilled	
sum	
surgery	
tone	

한국어	영어
명 본능	
형 꾸준한, 지속적인	
동 해결하다, 결심하다	
명 매출, 수입	
형 끝없는, 무한한	
명 마차, 객차	
형 상호간의, 서로의	
동 매료시키다, 황홀하게 하다	
명 장애, 장애물	
형 적당한, 중도의	
명 원조, 지원 동 돕다	
명 액수, 합계	
명 필요 조건, 요구	
형 먼, 외딴	
명 중력	
명 우울증, 우울함	
형 생산하는, 생산적인, 이익을 내는	
명 논리, 타당성	
형 숙련된, 능숙한	
동 간과하다, 눈감아주다	
명 향기, 향내	
명 평판, 명성	
형 열망하는, 열심인	
명 수술	
형 깊은, 심오한, 엄청난	
명 재료, 성분	
명 운명	
동 보호하다, 절약하다	
명 주의, 신중함	
명 어조, 말투	

Workbook

Day 11

| 월 일 |

영어 단어에 해당하는 한국어 뜻을 함께 적으세요.

property	성질	property	성질
specialize	전공하다, 전문화하다		
plain	분명한; 평원		
reliable	믿을만한, 신뢰할만한		
soaked	흠뻑 젖은		
justify	정당화하다, 해명하다		
probability	가능성, 개연성		
widespread	광범위한		
minor	중요하지 않은, 가벼운		
administration	관리, 경영		
abandon	버리다		
institution	기관, 제도		
commit	저지르다, 범하다		
scholarship	장학금		
spell out	~을 간결하게 설명하다		
charity	자선, 자선단체		
screw	나사; 나사로 고정시키다		
assemble	모으다, 조립하다		
accessible	접근 할 수 있는		
comprehend	이해하다		
bury	묻다, 매장하다		
hop	깡충깡충 뛰다		
cooperation	협력, 협동		
underlying	근본적인, 기초를 이루는		
mood	분위기, 기분		
notion	개념, 생각		
capture	포로로 잡다, 포착하다		
reserve	예약하다		
deserve	~받을 만 하다		
Pacific	태평양의; 태평양		

다음 단어에 해당하는 영어 단어 또는 우리말을 쓰세요. O____개 X____개

영어	한국어
deserve	
abandon	
accessible	
administration	
assemble	
bury	
capture	
charity	
commit	
comprehend	
cooperation	
hop	
institution	
justify	
minor	
mood	
notion	
Pacific	
plain	
probability	
property	
reliable	
reserve	
scholarship	
screw	
soaked	
specialize	
spell out	
underlying	
widespread	

한국어	영어
명 성질	
명 나사 동 나사로 고정시키다	
형 태평양의 명 태평양	
명 자선, 자선단체	
명 가능성, 개연성	
동 ~받을 만 하다	
동 모으다, 조립하다	
동 전공하다, 전문화하다	
형 분명한 명 평원	
동 묻다, 매장하다	
형 접근 할 수 있는	
~을 간결하게 설명하다	
동 정당화하다, 해명하다	
동 이해하다	
동 포로로 잡다, 포착하다	
형 믿을만한, 신뢰할만한	
명 분위기, 기분	
명 장학금	
형 흠뻑 젖은	
동 예약하다	
형 광범위한	
동 깡총깡총 뛰다	
명 중요하지 않은, 가벼운	
명 협력, 협동	
명 기관, 제도	
명 관리, 경영	
동 버리다	
동 저지르다, 범하다	
형 근본적인, 기초를 이루는	
명 개념, 생각	

Workbook

Day 12 | 월 일 |

영어 단어에 해당하는 한국어 뜻을 함께 적으세요.

expertise	전문적 기술	expertise	전문적 기술
automobile	자동차		
outer	외부의		
ratio	비율, 비		
psychology	심리학, 심리		
suburb	교외		
flip	휙 뒤집다, ~을 튀기다; 툭 던지기		
facial	얼굴의		
altitude	고도		
commute	통근하다		
squeeze	짜다, 짜내다; (손으로) 꼭 짜기		
abstract	추상적인		
meanwhile	한편, 그 동안에		
violate	위반하다, 침해하다		
Renaissance	문예 부흥기, 르네상스		
license	면허, 허가; (공식적으로) 허가하다		
permit	허용하다; 허가		
procedure	절차, 과정		
elaborate	정교한, 공들인; 자세히 설명하다		
solitary	혼자 하는, 단독의, 혼자 사는		
offend	기분 상하게 하다, 법규를 위반하다		
fulfill	이루다, 이행하다		
paw	(동물의) 발		
cattle	(집합적으로) 소		
innocence	결백, 무죄		
invisible	보이지 않는, 볼 수 없는		
addict	(약물, 오락거리 등의) 중독자		
botanical	식물(학)의		
genre	장르, 유형		
stroke	발작, 타법, (수영 등의) 스트로크		

다음 단어에 해당하는 영어 단어 또는 우리말을 쓰세요.

O____개 X____개

영어	한국어
elaborate	
expertise	
facial	
flip	
fulfill	
genre	
innocence	
invisible	
license	
meanwhile	
offend	
outer	
paw	
permit	
procedure	
psychology	
ratio	
Renaissance	
solitary	
squeeze	
stroke	
suburb	
violate	
abstract	
addict	
altitude	
automobile	
botanical	
cattle	
commute	

한국어	영어
명 면허, 허가 동 (공식적으로) 허가하다	
명 발작, 타법, (수영 등의) 스트로크	
명 고도	
동 통근하다	
명 장르, 유형	
명 절차, 과정	
명 자동차	
명 (집합적으로) 소	
형 교외	
동 허용하다 명 허가	
명 심리학, 심리	
형 정교한, 공들인 동 자세히 설명하다	
동 이루다, 이행하다	
명 전문적 기술	
형 식물(학)의	
명 문예 부흥기, 르네상스	
형 외부의	
형 혼자 하는, 단독의, 혼자 사는	
동 휙 뒤집다, ~을 튀기다 명 툭 던지기	
형 얼굴의	
명 비율, 비	
동 기분 상하게 하다, 법규를 위반하다	
형 추상적인	
명 (약물, 오락거리 등의) 중독자	
동 짜다, 짜내다 명 (손으로) 꼭 짜기	
명 결백, 무죄	
명 (동물의) 발	
동 위반하다, 침해하다	
부 한편, 그 동안에	
형 보이지 않는, 볼 수 없는	

Workbook

Day 13

| 월 일 |

영어 단어에 해당하는 한국어 뜻을 함께 적으세요.

aroma	향기, 방향	aroma	향기, 방향
crew	선원, 승무원		
vague	희미한, 막연한, 모호한		
toxic	유독성의		
reminder	상기시키는 것, 독촉장, 기념품		
spark	불꽃, 불똥; 촉발시키다, 유발하다		
molecule	분자		
depth	깊이		
misunderstanding	오해		
hesitate	망설이다, 주저하다		
opponent	반대의; 상대		
nevertheless	그럼에도 불구하고		
possession	소유, 재산		
military	군대; 군대의		
hormone	호르몬		
broad	넓은		
compliment	칭찬; 칭찬하다		
respectively	각자, 제각기		
heal	치유되다, 치유하다		
scout	정찰하다, 찾아내다; 정찰		
approve	찬성하다, 승인하다		
credit	신용, 학점		
lifestyle	생활 방식, 습관		
endure	견디다		
thorough	철저한, 완전한		
browse	둘러보다, 훑어보다		
flexible	유연한, 융통성 있는		
identical	동일한, 똑같은		
bounce	튀다, 튀기다		
useless	소용없는, 쓸모 없는		

다음 단어에 해당하는 영어 단어 또는 우리말을 쓰세요. O___개 X___개

영어	한국어
compliment	
credit	
crew	
endure	
flexible	
heal	
hesitate	
hormone	
identical	
lifestyle	
military	
misunderstanding	
molecule	
nevertheless	
opponent	
possession	
reminder	
respectively	
scout	
spark	
depth	
thorough	
toxic	
useless	
vague	
approve	
aroma	
bounce	
broad	
browse	

한국어	영어
명 향기, 방향	
형 넓은	
명 호르몬	
형 유연한, 융통성 있는	
형 소용없는, 쓸모 없는	
명 군대 형 군대의	
명 칭찬 동 칭찬하다	
명 상기시키는 것, 독촉장, 기념품	
형 동일한, 똑같은	
동 망설이다, 주저하다	
동 튀다, 튀기다	
명 선원, 승무원	
형 철저한, 완전한	
형 희미한, 막연한	
명 소유, 재산	
부 각자, 제각기	
명 분자	
동 치유되다, 치유하다	
동 찬성하다, 승인하다	
형 유독성의	
동 정찰하다, 찾아내다 명 정찰	
명 불꽃, 불똥 동 촉발시키다, 유발하다	
동 견디다	
명 신용, 학점	
명 깊이	
명 오해	
명 생활 방식, 습관	
형 반대의 명 상대, 적수, 반대자	
부 그럼에도 불구하고	
동 둘러보다, 훑어보다	

Workbook

Day 14 | 월 일 |

영어 단어에 해당하는 한국어 뜻을 함께 적으세요.

religious	종교의	religious	종교의
bush	덤불, 관목		
romantic	낭만적인, 공상적인		
evident	분명한, 명백한		
roast	굽다, 볶다		
bunch	다발, 송이		
sour	신, 시큼한		
oral	구두의, 입의		
distraction	집중을 방해하는 것, 주의 산만		
scatter	흩뿌리다, 흩어지다		
faith	믿음, 신념, 신앙(심)		
drown	익사하다, 물에 빠지다		
crime	범죄		
counter	계산대, 판매대		
pesticide	살충제, 농약		
conform	순응하다, 일치하다		
nerve	신경		
persistent	끊임없는, 끈질긴		
session	기간, 회의, 개정		
portray	묘사하다		
beverage	음료		
innate	타고난, 선천적인		
rectangular	직사각형의		
rear	뒤쪽		
inferior	하급의, 질 낮은		
manual	사용 설명서; 수동의		
conference	회의, 회견, 학회		
adversity	역경, 재난		
cease	중단하다, 그치다		
transaction	거래, 매매		

다음 단어에 해당하는 영어 단어 또는 우리말을 쓰세요.

O____개 X____개

영어	한국어
bunch	
cease	
conference	
conform	
counter	
crime	
distraction	
drown	
evident	
faith	
innate	
manual	
nerve	
oral	
persistent	
pesticide	
portray	
rear	
rectangular	
religious	
roast	
romantic	
scatter	
session	
sour	
transaction	
inferior	
adversity	
beverage	
bush	

한국어	영어
명 음료	
명 거래, 매매	
명 덤불, 관목	
동 순응하다, 일치하다	
동 중단하다, 그치다	
동 묘사하다	
명 신경	
명 기간, 회의, 개정	
동 흩뿌리다, 흩어지다	
형 끊임없는, 끈질긴	
형 타고난, 선천적인	
형 종교의	
명 집중을 방해하는 것, 주의 산만	
형 낭만적인, 공상적인	
명 뒤쪽	
형 분명한, 명백한	
명 회의, 회견, 학회	
형 직사각형의	
동 굽다, 볶다	
명 믿음, 신념, 신앙(심)	
명 다발, 송이	
명 살충제, 농약	
형 신, 시큼한	
형 하급의, 질 낮은	
명 계산대, 판매대	
형 구두의, 입의	
명 사용 설명서 형 수동의	
명 범죄	
동 익사하다, 물에 빠지다	
명 역경, 재난	

Workbook

Day 15 | 월 일 |

영어 단어에 해당하는 한국어 뜻을 함께 적으세요.

craft	수공예, 기술	craft	수공예, 기술
console	위로하다, 위안을 주다		
modify	수정하다		
naked	벌거벗은		
fragile	깨지기 쉬운, 취약한		
maintenance	유지, 보수		
on behalf of	~을 대신(대표)하여		
infer	추론하다, 뜻하다		
incorrect	부정확한, 틀린		
persuasive	설득력 있는		
plot	줄거리, 계략; ~을 계획하다		
orchard	과수원		
passionate	열정적인		
delicate	정교한, 섬세한, 미묘한		
container	용기, 그릇		
pitch	소리의 높이		
overwhelm	압도하다		
certainty	확실(성), 확신		
groom	신랑		
hook	갈고리, 걸이; 연결하다		
multiply	곱하다		
deadline	마감일, 최종 기한		
freshman	신입생, 1학년		
currency	통화, 화폐		
limitation	한계, 제한		
measurable	잴 수 있는, 주목할 만한		
fairly	꽤, 공정하게		
forehead	이마		
exaggerate	과장하다		
immune	면역의, 면역이 된		

다음 단어에 해당하는 영어 단어 또는 우리말을 쓰세요.

O____개 X____개

영어	한국어
certainty	
console	
container	
craft	
currency	
deadline	
delicate	
exaggerate	
fairly	
forehead	
fragile	
freshman	
groom	
hook	
immune	
incorrect	
infer	
limitation	
maintenance	
measurable	
modify	
multiply	
naked	
on behalf of	
orchard	
overwhelm	
passionate	
persuasive	
pitch	
plot	

한국어	영어
명 확실(성), 확신	
형 벌거벗은	
명 이마	
명 소리의 높이	
명 수공예, 기술	
동 수정하다	
동 압도하다	
형 면역의, 면역이 된	
동 위로하다, 위안을 주다	
형 잴 수 있는, 주목할 만한	
형 깨지기 쉬운, 취약한	
부 꽤, 공정하게	
~을 대신(대표)하여	
명 신랑	
명 용기, 그릇	
명 유지, 보수	
명 갈고리, 걸이 동 연결하다	
형 설득력 있는	
동 곱하다	
형 부정확한, 틀린	
동 추론하다, 뜻하다	
명 줄거리, 계략 동 ~을 계획하다	
명 마감일, 최종 기한	
명 통화, 화폐	
명 과수원	
형 열정적인	
명 신입생, 1학년	
동 과장하다	
명 한계, 제한	
형 정교한, 섬세한, 미묘한	

Workbook

Day 16

| 월 일 |

영어 단어에 해당하는 한국어 뜻을 함께 적으세요.

deposit	예금, 보증금; 예금(예치)하다	deposit	예금, 보증금; 예금(예치)하다
compassion	연민, 동정심		
costly	값이 비싼		
shrink	줄다, 줄어들게 하다		
dwell	살다, 거주하다		
eclipse	(일식, 월식의) 식		
democratic	민주적인		
concentration	집중, 농축		
carve	조각하다, 깎아서 만들다		
candidate	후보자		
shore	해안, 호숫가		
embrace	포용하다, 받아들이다		
thread	실; 실을 꿰다		
subjective	주관적인		
breakdown	고장, 쇠약, (기계, 차 등의) 고장		
despair	절망, 좌절; 절망하다, 체념하다		
grumble	투덜거리다		
economics	경제학		
priority	우선 순위 , 우선권		
coax	구슬리다, 달래다		
cushion	등 받침, 방석		
dental	치과의		
circuit	순환, 순회		
cheek	볼, 뺨		
dynamic	역동적인, 활발한		
privilege	특권, 특혜		
yawn	하품하다; 하품		
consonant	자음		
render	(어떤 상태가 되게) 만들다		
dye	염색하다		

다음 단어에 해당하는 영어 단어 또는 우리말을 쓰세요.

O____개 X____개

영어	한국어	한국어	영어
grumble		동 염색하다	
priority		명 특권, 특혜	
privilege		명 연민, 동정심	
shore		형 역동적인, 활발한	
shrink		동 (어떤 상태가 되게) 만들다	
coax		형 값이 비싼	
subjective		명 예금, 보증금 동 예금(예치)하다	
thread		명 볼, 뺨	
render		명 자음	
yawn		동 줄다, 줄어들게 하다	
breakdown		형 치과의	
candidate		명 집중, 농축	
carve		동 살다, 거주하다	
cheek		명 우선 순위 , 우선권	
circuit		명 (일식, 월식의) 식	
compassion		명 경제학	
concentration		형 민주적인	
consonant		명 절망, 좌절 동 절망하다, 체념하다	
costly		형 주관적인	
cushion		명 고장, 쇠약, (기계, 차 등의) 고장	
democratic		명 등 받침, 방석	
dental		명 실 동 실을 꿰다	
deposit		명 후보자	
despair		동 투덜거리다	
dwell		명 해안, 호숫가	
dye		명 순환, 순회	
dynamic		동 포용하다, 받아들이다	
eclipse		동 조각하다, 깎아서 만들다	
economics		동 하품하다 명 하품	
embrace		동 구슬리다, 달래다	

Workbook

Day 17

| 월 일 |

영어 단어에 해당하는 한국어 뜻을 함께 적으세요.

glow	(은은히) 빛나다, 타다; 부드러운 빛	glow	(은은히) 빛나다, 타다; 부드러운 빛
legitimate	타당한, 정당한		
motor	모터, 전동기, 발동기; 자동차의		
explicit	노골적인, 명백한		
loose	느슨해진, 헐렁한, (흙 등이) 단단하지 않은		
medieval	중세의		
illuminate	조명하다, 밝게 비추다		
masterpiece	걸작, 명작		
initiative	(목적 달성을 위한 새로운) 계획		
knot	매듭, 무리		
glorious	영광스러운		
mount	오르다, 시작하다; 산		
laundry	세탁물, 세탁, 빨래		
merit	장점, 이점, 가치; (칭찬, 관심 등을) 받을 만하다		
miserable	비참한, 고달픈		
optimist	낙관론, 낙천주의자		
framework	틀, 구조, 체계		
gum	껌, 잇몸		
execute	실시하다, 처형하다		
garage	차고, 주차장		
fierce	치열한, 사나운		
interrupt	가로막다, 중단시키다		
mad	미친, 몹시 화가 난		
homeless	집이 없는		
inward	안쪽으로; 내부의		
orbit	(천체, 인공 위성 등의) 궤도		
mimic	흉내 내다; 모방의, 모의의		
intimate	친밀한		
empathy	감정이입, 공감		
hay	건초		

다음 단어에 해당하는 영어 단어 또는 우리말을 쓰세요.

O____개 X____개

영어	한국어
empathy	
execute	
explicit	
fierce	
framework	
garage	
glorious	
glow	
gum	
hay	
homeless	
illuminate	
initiative	
interrupt	
intimate	
inward	
knot	
laundry	
legitimate	
loose	
mad	
masterpiece	
medieval	
merit	
mimic	
miserable	
motor	
mount	
optimist	
orbit	

한국어	영어
명 건초	
명 낙관론, 낙천주의자	
형 비참한, 고달픈	
명 틀, 구조, 체계	
형 타당한, 정당한	
동 실시하다, 처형하다	
명 장점, 이점, 가치 동 (칭찬, 관심 등을) 받을 만하다	
동 빛나다 명 부드러운 빛	
명 껌, 잇몸	
동 오르다, 시작하다 명 산	
명 감정이입, 공감	
명 모터, 전동기, 발동기 형 자동차의	
형 영광스러운	
명 차고, 주차장	
명 세탁물, 세탁, 빨래	
형 치열한, 사나운	
형 노골적인, 명백한	
명 매듭, 무리	
동 가로막다, 중단시키다	
형 느슨해진, 헐렁한, (흙 등이) 단단하지 않은	
동 흉내 내다 형 모방의, 모의의	
형 중세의	
동 조명하다, 밝게 비추다	
형 미친, 몹시 화가 난	
형 집이 없는	
명 걸작, 명작	
명 (목적 달성을 위한 새로운) 계획	
명 (천체, 인공 위성 등의) 궤도	
형 친밀한	
부 안쪽으로 형 내부의	

Workbook

Day 18

| 월 일 |

영어 단어에 해당하는 한국어 뜻을 함께 적으세요.

trustworthy	신뢰할 수 있는	trustworthy	신뢰할 수 있는
install	설치하다		
packet	통, 소포, 꾸러미		
toll	통행료; 종을 울리다		
complaint	불평, 불만		
anniversary	기념일		
democracy	민주주의		
beloved	가장 사랑하는, 소중한		
comet	혜성		
stove	(특정한 일, 계획이 있는) 시기		
canal	운하, 수로		
catalogue	목록, 카탈로그		
classify	분류하다		
barren	척박한, 황량한		
constructive	건설적인		
anchor	닻; 닻을 내리다		
chin	턱		
prejudice	편견		
realm	영역, 범위		
physiological	생리학의, 생리적인		
shortly	곧, 즉시		
apt	~하기 쉬운		
tariff	관세		
cone	원뿔, 솔방울		
dedicate	헌신하다, 바치다		
convict	유죄를 선고하다		
cope with	~에 대처하다, 대응하다		
detach	떼다, 분리하다		
representative	대표(자), 대리인; 대표하는, 전형적인		
tender	상냥한, 부드러운, 약한		

다음 단어에 해당하는 영어 단어 또는 우리말을 쓰세요. O____개 X____개

영어	한국어
packet	
install	
physiological	
prejudice	
realm	
representative	
shortly	
stove	
tender	
toll	
trustworthy	
anchor	
anniversary	
apt	
barren	
beloved	
canal	
catalogue	
chin	
classify	
tariff	
comet	
complaint	
cone	
constructive	
convict	
cope with	
dedicate	
democracy	
detach	

한국어	영어
형 상냥한, 부드러운, 약한	
동 떼다, 분리하다	
동 분류하다	
명 턱	
명 관세	
명 목록, 카탈로그	
명 닻 동 닻을 내리다	
형 척박한, 황량한	
명 운하, 수로	
명 편견	
동 ~에 대처하다, 대응하다	
형 신뢰할 수 있는	
명 영역, 범위	
형 건설적인	
형 생리학의, 생리적인	
명 통, 소포, 꾸러미	
형 ~하기 쉬운	
명 통행료 동 종을 울리다	
명 (특정한 일, 계획이 있는) 시기	
부 곧, 즉시	
명 불평, 불만	
동 유죄를 선고하다	
동 설치하다	
명 원뿔, 솔방울	
명 기념일	
명 혜성	
명 민주주의	
형 가장 사랑하는, 소중한	
명 대표(자), 대리인 형 대표하는, 전형적인	
동 헌신하다, 바치다	

Day 19

| 월 일 |

영어 단어에 해당하는 한국어 뜻을 함께 적으세요.

peel	껍질을 벗기다	peel	껍질을 벗기다
navy	해군; 남색의		
notorious	악명 높은		
neglect	등한시하다, ~을 무시하다		
dissolve	녹이다, 해산하다		
outstanding	두드러진, 뛰어난		
poisonous	독이 있는, 유독의		
gossip	소문, 수다		
liberate	해방시키다		
grace	우아함, 품위, 예의		
frown	눈살을 찌푸리다		
dismiss	무시하다, 해고하다		
leftover	나머지, 잔여		
halt	멈추다; 중단		
hydrogen	수소		
poetic	시의		
navigate	항해하다, 길을 찾다		
disability	장애		
fist	주먹		
lately	요즘, 최근에		
even	평평한, 고른		
harmonious	조화로운, 화목한		
faculty	능력, 재능, (대학의) 학부, 교수단		
foretell	예언하다		
immortal	불멸의, 불후의		
disposable	일회용의; 일회용품		
drill	연습, 훈련; 연습시키다		
fraction	부분, 일부		
motive	동기		
dissatisfied	불만스러워하는		

다음 단어에 해당하는 영어 단어 또는 우리말을 쓰세요. O___개 X___개

영어	한국어
disability	
dismiss	
disposable	
dissatisfied	
dissolve	
drill	
even	
faculty	
fist	
foretell	
fraction	
frown	
gossip	
grace	
halt	
harmonious	
hydrogen	
immortal	
lately	
leftover	
liberate	
motive	
navigate	
navy	
neglect	
notorious	
outstanding	
peel	
poetic	
poisonous	

한국어	영어
형 시의	
동 항해하다, 길을 찾다	
동 해방시키다	
명 능력, 재능, (대학의) 학부, 교수단	
형 불만스러워하는	
명 해군 형 남색의	
명 장애	
형 조화로운, 화목한	
동 껍질을 벗기다	
명 주먹	
명 소문, 수다	
부 요즘, 최근에	
형 악명 높은	
동 등한시하다, ~을 무시하다	
명 수소	
동 녹이다, 해산하다	
형 평평한, 고른	
형 두드러진, 뛰어난	
형 독이 있는, 유독의	
동 예언하다	
명 우아함, 품위, 예의	
명 부분, 일부	
형 불멸의, 불후의	
동 눈살을 찌푸리다	
형 일회용의 명 일회용품	
동 무시하다, 해고하다	
동 멈추다 명 중단	
명 나머지, 잔여	
명 연습, 훈련 동 연습시키다	
명 동기	

Workbook

Day 20 | 월 일 |

영어 단어에 해당하는 한국어 뜻을 함께 적으세요.

spit	뱉다; 침, 침 뱉기	spit	뱉다; 침, 침 뱉기
blast	폭발, 한 바탕 부는 바람; 폭파하다		
contaminate	오염시키다		
bathe	목욕하다, 세척하다		
thoughtful	사려 깊은, 생각이 깊은		
outrageous	너무나 충격적인, 터무니없는		
undo	풀다, 원상태로 돌리다		
collide	충돌하다, 부딪히다		
caterpillar	애벌레		
regulate	규제하다, 조절하다		
pollen	꽃가루, 화분		
skeptical	회의적인, 의심많은		
comprehensive	포괄적인, 종합적인		
commonplace	아주 흔한, 평범한		
compatible	호환이 되는, 양립될 수 있는		
suspect	의심하다; 혐의자, 용의자		
workout	운동, 연습		
progressive	진보적인, 점진적인		
vibrate	떨리다, 흔들리다		
coverage	보도(방송)		
province	지방, 분야		
steep	가파른		
deadly	치명적인; 극도로		
stroll	거닐다, 산책하다; 산책		
descend	내려오다, 내려가다		
tutor	가정교사		
storage	저장(소), 보관(소)		
bilingual	두 나라 말을 사용하는		
span	기간, 전 범위		
profession	직업, 직종		

다음 단어에 해당하는 영어 단어 또는 우리말을 쓰세요. O___개 X___개

영어	한국어
pollen	
profession	
progressive	
province	
outrageous	
skeptical	
span	
spit	
storage	
stroll	
suspect	
thoughtful	
tutor	
undo	
vibrate	
workout	
bathe	
bilingual	
blast	
caterpillar	
regulate	
collide	
commonplace	
compatible	
steep	
comprehensive	
contaminate	
coverage	
deadly	
descend	

한국어	영어
형 진보적인, 점진적인	
명 폭발, 한 바탕 부는 바람 동 폭파하다	
명 운동, 연습	
동 의심하다	
동 뱉다 명 침, 침 뱉기	
동 떨리다, 흔들리다	
동 목욕하다, 세척하다	
동 오염시키다	
명 지방, 분야	
명 보도(방송)	
형 사려 깊은, 생각이 깊은	
형 호환이 되는, 양립할 수 있는	
형 가파른	
형 너무나 충격적인, 터무니없는	
형 치명적인 부 극도로	
동 풀다, 원상태로 돌리다	
명 직업, 직종	
명 애벌레	
동 충돌하다, 부딪히다	
동 거닐다, 산책하다 명 산책	
동 내려오다, 내려가다	
동 규제하다, 조절하다	
명 저장(소), 보관(소)	
명 가정교사	
형 회의적인, 의심많은	
명 꽃가루, 화분	
형 두 나라 말을 사용하는	
형 포괄적인, 종합적인	
명 기간, 전 범위	
형 아주 흔한, 평범한	

Workbook

Day 21

| 월 일 |

영어 단어에 해당하는 한국어 뜻을 함께 적으세요.

fertilize	수정시키다, 땅을 비옥하게 하다	fertilize	수정시키다, 땅을 비옥하게 하다
ivory	상아, 상아색; 상아로 만든		
funeral	장례식		
fraud	사기		
insurance	보험		
drought	가뭄		
excel	뛰어나다, 두드러지다		
exotic	이국적인		
fasten	매다, 고정시키다		
disrupt	~을 혼란시키다, 해치다		
germ	세균		
encyclopedia	백과사전		
flatter	아첨하다		
effortless	쉬운, 노력이 필요 없는		
irony	모순, 예상외의 결과		
fabulous	(아주)멋진, 재미있는		
forbid	금지하다		
glamorous	매력적인, 화려한		
fossil	화석		
fiance	약혼자		
edible	식용의, 먹을 수 있는		
grind	갈다, 빻다		
entail	수반하다, 필요로 하다, 의미하다		
ethnic	민족의, 인종의		
gloomy	우울한, 비관적인		
imaginary	상상의, 가상적인		
blockbuster	블록버스터, 대작		
blackout	정전, 소등		
explosion	폭발, 급증		
feast	축제, 연회, 진수성찬		

다음 단어에 해당하는 영어 단어 또는 우리말을 쓰세요. O____개 X____개

영어	한국어
disrupt	
drought	
edible	
effortless	
encyclopedia	
entail	
ethnic	
excel	
exotic	
explosion	
fabulous	
fasten	
feast	
fertilize	
fiance	
flatter	
forbid	
blackout	
fossil	
fraud	
funeral	
germ	
glamorous	
gloomy	
grind	
imaginary	
blockbuster	
insurance	
irony	
ivory	

한국어	영어
명 화석	
명 약혼자	
형 (아주)멋진, 재미있는	
명 폭발, 급증	
동 금지하다	
동 수정시키다, 땅을 비옥하게 하다	
명 축제, 연회, 진수성찬	
형 매력적인, 화려한	
명 상아, 상아색 형 상아로 만든	
명 가뭄	
명 정전, 소등	
명 모순, 예상외의 결과	
명 블록버스터, 대작	
명 장례식	
형 식용의, 먹을 수 있는	
동 매다, 고정시키다	
동 갈다, 빻다	
명 사기	
명 보험	
동 뛰어나다, 두드러지다	
형 쉬운, 노력이 필요 없는	
동 아첨하다	
형 이국적인	
동 수반하다, 필요로 하다	
명 백과사전	
형 우울한, 비관적인	
동 ~을 혼란시키다, 해치다	
형 민족의, 인종의	
명 세균	
형 상상의, 가상적인	

Workbook

Day 22 | 월 일 |

영어 단어에 해당하는 한국어 뜻을 함께 적으세요.

reign	군림하다, 통치하다; 통치(기간)	reign	군림하다, 통치하다; 통치(기간)
quarrel	다툼, 언쟁; 다투다		
telescope	망원경		
recollect	기억하다, 회상하다		
literate	글을 읽고 쓸 줄 아는		
shallow	얕은		
meditation	명상, 묵상		
trade	거래하다, 무역하다		
monotonous	단조로운		
priceless	값을 매길 수 없는, 대단히 귀중한		
propel	나아가게 하다, 추진하다		
prohibit	금하다, 금지하다		
port	항구		
resign	물러나다, 사임하다		
crunch	아작아작 씹다		
qualification	(주로 복수형으로) 자격(증), 자질		
lantern	초롱, 호롱불, 손전등		
pendulum	(시계의) 추, 진자		
noble	고귀한, 숭고한		
resume	다시 시작하다, 재개하다		
pod	꼬투리; 껍질을 벗기다		
portion	부분, 일부		
kindergarten	유치원		
ladder	사다리		
prospective	장래의, 유망한		
marvelous	놀라운, 믿기 어려운		
refresh	상쾌하게하다, 재충전하다		
memorable	기억할만한, 주목할만한		
leather	가죽, 가죽상품		
resemble	닮다		

다음 단어에 해당하는 영어 단어 또는 우리말을 쓰세요.

O____개 X____개

영어	한국어
kindergarten	
telescope	
ladder	
lantern	
leather	
literate	
marvelous	
meditation	
memorable	
monotonous	
trade	
pendulum	
pod	
port	
portion	
crunch	
priceless	
prohibit	
propel	
prospective	
qualification	
quarrel	
noble	
recollect	
refresh	
reign	
resemble	
resign	
resume	
shallow	

한국어	영어
명 조롱, 호롱불, 손전등	
명 가죽, 가죽상품	
명 (주로 복수형으로) 자격(증), 자질	
동 닮다	
명 망원경	
명 (시계의) 추, 진자	
형 기억할만한, 주목할만한	
형 고귀한, 숭고한	
명 다툼, 언쟁 동 다투다	
동 상쾌하게하다, 재충전하다	
동 다시 시작하다, 재개하다	
동 군림하다, 통치하다 명 통치(기간)	
동 기억하다, 회상하다	
명 꼬투리 동 껍질을 벗기다	
동 금하다, 금지하다	
명 명상, 묵상	
형 얕은	
명 부분, 일부	
형 글을 읽고 쓸 줄 아는	
명 유치원	
명 사다리	
동 거래하다, 무역하다	
동 아작아작 씹다	
형 단조로운	
형 장래의, 유망한	
동 나아가게 하다, 추진하다	
형 값을 매길 수 없는, 대단히 귀중한	
형 놀라운, 믿기 어려운	
명 항구	
동 물러나다, 사임하다	

Workbook

Day 23 | 월 일 |

영어 단어에 해당하는 한국어 뜻을 함께 적으세요.

affair	일, 문제	affair	일, 문제
spine	척추, 등뼈		
divorce	이혼; 이혼하다		
treatment	치료, 치유		
stationary	움직이지 않는, 고정된		
alley	골목, 통로		
shortcut	지름길		
applause	박수 갈채		
decode	번역하다, 해독하다, 이해하다		
drainage	배수(시설)		
shed	흘리다, 떨구다		
ubiquitous	어디에나 있는, 아주 흔한		
bundle	꾸러미, 보따리		
considerable	상당한, 많은		
disclose	폭로하다, 공개하다		
supernatural	초자연적인		
crush	으깨다, 찧다		
combat	전투; 싸우다, 맞서다		
vice	악덕, 부도덕, 비행		
boast	자랑하다, 뽐내다		
uncertain	불확실한, 불투명한		
swift	신속한, 재빠른		
cucumber	오이		
debris	잔해, 파편		
therapy	치료, 요법		
suspicious	의심스러운		
clerk	점원, 사무원		
summit	산 꼭대기, 정상회담		
antique	골동품; 옛날의		
straightforward	간단한, 솔직한		

다음 단어에 해당하는 영어 단어 또는 우리말을 쓰세요.

O____개 X____개

영어	한국어
shed	
shortcut	
spine	
stationary	
summit	
supernatural	
suspicious	
swift	
therapy	
ubiquitous	
uncertain	
vice	
affair	
alley	
straightforward	
antique	
treatment	
boast	
bundle	
applause	
clerk	
combat	
considerable	
crush	
cucumber	
debris	
decode	
disclose	
divorce	
drainage	

한국어	영어
명 일, 문제	
동 으깨다, 찧다	
형 간단한, 솔직한	
형 초자연적인	
명 치료, 치유	
명 전투 동 싸우다, 맞서다	
동 폭로하다, 공개하다	
명 오이	
명 이혼 동 이혼하다	
명 악덕, 부도덕, 비행	
명 척추, 등뼈	
형 신속한, 재빠른	
형 상당한, 많은	
동 자랑하다, 뽐내다	
형 움직이지 않는, 고정된	
형 불확실한, 불투명한	
명 골목, 통로	
형 어디에나 있는, 아주 흔한	
형 의심스러운	
명 꾸러미, 보따리	
명 지름길	
명 박수 갈채	
명 잔해, 파편	
명 산 꼭대기, 정상회담	
동 흘리다, 떨구다	
동 번역하다, 해독하다, 이해하다	
명 배수(시설)	
명 점원, 사무원	
명 치료, 요법	
명 골동품 형 옛날의	

Workbook

Day 24

| 월 일 |

영어 단어에 해당하는 한국어 뜻을 함께 적으세요.

hollow	속이 빈, 움푹 꺼진	hollow	속이 빈, 움푹 꺼진
duplicate	복사하다; 복제한		
magnet	자석		
ash	재		
linear	직선의, 길이의, 선으로 된		
enforce	시행(집행)하다, 강요하다		
encode	암호로 바꾸다, 부호화하다		
limb	팔다리, 수족		
humid	습한, 눅눅한		
horizon	지평선, 수평선		
eminent	저명한, 탁월한		
asset	자산, 재산		
impair	손상시키다, 해치다		
incident	사건, 분쟁		
merchandise	상품		
hazardous	위험한		
guidance	지도, 안내		
goodwill	호의, 친선		
harden	단단하게 하다, 강화하다		
lively	활기 넘치는, 활발한		
infamous	악명 높은, 혐오할 만한		
instructive	유익한, 교훈적인		
mighty	강력한, 대단한		
lifespan	수명		
glaze	광택을 내다, 창에 유리를 끼우다		
gasp	숨이 막히다, 헐떡거리다		
hatred	증오, 혐오		
loyalty	충실, 충성		
kidnap	납치하다, 유괴하다		
drift	떠돌다, 표류하다		

다음 단어에 해당하는 영어 단어 또는 우리말을 쓰세요.

O____개 X____개

영어	한국어
drift	
duplicate	
eminent	
encode	
enforce	
gasp	
glaze	
goodwill	
guidance	
harden	
hatred	
hazardous	
hollow	
horizon	
humid	
ash	
impair	
incident	
asset	
infamous	
instructive	
kidnap	
lifespan	
limb	
linear	
lively	
loyalty	
magnet	
merchandise	
mighty	

한국어	영어
동 단단하게 하다, 강화하다	
동 복사하다 형 복제한	
명 호의, 친선	
형 속이 빈, 움푹 꺼진	
명 지도, 안내	
명 상품	
형 위험한	
명 자석	
형 유익한, 교훈적인	
명 재	
형 활기 넘치는, 활발한	
동 떠돌다, 표류하다	
형 직선의, 길이의, 선으로 된	
형 악명 높은, 혐오할 만한	
동 암호로 바꾸다, 부호화하다	
동 시행(집행)하다, 강요하다	
동 광택을 내다, 창에 유리를 끼우다	
명 증오, 혐오	
형 습한, 눅눅한	
형 강력한, 대단한	
명 팔다리, 수족	
명 수명	
명 사건, 분쟁	
명 지평선, 수평선	
동 숨이 막히다, 헐떡거리다	
명 자산, 재산	
형 저명한, 탁월한	
명 충실, 충성	
동 납치하다, 유괴하다	
동 손상시키다, 해치다	

Workbook

Day 25

| 월 일 | 영어 단어에 해당하는 한국어 뜻을 함께 적으세요.

reconsider	재고하다	reconsider	재고하다
treaty	조약, 협정, 의정서		
spacecraft	우주선		
pulse	맥박, 맥		
soothing	달래는, 위로하는		
staple	주된, 주요한		
outgoing	외향적인, 떠나가는		
scoop	한 숟갈의 양; 뜨다, 파다		
miniature	소형의, 아주 작은		
timid	소심한, 자신이 없는		
purity	순수성, 깨끗함		
mummy	미라		
sew	바느질하다, 꿰매다		
sprain	삐다, 접지르다		
ripe	익은, ~에 적합한		
milestone	획기적인 사건, 이정표		
superstition	미신		
prime	주요한, 뛰어난		
poll	여론 조사		
tournament	토너먼트, 경연대회		
sensible	분별 있는, 합리적인		
nap	낮잠		
multicultural	다문화의		
attain	달성하다, 얻다		
thermometer	온도계		
twinkle	반짝거리다, 반짝반짝 빛나다		
resolution	결의안, 해결, 결심		
sympathy	동정, 공감		
needle	바늘		
syndrome	증후군		

다음 단어에 해당하는 영어 단어 또는 우리말을 쓰세요. O____개 X____개

영어	한국어
milestone	
miniature	
multicultural	
mummy	
nap	
needle	
outgoing	
attain	
poll	
prime	
pulse	
purity	
reconsider	
resolution	
ripe	
scoop	
sensible	
sew	
soothing	
spacecraft	
sprain	
staple	
superstition	
sympathy	
syndrome	
thermometer	
timid	
tournament	
treaty	
twinkle	

한국어	영어
동 재고하다	
형 주요한, 뛰어난	
명 획기적인 사건, 이정표	
명 미신	
명 우주선	
명 여론 조사	
명 토너먼트, 경연대회	
형 소형의, 아주 작은	
형 소심한, 자신이 없는	
명 낮잠	
명 맥박, 맥	
명 한 숟갈의 양 동 뜨다, 파다	
형 분별 있는, 합리적인	
형 달래는, 위로하는	
형 다문화의	
형 주된, 주요한	
형 외향적인, 떠나가는	
동 달성하다, 얻다	
명 조약, 협정, 의정서	
동 반짝거리다, 반짝반짝 빛나다	
형 익은, ~에 적합한	
명 온도계	
명 순수성, 깨끗함	
동 삐다, 접지르다	
명 미라	
명 결의안, 해결, 결심	
명 증후군	
동 바느질하다, 꿰매다	
명 동정, 공감	
명 바늘	

Day 26

| 월 일 |

영어 단어에 해당하는 한국어 뜻을 함께 적으세요.

ethical	윤리적인, 도덕적인	ethical	윤리적인, 도덕적인
ascend	오르다, 상승하다		
audible	잘 들리는, 들을 수 있는		
by chance	우연히, 혹시		
compelling	강제적인, 강력한, 설득력있는		
unbelievable	믿기 어려운, 믿기 힘든		
blink	눈을 깜박이다		
unforgettable	잊을 수 없는		
ambassador	대사		
combination	조합, 결합		
blizzard	눈보라		
bomb	폭탄		
worship	예배, 숭배; 숭배하다, 흠모하다		
warfare	전쟁, 전투		
aptitude	소질, 적성		
committee	위원회		
boycott	구매, 참여를 거부하다; (구매, 사용 등의) 거부		
aggressive	공격적인, 적극적인		
destructive	파괴적인		
division	분할, 분배		
deliberately	의도적으로		
discourage	좌절시키다, (반대하여) 막다, 단념시키다		
be due to	~할 예정이다		
wrinkle	주름		
bold	용감한, 대담한		
critic	비평가		
seemingly	겉보기에는		
arbitrary	임의적인, 제멋대로인		
adore	아주 좋아하다, 숭배하다		
bald	대머리의, 머리가 벗겨진		

다음 단어에 해당하는 영어 단어 또는 우리말을 쓰세요.

O____개 X____개

영어	한국어
unbelievable	
unforgettable	
warfare	
worship	
wrinkle	
combination	
adore	
aggressive	
committee	
ambassador	
aptitude	
arbitrary	
ascend	
compelling	
audible	
critic	
deliberately	
bald	
be due to	
destructive	
blink	
blizzard	
bold	
bomb	
boycott	
discourage	
division	
ethical	
by chance	
seemingly	

한국어	영어
동 오르다, 상승하다	
형 대머리의, 머리가 벗겨진	
형 윤리적인, 도덕적인	
동 아주 좋아하다, 숭배하다	
형 강제적인, 강력한, 설득력 있는	
우연히, 혹시	
형 잘 들리는, 들을 수 있는	
형 공격적인, 적극적인	
형 임의적인, 제멋대로인	
동 눈을 깜박이다	
형 믿기 어려운, 믿기 힘든	
형 파괴적인	
명 위원회	
동 구매, 참여를 거부하다 명 (구매, 사용 등의) 거부	
부 겉보기에는	
형 잊을 수 없는	
명 분할, 분배	
형 의도적으로	
명 소질, 적성	
~할 예정이다	
동 좌절시키다, (반대하여) 막다, 단념시키다	
명 전쟁, 전투	
명 대사	
명 눈보라	
명 조합, 결합	
명 주름	
명 예배, 숭배 동 숭배하다, 흠모하다	
형 용감한, 대담한	
명 폭탄	
명 비평가	

Workbook

Day 27

| 월 일 |

영어 단어에 해당하는 한국어 뜻을 함께 적으세요.

crocodile	악어, 크로커다일	crocodile	악어, 크로커다일
demise	종말, 사망		
generalize	일반화하다		
tension	긴장(상태), 갈등		
significantly	크게, 상당히		
dampen	축축하게 하다, 무디게 하다		
cut down	~을 줄이다, 베어 쓰러뜨리다		
curable	치료 가능한		
fluent	유창한, 능통한		
mobile	이동하는		
consist	이루어지다, 구성되다		
marriage	결혼		
ferment	발효시키다, 발효되다		
debut	첫 출연, 데뷔		
figure out	이해하다, 해결하다, 알아내다		
resident	거주자		
carry out	~을 수행하다, 이행하다		
geology	지질학		
evacuate	비우다, 대피시키다		
excursion	여행, 소풍, 견학		
historical	역사적인		
forensic	법의학적인		
efficiency	효율		
famine	기아, 굶주림, 기근		
congress	의회, 국회		
expel	배출하다, 퇴학시키다		
defective	결함 있는, 불완전한		
creativity	창조성, 창의력		
crater	분화구		
conclude	결론을 내리다, 마치다		

다음 단어에 해당하는 영어 단어 또는 우리말을 쓰세요.

O____개 X____개

영어	한국어
resident	
carry out	
consist	
conclude	
congress	
marriage	
crater	
creativity	
crocodile	
curable	
cut down	
dampen	
debut	
defective	
demise	
mobile	
significantly	
evacuate	
excursion	
expel	
famine	
ferment	
figure out	
fluent	
forensic	
efficiency	
generalize	
geology	
tension	
historical	

한국어	영어
명 분화구	
명 악어, 크로커다일	
동 결론을 내리다, 마치다	
동 이루어지다, 구성되다	
형 이동하는	
명 지질학	
동 일반화하다	
~을 수행하다, 이행하다	
명 종말, 사망	
명 거주자	
동 비우다, 대피시키다	
~을 줄이다, 베어 쓰러뜨리다	
형 역사적인	
형 법의학적인	
형 유창한, 능통한	
명 긴장(상태), 갈등	
명 여행, 소풍, 견학	
부 크게, 상당히	
동 축축하게 하다, 무디게 하다	
이해하다, 해결하다, 알아내다	
명 효율	
형 치료 가능한	
명 창조성, 창의력	
명 첫 출연, 데뷔	
명 기아, 굶주림, 기근	
동 발효시키다, 발효되다	
형 결함 있는, 불완전한	
명 결혼	
명 의회, 국회	
동 배출하다, 퇴학시키다	

Workbook

Day 28 | 월 일 |

영어 단어에 해당하는 한국어 뜻을 함께 적으세요.

knight	기사	knight	기사
pale	창백한		
insist on	~을 고집하다, 주장하다		
insecure	불안정한		
ingenious	기발한, 독창적인		
gigantic	거대한		
grief	깊은 슬픔		
industrious	근면한, 부지런한		
formal	정중한, 공식적인		
have ~ in common	공통적으로 지니다, 공통점이 있다		
lava	용암		
hijack	납치하다; 납치 행위		
larva	유충, 애벌레		
misguided	잘못 이해한, 잘못 지도된		
humble	겸손한, 초라한, 소박한		
intentional	의도적인, 고의적인		
seldom	좀처럼 ~않다		
intercept	가로막다, 가로채다		
vendor	노점, 판매자		
implicate	관련시키다, 연루시키다		
hub	중심지		
in addition to	~에 더하여, ~일뿐 아니라		
inactive	활발하지 않은, 소극적인		
heir	후계자		
idle	게으른, 나태한		
clay	점토, 찰흙		
huddle	떼지어 몰리다, 옹기종기 모이다		
shade	그늘, 음영, 빛 가리개		
interfere with	방해하다, 간섭하다		
jeopardize	위태롭게 하다		

다음 단어에 해당하는 영어 단어 또는 우리말을 쓰세요.

O____개 X____개

영어	한국어
gigantic	
seldom	
shade	
pale	
grief	
vendor	
have ~ in common	
heir	
hijack	
hub	
huddle	
intentional	
humble	
idle	
implicate	
in addition to	
misguided	
inactive	
industrious	
ingenious	
insist on	
intercept	
interfere with	
jeopardize	
knight	
larva	
lava	
insecure	
formal	
clay	

한국어	영어
명 기사	
부 좀처럼 ~않다	
명 깊은 슬픔	
~을 고집하다, 주장하다	
명 중심지	
형 거대한	
형 의도적인, 고의적인	
형 창백한	
동 관련시키다, 연루시키다	
형 불안정한	
명 노점, 판매자	
형 기발한, 독창적인	
명 용암	
동 가로막다, 가로채다	
공통적으로 지니다, 공통점이 있다	
형 활발하지 않은, 소극적인	
형 정중한, 공식적인	
~에 더하여, ~일뿐 아니라	
형 겸손한, 초라한, 소박한	
명 점토, 찰흙	
형 근면한, 부지런한	
동 위태롭게 하다	
명 후계자	
동 납치하다 명 납치 행위	
형 게으른, 나태한	
형 잘못 이해한, 잘못 지도된	
명 유충, 애벌레	
명 그늘, 음영, 빛 가리개	
동 떼지어 몰리다, 옹기종기 모이다	
방해하다, 간섭하다	

Workbook

Day 29

| 월 일 | 영어 단어에 해당하는 한국어 뜻을 함께 적으세요.

obligate	강요하다, ~에게 의무를 지우다	obligate	강요하다, ~에게 의무를 지우다
peril	위험		
monk	수도승		
rubbish	쓰레기, 형편없는 것		
prominence	명성, 유명함		
maze	미로		
marine	바다의, 해양의		
malfunction	고장		
notify	알리다, 통지하다		
arrogant	오만한, 거만한		
railway	철로, 철도		
monarchy	군주제		
beneficial	유익한, 이로운		
pitiful	측은한, 가련한		
put off	연기하다		
paste	붙이다; 반죽		
oppressive	억압하는, 탄압하는		
memorial	기념비, 기념물, 기념일		
mansion	대저택		
masculine	남성의, 남자다운		
minister	장관, 성직자		
misty	안개 낀		
occupation	직업, 점령		
pebble	조약돌, 자갈		
open-minded	마음이 열린		
patent	특허권		
rifle	훔치다, 샅샅이 뒤지다		
pharmacy	약국, 조제실		
facade	정면, 앞면		
monologue	독백, 일인극		

다음 단어에 해당하는 영어 단어 또는 우리말을 쓰세요.

O____개 X____개

영어	한국어
malfunction	
mansion	
masculine	
maze	
memorial	
minister	
misty	
monarchy	
monk	
monologue	
facade	
rifle	
notify	
obligate	
occupation	
rubbish	
beneficial	
open-minded	
oppressive	
marine	
arrogant	
paste	
pebble	
peril	
pharmacy	
pitiful	
prominence	
put off	
patent	
railway	

한국어	영어
형 억압하는, 탄압하는	
명 고장	
명 정면, 앞면	
형 바다의, 해양의	
동 붙이다 명 반죽	
명 명성, 유명함	
동 훔치다, 샅샅이 뒤지다	
동 알리다, 통지하다	
명 대저택	
명 기념비, 기념물, 기념일	
명 미로	
명 장관, 성직자	
명 철로, 철도	
형 남성의, 남자다운	
형 오만한, 거만한	
명 쓰레기, 형편없는 것	
동 연기하다	
형 안개 낀	
명 위험	
명 수도승	
명 직업, 점령	
명 군주제	
명 조약돌, 자갈	
형 측은한, 가련한	
형 마음이 열린	
형 유익한, 이로운	
명 독백, 일인극	
동 강요하다, ~에게 의무를 지우다	
명 특허권	
명 약국, 조제실	

Workbook

Day 30

| 월 일 |

영어 단어에 해당하는 한국어 뜻을 함께 적으세요.

barely	간신히, 빠듯하게, 거의 ~아니게	barely	간신히, 빠듯하게, 거의 ~아니게
regardless of	~에 상관없이, 관계없이		
stumble	비틀거리다, 발을 헛디디다		
rebel	반역자, 저항세력		
revolve	돌다, 회전하다		
slope	경사지, 비탈		
paddle	노; 노를 젓다		
reptile	파충류		
inflation	물가 인상		
rapport	(친밀한) 관계		
rationalize	합리화하다		
sow	(씨를) 뿌리다, 심다		
speculate	추측하다, 짐작하다		
repertoire	연주곡 목록, 래퍼토리		
revolutionize	~에 혁명을 일으키다		
robber	강도		
scar	흉터		
sticky	끈적거리는, 달라붙는		
throne	왕위		
symbloize	상징하다, 기호화하다		
up-to-date	현대의, 최신 유행의		
sigh	한숨짓다; 한숨, 한숨소리		
misleading	오해의 소지가 있는, 오도하는		
renovate	혁신하다, ~을 보수하다		
tumble	굴러 떨어지다, 넘어지다		
talkative	말하기를 좋아하는, 수다스러운		
obesity	비만		
turn down	거절하다, 줄이다		
twilight	석양, 황혼		
riot	폭동, 시위		

다음 단어에 해당하는 영어 단어 또는 우리말을 쓰세요.

O____개 X____개

영어	한국어
barely	
inflation	
misleading	
obesity	
paddle	
repertoire	
rapport	
rationalize	
rebel	
regardless of	
renovate	
reptile	
revolutionize	
revolve	
riot	
robber	
scar	
sigh	
slope	
sow	
speculate	
sticky	
stumble	
symbloize	
talkative	
throne	
tumble	
turn down	
twilight	
up-to-date	

한국어	영어
명 흉터	
부 간신히, 빠듯하게, 거의 ~아니게	
명 강도	
동 혁신하다, ~을 보수하다	
동 비틀거리다, 발을 헛디디다	
형 오해의 소지가 있는, 오도하는	
전 ~에 상관없이, 관계없이	
형 끈적거리는, 달라붙는	
동 한숨짓다 명 한숨, 한숨소리	
명 노 동 노를 젓다	
명 왕위	
형 현대의, 최신 유행의	
명 반역자, 저항세력	
동 상징하다, 기호화하다	
동 돌다, 회전하다	
동 ~에 혁명을 일으키다	
명 경사지, 비탈	
동 굴러 떨어지다, 넘어지다	
동 추측하다, 짐작하다	
명 파충류	
형 말하기를 좋아하는, 수다스러운	
명 물가 인상	
명 비만	
명 (친밀한) 관계	
명 연주곡 목록, 래퍼토리	
동 합리화하다	
동 거절하다, 줄이다	
동 (씨를) 뿌리다, 심다	
명 석양, 황혼	
명 폭동, 시위	